ICTS
101-104

APT
Assessment of Professional Teaching
Teacher Certification Exam

By: Sharon Wynne, M.S
Southern Connecticut State University

"And, while there's no reason yet to panic, I think it's only prudent that we make preparations to panic."

XAMonline, INC.
Boston

To obtain permission(s) to use the material from this work for any purpose including workshops or seminars, please submit a written request to:

XAMonline, Inc.
21 Orient Ave.
Melrose, MA 02176
Toll Free 1-800-509-4128
Email: info@xamonline.com
Web www.xamonline.com
Fax: 1-781-662-9268

Library of Congress Cataloging-in-Publication Data

Wynne, Sharon A.
    APT Assessment of Professional Teaching 101-104: Teacher Certification / Sharon A. Wynne. - 2nd ed.   ISBN 978-1-58197-977-0
        1. APT Assessment of Professional Teaching 101-104.
        2. Study Guides.
        3. ICTS   4. Teachers' Certification & Licensure.
        5. Careers

Disclaimer:
The opinions expressed in this publication are the sole works of XAMonline and were created independently from the National Education Association, Educational Testing Service, or any State Department of Education, National Evaluation Systems or other testing affiliates.

Between the time of publication and printing, state specific standards as well as testing formats and website information may change that is not included in part or in whole within this product. Sample test questions are developed by XAMonline and reflect similar content as on real tests; however, they are not former tests. XAMonline assembles content that aligns with state standards but makes no claims nor guarantees teacher candidates a passing score. Numerical scores are determined by testing companies such as NES or ETS and then are compared with individual state standards. A passing score varies from state to state.

Printed in the United States of America

ICTS: APT Assessment of Professional Teaching 101-104
ISBN: 978-1-58197-293-1

Table of Contents

SUBAREA VI   EDUCATIONAL TECHNOLOGY

Study Tips:

1. <u>**Some foods aid the learning process.**</u> Foods such as milk, nuts, seeds, rice, and oats help your study efforts by releasing natural memory enhancers called CCKs (*cholecystokinin*) composed of *tryptophan*, *choline*, and *phenylalanine*. All of these chemicals enhance the neurotransmitters associated with memory. Before studying, try a light, protein-rich meal of eggs, turkey, and fish. All of these foods release the memory enhancing chemicals. The better the connections, the more you comprehend.

   Likewise, before you take a test, stick to a light snack of energy boosting and relaxing foods. A glass of milk, a piece of fruit, or some peanuts all release various memory-boosting chemicals and help you to relax and focus on the subject at hand.

2. <u>**Learn to take great notes.**</u> A by-product of our modern culture is that we have grown accustomed to getting our information in short doses (i.e. TV news sound bites or USA Today style newspaper articles.)

   Consequently, we've subconsciously trained ourselves to assimilate information better in neat little packages. If your notes are scrawled all over the paper, it fragments the flow of the information. Strive for clarity.

   Newspapers use a standard format to achieve clarity. Your notes can be much clearer through use of proper formatting. A very effective format is called the *Cornell Method.* Take a sheet of loose-leaf lined notebook paper and draw a line all the way down the paper about 1-2" from the left-hand edge. Draw another line across the width of the paper about 1-2" up from the bottom. Repeat this process on the reverse side of the page.

   Look at the highly effective result. You have ample room for notes, a left hand margin for special emphasis items or inserting supplementary data from the textbook, a large area at the bottom for a brief summary, and a little rectangular space for just about anything you want.

3. <u>**Dissect the material.**</u> Too often we focus on the details and don't gather an understanding of the concept. However, if you simply memorize only dates, places, or names, you may well miss the whole point of the subject.

   A key way to understand things is to put them in your own words. If you are working from a textbook, automatically summarize each paragraph in your mind. If you are outlining text, don't simply copy the author's words. *Rephrase* them in your own words. You remember your own thoughts and words much better than someone else's, and subconsciously tend to associate the important details to the core concepts.

4. **Turn every heading and caption in to a question.** Pull apart written material paragraph by paragraph and don't forget the captions under the illustrations.

   Example: If the heading is "Stream Erosion", flip it around to read "Why do streams erode?" Then answer the questions.

   If you train your mind to think in a series of questions and answers, not only will you learn more, but it also helps to lessen the test anxiety because you are used to answering questions.

5. **Read, Read, Read.** Even if you only have 10 minutes, put your notes or a book in your hand. Your mind is similar to a computer; you have to input data in order to have it processed. *By reading, you are storing data for future retrieval.* The more times you read something, the more you reinforce the storage of data.

   Even if you don't fully understand something on the first pass, *your mind stores much of the material for later recall.*

6. **Create the right study atmosphere.** Our bodies respond to an inner clock called biorhythms. Burning the midnight oil works well for some people, but not everyone. If possible, set aside a particular place to study that is free of distractions. Shut off the television, cell phone, pager and exile your friends and family during your study period.

   If you really are bothered by silence, try background music. Not rock, not hip-hop, not country, but classical. Light classical music at a low volume has been shown to aid in concentration. Don't pick anything with lyrics; you end up singing along. Try just about anything by Mozart, generally light and airy, it subconsciously evokes pleasant emotions and helps relax you.

7. **Limit the use of highlighters.** At best, it's difficult to read a page full of yellow, pink, blue, and green streaks. Try staring at a neon sign for a while and you'll soon see my point, the horde of colors obscure the message. A quick note, a brief dash of color, an underline, and an arrow pointing to a particular passage is much clearer than a horde of highlighted words.

8. **Budget your study time.** Although you shouldn't ignore any of the material, *allocate your available study time in the same ratio that topics may appear on the test.*

Testing Tips:

1. **Don't outsmart yourself.** Don't read anything into the question. Don't make an assumption that the test writer is looking for something else than what is asked. Stick to the question as written and don't read extra things into it.

2. **Read the question and all the choices _twice_ before answering the question.** You may miss something by not carefully reading, and then re-reading both the question and the answers. If you really don't have a clue as to the right answer, leave it blank on the first time through. Go on to the other questions, as they may provide a clue as to how to answer the skipped questions. If later on, you still can't answer the skipped ones . . . **_Guess._** The only penalty for guessing is that you _might_ get it wrong. Only one thing is certain; if you don't put anything down, you will get it wrong!

3. **Turn the question into a statement.** Look at the way the questions are worded. The syntax of the question usually provides a clue. Does it seem more familiar as a statement rather than as a question? Does it sound strange? By turning a question into a statement, you may be able to spot if an answer sounds right, and it may also trigger memories of material you have read.

4. **Look for hidden clues.** It's actually very difficult to compose multiple-foil (choice) questions without giving away part of the answer in the options presented. In most multiple-choice questions you can often readily eliminate one or two of the potential answers. This leaves you with only two real possibilities and automatically your odds go to fifty-fifty for very little work.

5. **Trust your instincts.** For every fact that you have read, you subconsciously retain something of that knowledge. On questions that you aren't really certain about, go with your basic instincts, **your first impression on how to answer a question is usually correct.**

6. **Mark your answers directly on the test booklet.** Don't bother trying to fill in the optical scan sheet on the first pass through the test. Just be very careful not to miss-mark your answers when you eventually transcribe them to the scan sheet.

7. **Watch the clock!** You have a set amount of time to answer the questions. Don't get bogged down trying to answer a single question at the expense of 10 questions you can more readily answer.

SUBAREA I   FOUNDATIONS, CHARACTERISTICS, AND ASSESSMENT

COMPETENCY 1.0   UNDERSTANDS HOW CHILDREN LEARN AND DEVELOP.

Skill 1.1   Demonstrates knowledge of human development, learning theory, neural science, and the ranges of individual variation within each domain.

It is important for teachers to consider students' development and readiness when making instructional decisions. If an educational program is child-centered, it will surely address the developmental abilities and needs of the students because it will take its cues from students' interests, concerns, and questions. Making an educational program child-centered involves building on the natural curiosity children bring to school and asking children what they want to learn.

Teachers help students to identify their own questions, puzzles, and goals, and they then structure for them widening circles of experiences and investigations of those topics. Teachers manage to infuse all of the skills, knowledge, and concepts that society mandates into a child-driven curriculum. This does not mean to imply that teachers are passive and only respond to students' explicit cues. Teachers also draw on their understanding of children's developmental characteristic needs and individual enthusiasms to design experiences that lead children into areas they might not otherwise choose, but that they do enjoy and find engaging. Teachers also bring their own interests and enthusiasms into the classroom to share and act as a motivational means of guiding children.

Implementing such a child-centered curriculum is the result of very careful and deliberate planning. Planning serves as a means of organizing instruction and influences classroom teaching. Well thought-out planning includes: specifying behavioral objectives, specifying students' entry behavior (knowledge and skills), selecting and sequencing learning activities so as to move students from entry behavior to objective, and evaluating the outcomes of instruction in order to improve planning.

Development in one domain affects learning and development in other domains

Elementary age children face many changes during their early school years, and these changes will impact how learning occurs in either a positive or negative manner. Some cognitive developments (i.e., learning to read) may broaden their areas of interest as students realize the amount of information (i.e., novels, magazines, non-fiction books) that is available. On the other hand, a young student's limited comprehension may inhibit some of their confidence (emotional) or conflict with values taught at home (moral). Joke telling (linguistic) becomes popular with children aged six or seven, and children may use this newly discovered "talent" to gain friends or social "stature" in their class (social). Learning within one domain often spills over into other areas for young students.

Likewise, learning continues to affect all domains as a child grows. Adolescence is a complex stage of life. While many people joke about the awkwardness of adolescence, it is particularly important to remember that this stage of life is the stage just before adulthood. While people do indeed develop further in adulthood, the changes are not as quick or significant as they are in adolescence.

Development within domains refers to the fact that different aspects of a human change as they mature. For example, physical changes take place (e.g., body growth, sexuality); cognitive changes take place (e.g., better ability to reason); linguistic changes take place (e.g., a child's vocabulary develops further); social changes take place (e.g., figuring out identity); emotional changes take place (e.g., changes in ability to be concerned about other people); and moral changes take place (e.g., testing limits).

The important thing to remember about adolescent development within each of these domains is that they are not exclusive. For example, physical and emotional development are tied intricately, particularly when one feels awkward about his or her body; when emotional feelings are tied to sexuality; or when one feels that he or she does not look old enough (as rates of growth are obviously not similar). Moral and cognitive development often go hand-in-hand when an adolescent begins to identify reasons for behavior or searches for role models.

It is important, as an educator, to be sensitive to changes in adolescents. Just because a change in one area is not apparent does not mean there aren't changes in another area, hidden beneath the surface.

Another area of extreme importance when dealing with adolescents is to realize that they may be deeply hurt over certain issues which may or may not be directly related to the changes they are going through at a specific time. It is particularly important for educators to be on the lookout for signs of depression, drug use, or other damaging activities, behaviors, or symptoms.

Range of individual development differences in students

Knowledge of age-appropriate expectations is fundamental to the teacher's positive relationship with students and being able to utilize effective instructional strategies. Equally important is the knowledge of what is individually appropriate for the specific children within a classroom. In this way, teachers are able to approach classroom groups and individual students with a respect for their emerging capabilities and meet the developmental needs of their students.

Developmentalists recognize the fact that children progress through common patterns, but may do so at different rates. These rates cannot typically be accelerated by adult pressure or input. Developmentally oriented teachers understand that variances in the school performance of different children often results from differences in their general developmental growth. With the establishment of inclusion classes throughout the schools, it is vital for all teachers to have a complete understanding of the characteristics of students' various disabilities and the possible implications on learning.

The effective teacher selects learning activities based on specific learning objectives. Ideally, teachers should not plan activities that fail to augment the specific objectives of the lesson. Learning activities should be planned with a learning objective in mind. Objective driven learning activities tend to serve as a tool to reinforce the teacher's lesson presentation. Additionally, teacher selected learning objectives should be aligned with state and district educational goals. State and district goals should focus on National Educational Goals (Goals 2000) and the specific strengths and weaknesses of individual students assigned to their class.

The effective teacher is cognizant of students' individual learning styles as well as human growth and development theory. S/he then applies these principles to the selection and implementation of appropriate classroom instructional activities.

Learning activities selected for younger students (below age eight) should focus on short time frames and be in a highly simplified form. The nature of the activity and the content in which the activity is presented effects the approach the students will use to process the information. Younger children tend to process information at a slower pace than children aged eight and older.

On the other hand, when selecting and implementing learning activities for older children, teachers should focus on more complex ideas. Older students are capable of understanding more complex instructional activities. Moreover, effective teachers maintain a clear understanding of the developmental appropriateness of activities selected.

Skill 1.2   Demonstrates knowledge of how students construct knowledge, acquire skills, and develop habits of mind.

Historically, there are two main theories which readily help to describe how students construct knowledge, acquire skills and develop habits of mind. The first theory is behavioral learning. Behavioral learning theory suggests that people learn socially, by stimulation, or through repetition. For example, when a person touches a hot stove, they learn not to repeat that action. Another example would be when a person makes a social error which leads to teasing or taunting, they learn acceptable social conventions. Learning by watching another complete an activity would be a third example of behavioral learning theory.

The second broad theory is cognitive learning. Cognitive learning theories suggest that learning takes place within the mind. It goes further to explain that the mind processes ideas through brain mapping and connections with other material and experiences. In other words, with behaviorism, learning is somewhat external. We see something, for example, and then we copy it. With cognitive theories, learning is internal. For example, we see something, analyze it in our minds, and make sense of it for ourselves. Then, if we choose to copy it, we do, but we do so having internalized (or thought about) the process.

Today, even though behavioral theories exist, most educators believe that children learn cognitively. Based on this information, teachers introduce new topics by relating those topics to information students may have already received exposure or that with which they are already familiar. In this way, the teacher is expecting that students will be able to better integrate this new information into their memories by attaching it to something that is already there. Or, when teachers apply new learning to real-world situations, they are expecting that the information will make more sense because it has been related to a more real situation.

In all of the examples given in this standard, the importance is the application of new learning to something concrete. In essence, what is going on with these examples is that the teacher is slowing building on knowledge or adding knowledge to what students already know. Cognitively, this makes a great deal of sense. Think of a file cabinet. When we already have files for certain things, it's easy for us to find a file and throw new information into it. When we're given something that doesn't fit into one of the pre-existing files, we struggle to know what to do with it. The same is true with human minds.

Skill 1.3   Identifies differences in approaches to learning and performance, including different learning styles, multiple intelligences, and performance modes.

There are many factors that affect student learning including: how students learn, how learning is presented, amount of background knowledge and/or experiences. There are several educational learning theories which can be applied to classroom practices. One classic learning theory is Piaget's stages of development which consist of four learning stages:

- Sensory motor stage (from birth to age 2)
- Pre-operation stages (ages 2 to 7 or early elementary)
- Concrete operational (ages7 to 11 or upper elementary)
- Formal operational (ages 7-15 or late elementary/high school).

Piaget believed children passed through this series of stages as they developed from the most basic forms of concrete thinking to the most sophisticated levels of abstract thinking.

Two of the most prominent learning theories in education today are Brain-Based Learning and the Multiple Intelligence Theory. Recent brain research suggests that increased knowledge about the way the brain retains information will enable educators to design the most effective learning environments. As a result, researchers have developed twelve principles that relate knowledge about the brain to teaching practices. These twelve principles of Brain-based Learning Theory are:

- The brain is a complex adaptive system
- The brain is social
- The search for meaning is innate
- We use patterns to learn more effectively
- Emotions are crucial to developing patterns
- Each brain perceives and creates parts and whole simultaneously
- Learning involves focused and peripheral attention
- Learning involves conscious and unconscious processes
- We have at least two ways of organizing memory
- Learning is developmental
- Complex learning is enhanced by challenged (and inhibited by threat)
- Every brain is unique
  (Caine & Caine, 1994, Mind/Brain Learning Principles)

Educators can use these principles to help design methods and environments in their classrooms to maximize student learning.

The Multiple Intelligence Theory, developed by Howard Gardner, suggests that students learn in (at least) seven different ways. These include: visually/spatially, musically, verbally, logically/mathematically, interpersonally, intrapersonally, and bodily/kinesthetically.

Another learning theory is that of Constructivism. The theory of constructivist learning allows students to construct learning opportunities. For constructivist teachers, the belief is that students create their own reality of knowledge and how to process and observe the world around them. Students are constantly constructing new ideas, which serve as frameworks for learning and teaching. Researchers have shown that the constructivist model is comprised of the following four components:

- Learner creates knowledge
- Learner constructs and makes meaningful new knowledge to existing knowledge
- Learner shapes and constructs knowledge by life experiences and social interactions
- In constructivist learning communities, the student, teacher and classmates establish knowledge cooperatively on a daily basis.

Kelly (1969) states "human beings construct knowledge systems based on their observations; this parallels Piaget's theory that individuals construct knowledge systems as they work with others who share a common background of thought and processes." Constructivist learning for students is dynamic and ongoing. For constructivist teachers, the classroom becomes a place where students are encouraged to interact with the instructional process by asking questions and posing new ideas to old theories. The use of cooperative learning which encourages students to work in supportive learning environments using their own ideas to stimulate questions and propose outcomes is a major aspect of a constructivist classroom.

Yet another learning theory is that of metacognition. The metacognition learning theory deals with "the study of how to help the learner gain understanding about how knowledge is constructed and about the conscious tools for constructing that knowledge" (Joyce and Weil 1996). The metacognitive approach to learning involves the teacher's understanding that teaching the student to process his/her own learning and mastery of skill provides the greatest learning and retention opportunities in the classroom. Students are taught to develop concepts and teach themselves skills in problem solving and critical thinking. The student becomes an active participant in the learning process and the teacher facilitates that conceptual and cognitive learning process.

Finally, social and behavioral theories look at the social interactions of students in the classroom that instruct or impact learning opportunities in the classroom. The psychological approaches behind both theories are subject to individual variables that are learned and applied either proactively or negatively in the classroom. The stimulus of the classroom can promote conducive learning or evoke behavior that is counterproductive for both students and teachers. Students are social beings that normally gravitate to action in the classroom, so teachers must be cognizant in planning classroom environments that provide both focus and engagement in maximizing learning opportunities.

Skill 1.4 **Demonstrates understanding of the cognitive processes associated with various kinds of learning and how these processes can be stimulated and developed.**

Students learn through a variety of methods. Efficient teachers are able to alter their instructional methods to present material using range of methods in order to meet the needs of students. Below are some of the diverse ways teachers can implement instruction.

Direct Instruction
Siegfried Engelmann and Dr. Wesley Becker, and several other researchers proposed the direct instruction method. Direct Instruction (DI) is a teaching method that emphasizes well-developed and carefully-planned lessons with small learning increments. DI assumes that the use of clear instruction eliminates misinterpretations will therefore improve outcomes. Their approach is being used by thousands of schools. It recommends that the popular valuing of teacher creativity and autonomy be replaced by a willingness to follow certain carefully prescribed instructional practices. At the same time, it encourages the retention of hard work, dedication, and commitment to students. It demands that teachers adopt and internalize the belief that all students, if properly taught, can and will learn.

Discovery Learning

Beginning at birth, discovery learning is a normal part of the growing-up experience. This naturally occurring phenomenon can be used to improve the outcomes within classrooms. Discovery learning, in the classroom, is based upon inquiry, and it has been a factor in many of the advances mankind has made through the years. For example, Rousseau constantly questioned his world, particularly the philosophies and theories that were commonly accepted. Dewey, himself a great discoverer, wrote, "There is an intimate and necessary relation between the processes of actual experience and education." Piaget, Bruner, and Papert have all recommended this teaching method as well. In discovery learning, students solve problems by using their own experiences and their prior knowledge to determine what truths can be learned. Bruner wrote "Emphasis on discovery in learning has precisely the effect on the learner of leading him to a constructionist, to organize what he is encountering in a manner not only designed to discover regularity and relatedness, but also to avoid the kind of information drift that fails to keep account of the uses to which information might have to be put."

Whole Group Discussion

Whole group discussion can be used in a variety of settings, but the most common is in the discussion of an assignment. Since learning is peer-based with this strategy, students gain a different perspective on the topic, as well as learn to respect the ideas of others. One obstacle that can occur with this teaching method is that the same students tend to participate over and over while the same students also do not participate time after time. However, with proper teacher guidance during this activity, whole group discussions are highly valuable.

Case Method Learning

Providing an opportunity for students to apply what they learn in the classroom to real-life experiences has proven to be an effective way of both disseminating and integrating knowledge. The case method is an instructional strategy that engages students in active discussion about issues and the problems inherent in practical application. It can highlight fundamental dilemmas or critical issues and provide a format for role playing ambiguous or controversial scenarios. Obviously, a successful class discussion involves planning on the part of the instructor and preparation on the part of the students. Instructors should communicate this commitment to the students on the first day of class by clearly articulating course expectations. Just as the instructor carefully plans the learning experience, the students must comprehend the assigned reading and show up for class on time, ready to learn.

Concept Mapping

Concept mapping is a common tool used by teachers in various disciplines. There are many different kinds of maps which have been developed. They are useful devices, but each teacher must determine which is appropriate for use in his/her own classroom. Following is a common one used in writing courses:

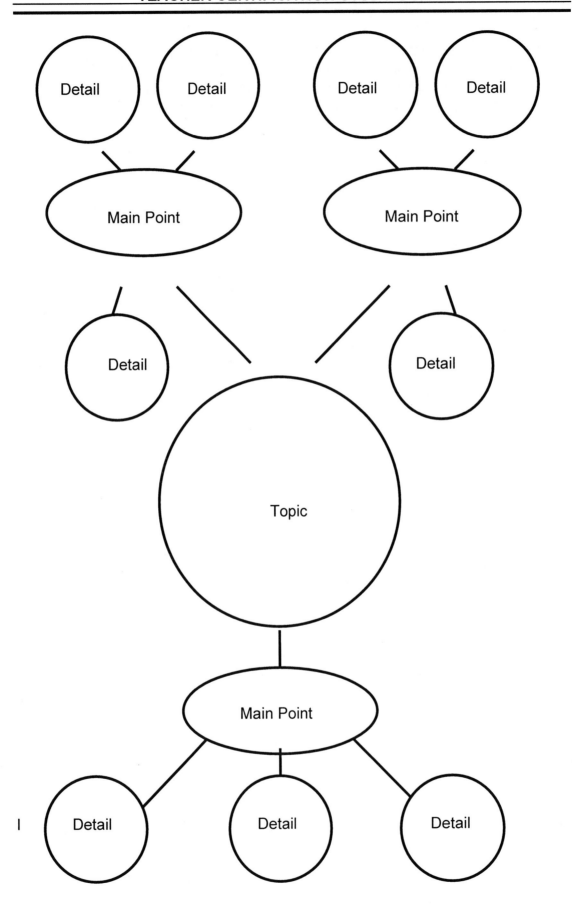

Inquiry

All learning begins with the learner. What children know and what they want to learn are not just constraints on what can be taught; they are the very foundation for learning. Dewey's descriptions of the four primary interests of the child are still appropriate starting points. These starting points are:

- The child's instinctive desire to find things out
- In conversation, the propensity children have to communicate
- In construction, their delight in making things
- In their gifts of artistic expression.

Questioning

Questioning is a teaching strategy as old as Socrates. The most important factor for the teacher to remember is that questioning must be deliberative and carefully planned. This is an important tool for leading students into critical thinking. Bloom's Taxonomy provides a hierarchy for increasing the critical thinking levels of question posed.

Play

There are so many useful games available that the most difficult task is choosing which will fit into your classroom. Some are electronic, some are board games, and some are designed to be played by a child individually. Even in those cases, a review of the results by the entire classroom can be used to provide a useful learning experience.

Learning centers

In a flexible classroom where students have some time when they can choose which activity they will complete, learning centers are extremely important. They take out-of-class time for creating them, collecting the items that will make them up, and then setting up the center. In some classes, the students might participate in creating a learning center.

Small group work

In today's diverse classrooms, small group work is vital. Children can be grouped according to their level of development or the small groups themselves can be diverse, giving the students who are struggling an opportunity to learn from a student who is already proficient. The better prepared student will learn from becoming a source for the weaker student, and the weaker student may be more likely to accept help from another student sometimes than from the teacher.

Revisiting

Revisiting should occur during a unit, at the end of a unit, and at the end of a semester. In other words, giving students more than one opportunity to grasp principles and skills and to integrate them is practical teaching theory.

Reflection

Teaching can move along so rapidly sometimes that students fail to incorporate what they've learned and to think about it in terms of what they bring to the topic in the first place. Providing time for reflection and guiding students in developing tools for it is a wise teaching method.

Projects

Seeing a unit as a project is also very useful. It opens the door naturally to a multi-task approach to learning. Not only will the students learn about birds, they will have an opportunity to observe them, they can try their hands at drawing them, and they can learn to differentiate one from the other. It's easy to see how a lifetime interest in bird watching can take root in such a project, which is more effective than in simply reading about the topic and talking about it.

Skill 1.5 **Demonstrates knowledge of the interaction among students' physical, social, emotional, ethical, and cognitive development and students' approaches to learning and performance.**

The teacher needs a broad knowledge and thorough understanding of the development that typically occurs during the students' current period of life. More importantly, the teacher needs to understand how children learn best during each period of development. The most important premise of child development is that all domains of development (physical, social, and academic) are integrated. Development in each dimension is influenced by the other dimensions. Moreover, today's educator must also have knowledge of disabilities and how these disabilities affect all domains of a child's development.

Physical Development

It is important for the teacher to be aware of the physical stage of development and how the child's physical growth and development affect the child's learning. Factors determined by the physical stage of development include: ability to sit and attend, the need for activity, the relationship between physical skills and self-esteem, and the degree to which physical involvement in an activity (as opposed to being able to understand an abstract concept) affects learning.

Cognitive (Academic) Development

Children progress through patterns of learning beginning with pre-operational thought processes and moving to concrete operational thoughts. Eventually, they begin to acquire the mental ability to think about and solve problems in their head because they can manipulate objects symbolically. Children of most ages can use symbols such as words and numbers to represent objects and relations, but they need concrete reference points. It is essential children be encouraged to use and develop the thinking skills that they possess in solving problems that are of interest to them. The content of the curriculum must be relevant, engaging, and meaningful to the students.

Social Development

Children progress through a variety of social stages beginning with an awareness of peers but a lack of concern for the presence of these peers. Young children engage in "parallel" activities (playing alongside their peers without directly interacting with one another). During the primary years, children develop an intense interest in peers. They establish productive, positive, social, and working relationships with one another. This stage of social growth continues to increase in importance throughout the child's school years.. It is necessary for the teacher to recognize the importance of developing positive peer group relationships and to provide opportunities and support for cooperative small group projects which not only develop cognitive ability but promote peer interaction. The ability to work and relate effectively with peers is of major importance and contributes greatly to the child's sense of competence. In order to develop this sense of competence, children need to be successful in acquiring the knowledge and skills recognized by our culture as important, especially those skills which promote academic achievement.

Skill 1.6   Recognizes key aspects of the disciplinary and interdisciplinary approaches to learning and how they relate to life and career experiences.

Keeping in mind what is understood about the students' abilities and interests, the teacher needs to design a course of study that presents units of instruction in an orderly sequence. The instruction should be planned so as to advance all students toward the next level of instruction, although exit behaviors need not be identical due to the inevitability of individual differences.

Studies have shown students learn best when what is taught in lecture and textbook reading is presented more than once in a variety of formats. In some instances, students themselves may be asked to reinforce what they have learned by completing some original production—for example, by drawing pictures to explain some scientific process, by writing a monologue or dialogue to express what some historical figure might have said on some occasion, by devising a board game to challenge the players' mathematical skills, or by acting out (and perhaps filming) episodes from a classroom reading selection. Students usually enjoy having their work displayed or presented to an audience of peers. Thus, their productions may supplement and personalize the learning experiences that the teacher has planned for them.

The effective teacher takes care to select appropriate activities and classroom situations in which learning is optimized. The classroom teacher should manipulate instructional activities and classroom conditions in a manner that enhances group and individual learning opportunities. For example, the classroom teacher can organize group learning activities in which students are placed in a situation in which cooperation, sharing ideas, and discussion occurs. Cooperative learning activities can assist students in learning to collaborate, share personal and cultural ideas, and values in a classroom learning environment.

The effective teacher plans his/her learning activities to introduce them in a meaningful instructional sequence. Teachers should combine instructional activities as to reinforce information by providing students with relevant learning experiences throughout instructional activities.

Educators have recognized the necessity to more closely integrate academic and vocational learning, as the transition from school to work has proven a rocky road for students of the 21st century. With heavy academic loads and pressures to perform well on mandated tests, students are finding it increasingly difficult to find relevance in or connect to the instructional content and apply it to their own lives..

For some students, the pressures of preparing for college, succeeding academically, volunteering in community service, participating in extracurricular activities overshadows the actual purpose of college: to train for a career. They may reach their senior year of high school academically ready but largely unaware of and unprepared for the breadth of career choices available to them.

It's never too early to begin incorporating information about the working world into instruction and curriculum. One or more of a child's parents or caregivers likely has a job outside of the home, so the working world is already a part of the child's life and s/he has a context with which to discuss it.

In general, the effective teacher takes every opportunity to make real-world associations within all subjects and lessons. The teacher should also explicitly make connections between an academic skill and the working world, and not simply assume the students will be able to make these connections on their own.

Authentic learning/work experiences

Exposing students to key facets of the working world is an important aspect of authentic learning experiences. It is important to take every opportunity to show an active relationship between the students' textbooks and the world around them. Below are some examples of ways to incorporate authentic learning and work experiences into the classroom.

- Invite business and community leaders to speak about their careers. Have students prepare questions ahead of time: What does it take to perform their jobs, in terms of education and experience? How did they get started on their career path? What advice can they share with someone considering such a career?
- Arrange a field trip to a local business where students can observe the environment and speak with employees about their typical days. Ask a representative to describe the various jobs available within the company.
- Incorporate news and published works from the working world that are related to a lesson. When reading a novel in language arts class, include an interview with the author about the writing process. For a unit in microbiology, include news of the latest scientific findings.

Expanding students' knowledge of career opportunities

- Find magazine or Internet articles listing different types of job groupings (e.g., the top paying jobs, the "hottest" jobs, hot jobs of the future) and use them as discussion points – why are they top paying/hot jobs, what skills do those jobs require, where can one obtain those skills, etc.
- During a larger lesson unit, make time to include a discussion about what jobs exist related to the instructional content. In a government class, a lesson on the U.S. Constitution can incorporate a discussion of jobs that maintain, enforce and protect the Constitution, such as Congress, the Senate, justices and judges, law enforcement officers, lawyers and paralegals.

COMPETENCY 2.0   UNDERSTANDS FACTORS THAT MAY AFFECT STUDENTS' DEVELOPMENT AND LEARNING.

Skill 2.1   Demonstrates understanding of how students' development, behavior, and learning are influenced by individual experiences, talents, and prior learning, as well as language, culture, family background, and community values.

Often, students absorb the culture and social environment around them without deciphering contextual meaning of the experiences. When provided with a diversity of cultural contexts, students are able to adapt and incorporate multiple meanings from cultural cues vastly different from their own socioeconomic backgrounds. Socio-cultural factors provide a definitive impact on a students' psychological, emotional, affective, and physiological development, along with a students' academic learning and future opportunities.

The educational experience for most students is a complicated and complex experience with a diversity of interlocking meanings and inferences. If one aspect of the complexity is altered, it affects other aspects. These changes may impact how a student or teacher views an instructional or learning experience. With the current demographic profile of today's school communities, the complexity of understanding, interpreting, and synthesizing the nuances from the diversity of cultural lineages can provide difficulties in both communication and learning that could impede the acquisition of skills for students.

Teachers should create personalized learning communities where every student is a valued member and contributor of the classroom experiences. In classrooms where socio-cultural attributes of the student population are incorporated into the fabric of the learning process, dynamic interrelationships are created that enhance the learning experience and the personalization of learning. When students are provided with numerous academic and social opportunities to share cultural incorporations into the learning, everyone in the classroom benefits from bonding through shared experiences and having an expanded viewpoint of a world experience and culture that vastly differs from their own.

Researchers continue to show that personalized learning environments increase the learning effect for students; decrease drop-out rates among marginalized students; and decrease unproductive student behavior which can result from constant cultural misunderstandings or miscues between students. Promoting diversity of learning and cultural competency in the classroom for students and teachers creates a world of multicultural opportunities and learning. When students are able to step outside their comfort zones and share themselves, then students grow exponentially in social understanding and cultural connectedness. Examining the world of a homeless student or empathizing with an English Language Learner (ELL) student who has just immigrated to the United States can be important lessons for students to experience.

Personalized learning communities provide supportive learning environments that address the academic and emotional needs of students. As socio-cultural knowledge is conveyed continuously in the interrelated experiences, shared cooperatively, and collaboratively in student groupings or individualized learning, the current and future benefits will continue to present the case and importance of understanding the "whole" child, inclusive of the social and the cultural context.

Skill 2.2 **Analyzes how variance in cognitive, emotional, physical, and sensory abilities affects development, learning, behavior, and communication.**

SEE Skill 1.1

Skill 2.3 **Recognizes the effects of behavior on learning and the differences between behavioral and emotional disorders.**

Classroom management plans should be in place when the school year begins. Developing a management plan requires a proactive approach. A proactive approach involves: deciding what behaviors will be expected of the class as a whole, anticipating possible problems, teaching the behaviors early in the school year, and implementing behavior management techniques which focus on positive procedures that can be used at home as well at school. It is important to involve the students in the development of the classroom rules. The benefits include:

- It lets the students understand the rationale for the rules
- It allows the students to assume responsibility for the rules because they had a part in developing them. When students get involved in helping establish the rules, they will be more likely to assume responsibility for following them.

Once the rules are established, enforcement and reinforcement for following the rules should begin right away.

Consequences should be introduced when the rules are introduced, clearly stated, and understood by all of the students. The severity of the consequence should match the severity of the offense and must be enforceable. The teacher must apply the consequence consistently and fairly; so the students will know what to expect when they choose to break a rule.

Like consequences, students should understand what rewards to expect for following the rules. The teacher should never promise a reward that cannot be delivered, and follow through with the reward as soon as possible. Consistency and fairness is also necessary for rewards to be effective. Students will become frustrated and give up if they see that rewards and consequences are not delivered timely and fairly.

About four to six classroom rules should be posted where students can easily see and read them. These rules should be stated positively, and describe specific behaviors so they are easy to understand. Certain rules may also be tailored to meet target goals and IEP requirements of individual students. (For example, a new student who has had problems with leaving the classroom may need an individual behavior contract to assist him or her with adjusting to the class rule about remaining in the assigned area.) As the students demonstrate the behaviors, the teacher should provide reinforcement and corrective feedback. Periodic "refresher" practice can be done as needed, for example, after a long holiday or if students begin to "slack off." A copy of the classroom plan should be readily available for substitute use, and the classroom aide should also be familiar with the plan and procedures.

The teacher should clarify and model the expected behavior for the students. In addition to the classroom management plan, a management plan should be developed for special situations, (i.e., fire drills) and transitions (i.e., going to and from the cafeteria). Periodic review of the rules, as well as modeling and practice, may be conducted as needed, such as after an extended school holiday.

Procedures that use social humiliation, withholding of basic needs, pain, or extreme discomfort should never be used in a behavior management plan. Emergency intervention procedures used when the student is a danger to himself or others are not considered behavior management procedures. Throughout the year, the teacher should periodically review the types of interventions being used, assess their effectiveness, and make revisions as need.

Many safe and helpful interventions are available to the classroom teacher when dealing with a student who is suffering from a serious emotional disturbance. First, and foremost, the teacher must maintain open communication with the parents and other professionals who are involved with the student whenever overt behavior characteristics are exhibited. Students with behavior disorders need constant behavioral interventions , which may involve two-way communication between the home and school on a daily basis.

The teacher must establish an environment that promotes appropriate behavior for all students, as well as respect for one another. Classmates may need to be informed of any special needs that their fellow students have to better understand behavioral interventions and outbursts which may occur in the classroom. The teacher should also initiate a behavior intervention program for any student that might demonstrate emotional or behavioral disorders. Such behavior modification plans can be effective means of preventing deviant behavior. If deviant behavior does occur, the teacher needs to have previously arranged for a safe and secure time-out place where the student can go for a respite and an opportunity to regain self-control.

Often when a behavior disorder is more severe, the student must be involved in a more concentrated program aimed at alleviating deviant behavior, such as psychotherapy. In such instances, the school psychologist, guidance counselor, or behavior specialist should be directly involved with the student and provide counseling and/or therapy on a regular basis. Frequently they are also involved with the student's family.

As a last resort, many families are turning to drug therapy. Once viewed as a radical step, administering drugs to children to balance their emotions or to control their behavior has become a widely used form of therapy. Of course, only a medical doctor can recommend or prescribe such drugs. Great care must be exercised when giving pills to children in order to change their behavior, especially since so many medicines have undesirable side effects. It is important to know that these drugs relieve only the symptoms of behavior and do not always eliminate the underlying causes. Parents and teachers need to be educated as to the side effects of these medications.

Skill 2.4   Demonstrates knowledge of the effects of sensory input on the development of language and cognition of students with sensory impairments, including the effects on cultural development and familial structures

From high school and college, most of us think that learning a language strictly involves drills, memorization, and tests. While this is a common method used (some people call it a structural, grammatical, or linguistic approach). While this works for some students, it certainly does not work for all.

Although there are dozens of methods that have been developed to help people learn additional languages, these are some of the more common approaches used in today's K-12 classrooms. Cognitive approaches to language learning focus on concepts. While words and grammar are important, when teachers use the cognitive approach, they focus on using language for conceptual purposes—rather than learning words and grammar for the sake of simply learning new words and grammatical structures. This approach focuses heavily on students' learning styles, and it cannot necessarily be pinned down as having specific techniques. Rather, it is more of a philosophy of instruction.

There are many approaches that are noted for their motivational purposes. In a general sense, when teachers work to motivate students to learn a language, they do things to help reduce fear and to assist students in identifying with native speakers of the target language. A very common method is often called the functional approach. In this approach, the teacher focuses on communicative elements. For example, a first grade English as a Second Language (ESOL) teacher might help students learn phrases that will assist them in finding a restroom, asking for help on the playground, etc. Many functionally-based adult ESOL programs help learners with travel-related phrases and words.

Another very common motivational approach is Total Physical Response. This is a kinesthetic approach that combines language learning and physical movement. In essence, students learn new vocabulary and grammar by responding with physical motion to verbal commands. Some people say it is particularly effective because the physical actions help to create good brain connections with the words.

In general, the best methods do not treat students as if they have a language deficit. Rather, the best methods build upon what students already know, and they help to instill the target language as a communicative process rather than a list of vocabulary words that have to be memorized.

Students with sensory disabilities such as those who are blind, visually impaired, deaf, or hearing impaired often bring auxiliary aids and adaptive equipment to the classroom (e.g., dog, cane, interpreter, Type-N-Speak, etc).

Often students who are blind or visually impaired use Braille; others make use of adaptive technology, especially print to voice conversion using a scanner and voice production software. Students with visual impairments will likely need all print material in alternative format, which means that they need print material converted to audio tapes, scanned onto disks, Braille, enlarged or image enhanced. Students with visual impairments may need preferential seating since they depend upon listening.

Some students who are deaf or hard of hearing are extremely adept at speech-reading, while others have very limited ability to "read lips". Sign language and/or finger spelling are the preferred means of communication for other students. Individuals who are deaf or hard of hearing rely upon visual input rather than auditory input when communicating. It is important for the teacher to make sure they have a deaf student's attention before speaking. Teachers can learn to communicate effectively with students who are deaf or hard of hearing, by using visual aspects of communication (body language, gestures, and facial expression).

COMPETENCY 3.0 **UNDERSTANDS HUMAN DIVERSITY, CREATE LEARNING OPPORTUNITIES AND ENVIRONMENTS THAT RESPOND TO DIFFERENCES AMONG STUDENTS, AND FOSTERS AN APPRECIATION OF AND RESPECT FOR DIVERSITY IN THE CLASSROOM AND IN THE COMMUNITY.**

Skill 3.1 **Demonstrates understanding of variations in beliefs, traditions, and values across cultures within society and the effects of the relationships among child, family, and schooling on behavior and learning.**

Effective teaching and learning for students begins with teachers who can demonstrate sensitivity for diversity in teaching and relationships within school communities. Student portfolios should include work that includes a multicultural perspective. Teachers also need to be responsive to including cultural and diverse resources in their curriculum and instructional practices.

Exposing students to culturally sensitive room decorations or posters that show positive and inclusive messages is one way to demonstrate inclusion of multiple cultures. Teachers should also continuously make cultural connections that are relevant and empowering for all students while communicating academic and behavioral expectations. Cultural sensitivity is communicated beyond the classroom with parents and community members to establish and maintain relationships.

Diversity can be further defined as the following:

- Differences among learners, classroom settings and academic outcomes
- Biological, sociological, ethnicity, socioeconomic status psychological needs, learning modalities and styles among learners
- Differences in classroom settings that promote learning opportunities such as collaborative, participatory, and individualized learning groupings
- Expected learning outcomes that are theoretical, affective and cognitive for students

Teachers should establish a classroom climate that is culturally respectful and engaging for students. In a culturally sensitive classroom, teachers maintain equity and fairness in student interactions and curriculum implementation. Assessments include cultural responses and perspectives that become further learning opportunities for students. Other artifacts that could reflect teacher/student sensitivity to diversity might consist of the following:

- Student portfolios reflecting multicultural/multiethnic perspectives
- Journals and reflections from field trips/ guest speakers from diverse cultural backgrounds
- Printed materials and wall displays from multicultural perspectives
- Parent/guardian letters in a variety of languages reflecting cultural diversity
- Projects that include cultural history and diverse inclusions
- Disaggregated student data reflecting cultural groups
- Classroom climate of professionalism that fosters diversity and cultural inclusion

The encouragement of diversity education allows teachers a variety of opportunities to expand their experiences with students, staff, community members and parents from culturally diverse backgrounds. These experiences can be proactively applied to promote cultural diversity inclusion in the classroom. Teachers are able to engage and challenge students to develop and incorporate their own diversity skills in building character and relationships with cultures beyond their own. In changing the thinking patterns of students to become more cultural inclusive in the 21st century, teachers are addressing the globalization of our world.

Skill 3.2   Demonstrates knowledge of cultural and community diversity through a well-grounded framework, and demonstrate understanding of how to learn about and incorporate students' experiences, cultures, and community resources into instruction.

The student's capacity and potential for academic success within the overall educational experience are products of her or his total environment: classroom and school system; home and family; neighborhood and community in general. All of these segments are interrelated and can be supportive, one of the other, or divisive, one against the other. As a matter of course, the teacher will become familiar with all aspects of the system, the school and the classroom pertinent to the students' educational experience. This would include not only process and protocols but also the availability of resources provided to meet the academic, health and welfare needs of students. But it is incumbent upon the teacher to look beyond the boundaries of the school system to identify additional resources as well as issues and situations which will effect (directly or indirectly) a student's ability to succeed in the classroom.

Examples of Resources

Libraries, museums, zoos, planetariums, etc.
Clubs, societies and civic organizations, community outreach programs of private businesses and corporations and of government agencies These programs can provide a variety of materials and media as well as possible speakers and presenters to help address diversity issues.

Departments of social services operating within the local community
These agencies can provide background and program information relevant to social issues which may be impacting individual students. This information can be used as a resource for classroom instruction regarding life skills, at-risk behaviors, etc.

Initial contacts for resources outside of the school system will usually come from within the system itself: from administration; teacher organizations; department heads; and other colleagues.

Examples of Issues/Situations

Students from multicultural backgrounds: Curriculum objectives and instructional strategies may be inappropriate and unsuccessful when presented in a single format which relies on the student's understanding and acceptance of the values and common attributes of a specific culture which is not his or her own.

Parental/family influences: Attitude, resources and encouragement available in the home environment may be attributes for success or failure.

Families with higher incomes are able to provide increased opportunities for students. Students from lower income families will need to depend on the resources available from the school system and the community. These resources should be orchestrated by the classroom teacher in cooperation with school administrators and educational advocates in the community.

Family members with higher levels of education often serve as models for students, and have high expectations for academic success. And families with specific aspirations for children (often, regardless of their own educational background) encourage students to achieve academic success, and are most often active participants in the process.

A family in crisis (caused by economic difficulties, divorce, substance abuse, physical abuse, etc.) creates a negative environment which may profoundly impact all aspects of a student's life, and particularly his or her ability to function academically. The situation may require professional intervention. It is often the classroom teacher who will recognize a family in a crisis situation and instigate an intervention by reporting this to school or civil authorities.

Regardless of the positive or negative impacts on the students' education from outside sources, it is the teacher's responsibility to ensure that all students in the classroom have an equal opportunity for academic success. This begins with the teacher's statement of high expectations for every student, and develops through planning, delivery and evaluation of instruction which provides for inclusion and ensures that all students have equal access to the resources necessary for successful acquisition of the academic skills being taught and measured in the classroom.

SEE also Skill 3.3

Skill 3.3 **Recognizes personal attitudes and biases that affect acceptance of individuals with disabilities, individuals of differing gender and sexual orientation, and individuals with various cultural, racial, linguistic, religious, and socioeconomic backgrounds**

When diversity is promoted in learning environments and curriculum, both students and teachers are the beneficiaries of increased academic success. Using classrooms as vital resources for cultural and ethnic inclusion can assist students in contributing cultural norms and artifacts to the acquisition of learning. Teachers who are able to create global thinkers are helping students identify cultural assumptions and biases that may direct the type of social and academic groupings. These groupings are occurring in the classroom and influence the type of thinking and ability of students to construct appropriate learning experiences. For example, if a student is struggling in math, a teacher can examine the cultural aspect of learning math. For some students, math is insignificant when socioeconomic issues of poverty and survival are the daily reality of existence. When students see parents juggling finances, the only math that becomes important for them is that less is never enough to keep the lights on and mortgage paid.

When there is equity in pedagogy, teachers are able to use a variety of instructional styles to facilitate diversity in both cooperative learning and individualized instruction that will provide more opportunities for positive student experiences and lead to future academic success. Empowering the school culture and climate by establishing an anti-bias learning environment as well as promoting multicultural learning activities will discourage disproportional and unfair labeling of certain students.

Teachers can use various toolkits to evaluate the ethnic and cultural inclusion in classroom. Effective promotion of diversity should translate into increased academic success and opportunities for all students. Looking at diverse or homogenous groupings in the classroom can provide teachers with opportunities to restructure cooperative learning groupings and increase diverse student interactions, which can provide increased improvements for school communities.

Using culture grams to help students understand different cultures and research cultural diversity is a useful tool for helping teachers profile students' learning styles and engagement in the classroom. Students can also use technology to network and learn how students in other cultures or other states learn. The ability to communicate with other learners provides another way of compiling and categorizing cultural profiles that may assist teachers in identifying learning styles and how students acquire learning. An interesting aspect of using culture grams is the manner in which it helps students connect to other cultures and their perceptions of students who identify with different cultures.

SEE also Skill 11.2

Skill 3.4 **Identifies a variety of instructional approaches that promote social interaction between students with disabilities and students without disabilities.**

Per federal law, students with disabilities should be included as much as possible in the general education curriculum of their schools. While this may be difficult for new teachers (likewise, it may be difficult for new teachers to include gifted students in the general education curriculum), it is extremely important to do so.

Flexible grouping is a unique strategy to ensure that students with special needs are fully accommodated. While flexible grouping can indeed involve groups for various learning activities that will change (depending on the activity, or just depending on the need to rotate groups), when teachers consistently build in various group structures in order to accommodate various learning needs, their students will get varied and multiple opportunities to talk about, reflect upon, and question new learning. In some cases, teachers may wish to pair students with special needs with other students who are proficient in particular subjects; at other times, they may desire to pair students with others who have similar levels of proficiency.

Behavior issues often cause students with special needs to be excluded from full class participation. It is important for teachers to note that often, students with special needs do not want to be excluded, and often, they do not want to be "bad." Rather, they are seeking attention, or they are bored. In either case, classroom activities must be developed with these concerns in mind. All students, in fact, will be more engaged with hands-on, real-world learning activities. Often, when teachers give students even small amounts of choice, such as letting them choose one of three topics to write about, students feel empowered. Students with special needs are no different.

Finally, many students with special needs want to stay "caught up" with the rest of the class, but occasionally, they cannot. In such cases, it is imperative that teachers find ways that will allow these students to know that they are on the same page as the rest of the class. Reducing the amount of work for students with special needs is often productive; pairing such students with more proficient students can also be assistive.

Students with exceptional abilities can be a great challenge for teachers. It is very unfair to assume that since these students already "get it" that they can be ignored. These students need to continue to learn, even if it is above and beyond the rest of the class. Furthermore, they will often resent being so much smarter than the rest of the class because they are "called on" more or they are treated as if they do not need any attention. First, while these students are a fantastic resource for the rest of the class, being a resource is not their role in the classroom. They are there to learn, just like the rest of the class. They occasionally need different work to engage them and stimulate their minds. They do not simply need more work; this is unfair to them, and it is insulting.

Strategies and Resources

Special education teachers, resource specialists, school psychologists, and other special education staff are present on school campuses to be resources for students who have special educational needs. Occasionally, new teachers fear that when a resource specialist seeks to work with them, it means that the resource specialist does not think they are doing an adequate job in dealing with students with IEPs. Quite the contrary is true. Many IEPs require that resource specialists work in students' general education classrooms. Indeed, the law for special education ("IDEA") states that students should receive education in the "least restrictive environment." This means that if a student can function in a regular education classroom, even if the assistance of a specialist is required, the student should be in that regular education classroom. Considering that school is more than just about the learning of content standards—that it is often about socialization and the development of citizens for a democratic society—it is both counterproductive and unfair to exclude students from regular classrooms, even if they need some individualized assistance from a special education resource teacher.

First and foremost, teachers must be familiar with what is stated in their students' IEPs. For example, some IEPs have explicit strategies that teachers should use to help the students learn effectively. Additionally, teachers may want to provide additional attention to these students to ensure that they are progressing effectively. Sometimes, it may be necessary to reduce or modify assignments for students with disabilities. For example, if a teacher were to assign fifteen math problems for homework for most students, the assignment might be more effective if it is five problems for the students with disabilities. Teachers can use multiple strategies, group students in flexible situations, and pair them with others who can be of greater assistance.

Finally, welcome and include the suggestions and assistance of the special education staff. Most resource specialists are trained particularly to work with general education teachers, and most want to be able to do that in the most effective, non-threatening way.

Skill 3.5 **Demonstrates knowledge of strategies for facilitating a learning community in which individual differences of students and their families are respected, regardless of race, culture, religion, gender, sexual orientation, socioeconomic background, and/or varying abilities.**

A positive environment, where open, discussion-oriented, non-threatening communication among all students can occur, is a critical factor in creating an effective learning culture. The teacher must take the lead and model appropriate actions and speech, while intervening quickly when a student makes a misstep and offends (often inadvertently) another.

Communication issues that the teacher in a diverse classroom should be aware of include:

- Being sensitive to terminology and language patterns that may exclude or demean students. Regularly switch between the use of "he" and "she" in speech and writing. Know and use the current terms that ethnic and cultural groups use to identify themselves (e.g., "Latinos" (favored) vs. "Hispanics").
- Being aware of body language that is intimidating or offensive to some cultures, such as direct eye contact, and adjust accordingly.
- Monitoring your own reactions to students to ensure equal responses to males and females, as well as differently-performing students.
- Don't "protect" students from criticism because of their ethnicity or gender. Likewise, acknowledge and praise all meritorious work without singling out any one student. Both actions can make all students hyper-aware of ethnic and gender differences and cause anxiety or resentment throughout the class.

- Emphasize the importance of discussing and considering different viewpoints and opinions. Demonstrate and express value for all opinions and comments and lead students to do the same

When teaching in diverse classrooms, teachers must also expect to be working and communicating with all kinds of students. The first obvious difference among students is gender. Interactions with male students are often different than those with female students. Depending on the lesson, female students are more likely to be interested in working with partners or perhaps even individually. On the other hand, male students may enjoy a more collaborative or hands-on activity. The gender of the teacher may also come into play when working with male and female students. Of course, every student is different and may not fit into a stereotypical role, and getting to know their students' preferences for learning will help teachers to truly enhance learning in the classroom.

Most class rosters will consist of students from a variety of cultures, as well. Teachers should get to know their students (of all cultures) so that they may incorporate elements of their cultures into classroom activities and planning. Also, getting to know about a student's background/cultural traditions helps to build a rapport with each student, as well as further educate the teacher about the world in which he or she teaches.

See Skill 3.5 for more information about a culturally diverse classroom.

For students still learning English, teachers must make every attempt to communicate with that student daily. Whether it's with another student who speaks the same language, word cards, computer programs, drawings or other methods, teachers must find ways to encourage each student's participation. Of course, the teacher must also be sure the appropriate language services begin for the student in a timely manner, as well.

Teachers must also consider students from various socioeconomic backgrounds. These students are just as likely as anyone else to work well in a classroom; unfortunately, sometimes difficulties occur with these children when it comes to completing homework consistently. These students may need help deriving a homework system or perhaps need more attention on study or test-taking skills. Teachers should encourage these students as much as possible and offer positive reinforcements when they meet or exceed classroom expectations. Teachers should also watch these students carefully for signs of malnutrition, fatigue or possible learning disorders.

COMPETENCY 4.0 **UNDERSTANDS ASSESSMENT AND USES A VARIETY OF ASSESSMENT STRATEGIES TO EVALUATE STUDENTS' DEVELOPMENT AND LEARNING, MONITOR PROGRESS, AND GUIDE TEACHING DECISIONS.**

Skill 4.1 **Demonstrates understanding of assessment as an educational process; measurement theory and assessment-related issues such as validity, reliability, bias, and scoring; the purposes, characteristics, strengths, and limitations of different kinds of assessments; and terminology used in assessments.**

Purposes for Assessment
There are a number of different classification systems used to identify the various purposes for assessment. A compilation of several lists identifies some common purposes such as the following:

1. Diagnostic assessments are used to determine individual weakness and strengths in specific areas.
2. Readiness assessments measure prerequisite knowledge and skills.
3. Interest and Attitude assessments attempt to identify topics of high
4. interest or areas in which students may need extra motivational activities.
5. Evaluation assessments are generally program or teacher focused and help to determine progress made.
6. Placement assessments are used for purposes of grouping students or determining appropriate beginning levels in leveled materials.
7. Formative assessments provide on-going feedback on student progress and the success of instructional methods and materials.
8. Summative assessments define student accomplishment with the intent to determine the degree of student mastery or learning that has taken place.

For most teachers, assessment purposes vary according to the situation. It may be helpful to consult several sources to help formulate an overall assessment plan. Kellough and Roberts (1991) identify six purposes for assessment. These are:

1. To evaluate and improve student learning
2. To identify student strengths and weaknesses
3. To assess the effectiveness of a particular instructional strategy
4. To evaluate and improve program effectiveness
5. To evaluate and improve teacher effectiveness
6. To communicate to parents their children's progress

Validity and Reliability

A desirable assessment is both reliable and valid. Without adequate reliability and validity, an assessment provides unusable results. A reliable assessment provides accurate and consistent results; there is little error from one time it is given to the next. A valid assessment is one which tests what it intends to test.

Reliability can be sometimes described by a correlation. A perfect positive correlation equals + 1.00 and a perfect negative correlation equals -1.00. The reliability of an assessment tool is generally expressed as a decimal to two places (e.g. 0.85). This decimal number describes the correlation that would be expected between two scores if the same student took the test two times.

Actually, there are several ways to estimate the reliability of an instrument. The method which is conceptually the most clear is the test-retest method. When the same test is administered again to the same students, if the test is perfectly reliable, each student will receive the same score each time. Even as the scores of individual students vary some from one time to the next, it is desirable for the rank order of the students to remain unchanged. Other methods of estimating reliability operate off of the same conceptual framework.

Split-half methods divide a single test into two parts and compare them. Equivalent form methods use two versions of the same test and compare results. With some types of assessment, such as essays and observation reports, reliability concerns also deal with the procedures and criteria used for scoring. The inter-rater reliability asks the question: How much will the results vary depending on who is scoring or rating the assessment data?

There are three commonly described types of validity: content validity, criterion validity, and construct validity. Content validity describes the degree to which the assessment actually measures the skills it was designed to measure, say, arithmetic. Story problems on an arithmetic test will lower its validity as a measure of arithmetic since reading ability will also be reflected in the results. However, note that it remains a valid test of the ability to solve story problems.

Criterion validity is so named because of the concern with the test's ability to predict performance on another measure or test. For example, a college admissions test is highly valid if it predicts very accurately those students who will attain high GPAs at that college. The criterion in this case is college GPA.

Construct validity is concerned with describing the usefulness or reality of what is being tested. The recent interest in multiple intelligences, instead of a single IQ score, is an example of the older construct of intelligence being reexamined as potentially several distinct constructs.

See also Skill 4.2

Skill 4.2   Demonstrates knowledge of how to select, construct, and use a variety of formal and informal assessment instruments, technologies, and strategies, including self-assessment, to diagnose and evaluate students' learning needs and progress, align and modify instruction, design and evaluate teaching strategies, and match the purposes of assessment.

Examples of Formal Assessments

Norm-referenced Assessments

Norm-referenced tests (NRT) are used to classify student learners for homogenous groupings based on ability levels or basic skills into a ranking category. In many school communities, NRTs are used to classify students into AP (Advanced Placement), honors, regular or remedial classes that can significantly impact student future educational opportunities or success. NRTs are also used by national testing companies such as Iowa Test of Basic Skills (Riverside), Florida Achievement Test (McGraw-Hill) and other major test publishers to test a national sample of students which are used to develop norms against standard test-takers. Stiggins (1994) states "Norm-referenced tests (NRT) are designed to highlight achievement differences between and among students to produce a dependable rank order of students across a continuum of achievement from high achievers to low achievers."

Educators may use the information from NRTs to provide students with academic learning that accelerates student skills from the basic level to higher skill applications and thereby able to meet the requirements of state assessments and/or core subject expectations. NRT ranking ranges from 1-99 with 25% of students scoring in the lower ranking of 1-25 and 25% of students scoring in the higher ranking of 76-99. Florida uses a variety of NRTs for student assessments that range from Iowa Basic Skills Testing to California Battery Achievement testing to measure student learning in reading and math.

Criterion-referenced Assessments

Criterion-referenced assessments examine specific student learning goals and performance compared to a norm group of student learners. According to Bond (1996) "Educators or policy makers may choose to use a Criterion-referenced test (CRT) when they wish to see how well students have learned the knowledge and skills which they are expected to have mastered." Many school districts and state legislation use CRTs to ascertain whether schools are meeting national and state learning standards. The latest national educational mandate of "No Child Left Behind" (NCLB) and Adequate Yearly Progress (AYP) use CRTs to measure student learning, school performance, and school improvement goals as structured accountability expectations in school communities. CRTs are generally used in learning environments to reflect the effectiveness of curriculum implementation and learning outcomes.

Performance-based Assessments

Performance-based assessments are currently being used in a number of state testing programs to measure the learning outcomes of individual students in subject content areas. Washington state uses performance-based assessments for the WASL (Washington Assessment of Student Learning) in reading, writing, math and science to measure student-learning performance. Attaching a graduation requirement to passing the required state assessment for the class of 2008 has created high-stakes testing and educational accountability for both students and teachers in meeting the expected skill based requirements for 10th grade students taking the test.

In today's classrooms, performance-based assessments in core subject areas must have established and specific performance criteria that start with pre-testing in the subject area and maintaining of daily or weekly testing to gauge student progress toward learning goals and objectives. To understand a student's learning is to understand how a student processes information. Effective performance assessments will show the gaps or holes in student learning which allows for an intense concentration on providing fillers to bridge non-sequential learning gaps. Typical performance assessments include oral and written student work in the form of research papers, oral presentations, class projects, journals, student portfolio collections of work, and community service projects.

Examples of Informal Assessments

Anecdotal records
These are notes recorded by the teacher concerning an area of interest or concern with a particular student. These records should focus on observable behaviors and should be descriptive in nature. They should not include assumptions or speculations regarding effective areas such as motivation or interest. These records are usually compiled over a period of several days to several weeks.

Rating Scales & Checklists
These assessments are generally self-appraisal instruments completed by the students or observations-based instruments completed by the teacher. The focus of these is frequently on behavior or effective areas such as interest and motivation.

Portfolio Assessment
The use of student portfolios for some aspect of assessment has become quite common. The purpose, nature, and policies of portfolio assessment vary greatly from one setting to another. In general, though, a student's portfolio contains samples of work collected over an extended period of time. The nature of the subject, age of the student, and scope of the portfolio, all contribute to the specific mechanics of analyzing, synthesizing, and otherwise evaluating the portfolio contents.

In most cases, the student and teacher make joint decisions as to which work samples will go into the student's portfolios. A collection of work compiled over an extended time period allows teacher, student, and parents to view the student's progress from a unique perspective. Qualitative changes over time can be readily apparent from work samples. Such changes are sometimes difficult to establish with strictly quantitative records, such as those typical of the scores recorded in the teacher's grade book.

Questioning

One of the most frequently occurring forms of assessment in the classroom is oral questioning by the teacher. As the teacher questions the students, s/he collects a great deal of information about the degree of student learning and potential sources of confusing for the students. While questioning is often viewed as a component of instructional methodology, it is also a powerful assessment tool.

Tests

Tests and similar direct assessment methods represent the most easily identified types of assessment. Thorndike (1997) identifies three types of assessment instruments:

1. Standardized achievement tests
2. Assessment material packaged with curricular materials
3. Teacher-made assessment instruments

   - Pencil and paper test
   - Oral tests
   - Product evaluations
   - Performance tests
   - Effective measures

Kellough and Roberts (1991) take a slightly different perspective. They describe "three avenues for assessing student achievement:

- What the learner says
- What the learner does
- What the learner writes..."

Types of Tests

Formal tests are those tests that have been standardized using a large sample population. The process of standardization provides various comparative norms and scales for the assessment instrument.

The term <u>informal test</u> includes all other tests. Most publisher-provided tests and teacher-made tests are informal tests using this definition. Note clearly that an informal test is not necessarily unimportant. A teacher-made final exam, for example, is informal by definition simply because it has not been standardized.

Assessment Terminology

Assessment language has been deeply rooted in key terms such as the following:

- *Formative*-sets targets for student learning and creates an avenue to provide data on whether students are meeting the targets
- *Diagnostic testing*- is used to determine students; skill levels and current knowledge
- *Normative*-establishes rankings and comparatives of student performances against an established norm of achievement.
- *Alternative*-non-traditional method of helping students construct responses to problem-solving
- *Authentic*-real life assessments that are relevant and meaningful in a student's life. (For example, calculating a 20% discount on a Texas Instrument calculator, for a student learning math percentages creates a more personalized approach to learning).
- *Performance based*-judged according to pre-established standards
- *Traditional*-diversity of teacher assessments that either come with the textbooks or ones that are directly created from the textbooks.

Using Assessment to Adjust Instruction

Assessment skills should be an integral part of teacher training. Teachers need to: be able to monitor student learning using pre and post assessments of content areas; analyze assessment data in terms of individualized support for students and instructional practice for teachers; and design lesson plans that have measurable outcomes and definitive learning standards. Assessment information should be used to provide performance-based criteria and academic expectations for all students in evaluating whether students have learned the expected skills and content of the subject area.

For example in an Algebra I class, teachers can use assessment to see whether students have acquired enough prior knowledge to engage in the subject area. If the teacher provides students with a pre-assessment on algebraic expression and can then ascertain whether the lesson plan should be modified to include a pre-algebraic expression lesson unit to refresh student understanding of the content area, then the teacher can create if needed, quantifiable data to support the need of additional resources to support student learning. Once the teacher has taught the unit on algebraic expression, a post assessment test can be used to test student learning and a mastery exam can be used to test how well students understand and can apply the knowledge to the next unit of math content learning.

Teachers can use assessment data to inform and impact instructional practices by making inferences on teaching methods and gathering clues for student performance. By analyzing the various types of assessments, teachers can gather more definitive information on projected student academic performance. Instructional strategies for teachers would provide learning targets for student behavior, cognitive thinking skills, and processing skills that can be employed to diversify student learning opportunities.

SEE also Skill 4.6

Skill 4.3   **Demonstrates knowledge of appropriate methods and technologies for monitoring and analyzing changes in individual and group behavior and performance across settings, curricular areas, and activities; gathering background information regarding academic history; creating and maintaining useful and accurate records of students' work and performance; and communicating students' progress knowledgeably and responsibly to students, parents/guardians, and colleagues.**

Assessment is the key to providing differentiated and appropriate instruction to all students. Teachers should use a variety of assessment techniques to determine a student's existing knowledge and skills, as well as the needs. Depending on the age of the student and the subject matter under consideration, diagnosis of readiness may be accomplished through pre-test, checklists, teacher observation, or student self-report. Diagnosis serves two related purposes—to identify those students who are not ready for the new instruction, and to identify for each student what prerequisite knowledge is lacking.

Student assessment is an integral part of the teaching and learning process. Identifying student, teacher, or program weaknesses is only significant if the information so obtained is used to remedy the concerns. Lesson materials and lesson delivery must be evaluated to determine relevant prerequisite skills and abilities. The teacher must be capable of determining whether a student's difficulties lie with the new information or with a lack of significant prior knowledge. The ultimate goal of any diagnostic or assessment endeavor is improved learning. Thus, instruction is adapted to the needs of the learner based on assessment information.

As is the case with purposes of assessment, there are a number of lists identifying principles of assessment. Linn and Gronlund (1995) identify five principles of assessment.

1. Clearly specifying what is to be assessed has priority in the assessment process
2. An assessment procedure should be selected because of its relevance to the characteristics or performance to be measured
3. Comprehensive assessment requires a variety of procedures
4. Proper use of assessment procedures requires an awareness of their limitations
5. Assessment is a means to an end, not an end in itself

Stiggins (1997) introduces seven guiding principles for classroom assessment.

1. Assessments require clear thinking and effective communication.
2. Classroom assessment is key.
3. Students are assessment users.
4. Clear and appropriate targets are essential.
5. High-quality assessment is a must.
6. Understand personal implication
7. Assessment as teaching and learning.

Skill 4.4 Demonstrates knowledge of nondiscriminatory assessment strategies and instruments that take into consideration the effect of disabilities, methods of communication, cultural background, and primary language on measuring knowledge and performance of students

Assessments can be discriminatory—or biased—when they rely on cultural knowledge and heavy language descriptions (when the assessment is not on language). As an example, let us consider that to answer correctly a question on a reading comprehension test, a student would have to know something about American culture. If a student is not native to this country, the reading comprehension score would be biased against the student. Alternatively, an English Language Learner may be very good at math. On a math test that over-utilizes specific, detailed directions simply to complete various problems, the student may not be able to demonstrate her or his math skill.

Generally, there are three ways in which assessments can become nondiscriminatory:

1. Compare assessment results with results from multiple assessments of different styles. Perhaps one assessment is slightly biased. Teachers, schools, and districts should not make decisions on one assessment alone. It is entirely possible that with all best intentions, an assessment that is biased may never be realized as such. Therefore, it is simply better practice to use multiple types of assessments to get a more complete picture.

2. Scaffold informal assessments (as opposed to official, state- or district-mandated assessments) so that students can understand exactly what is being asked of them.

3. Design assessments that consider the learning objective as closely as possible, with as little superfluous information as necessary. This way, assessments will test exactly what a student knows in regard to the material, rather than confounding an understanding of the student's skill or knowledge with unrelated concerns.

Skill 4.5   Applies strategies for modifying and adapting formal tests, including accommodations and modifications of national, state, and local assessments and the Illinois Alternative Assessment

Formal tests, used for classroom purposes (as opposed to national, state, and local assessments) can be adapted and modified for students with disabilities. Such information typically is included in a student's Individualized Education Plan. Furthermore, specific details about how tests should be modified for students with disabilities should be obtained from the special education teacher. Yet, in general, a variety of strategies for modification exist. Some are described below:

- Extending test period. Many students can perform well on assessments, provided they have extended time. Usually, such time can be provided in other class times, before or after the school day, or during enrichment periods.

- Reducing test questions. Some students can still demonstrate proficiency on fewer questions or problems.

- Providing support. Some students need the support of a classroom aide, technology, or a peer in order to convey knowledge.

- Presentation modification. Often, some students need assessments provided to them in alternative ways so that they can understand the assessments better.

- Setting modification. Some settings, such as large classrooms, may be distracting to some students. Therefore, alternative rooms may be necessary for some students.

- Response modification. The ways in which students with disabilities can effectively respond and demonstrate capacity may vary, therefore, formats for responding may very considerably.

Accommodations may be given for official state, national, or local assessments, however, such accommodates must be approved and/or documented. The types of modifications above may be listed directly on a student's Individualized Education Plan. Consult with that plan, the special education teacher, and the district testing coordinator before making any accommodations for an official assessment.

Skill 4.6   Develops individualized assessment strategies for instruction

Alternative Assessments

Alternative assessment is an assessment where students create an answer or a response to a question or task. This is as opposed to traditional, inflexible assessments where students choose a prepared response from among a selection of responses, such as matching, multiple-choice or true/false.

When implemented effectively, an alternative assessment approach will exhibit these characteristics, among others:

- Requires higher-order thinking and problem-solving
- Provides opportunities for student self-reflection and self-assessment
- Uses real world applications to connect students to the subject
- Provides opportunities for students to learn and examine subjects on their own, as well as to collaborate with their peers.
- Encourages students to continuing learning beyond the requirements of the assignment
- Clearly defines objective and performance goals

Teachers realize the value of giving assignments that meet the individual abilities and needs of students. After instruction, discussion, questioning, and practice have been provided, rather than assigning one task to all students—teachers are asking students to generate tasks that will show their knowledge of the information presented. Students are given choices and thereby have the opportunity to demonstrate more effectively the skills, concepts, or topics that they as individuals have learned. It has been established that student choice increases student originality, intrinsic motivation, and higher mental processes.

Rubrics

Subjective tests put the student in the driver's seat. These types of assessments usually consist of short answer, longer essays or problem solving that requires more critical thinking skills. Sometimes teachers provide rubrics that include assessment criteria for high scoring answers and projects. Sometimes, the rubric is as simple as a checklist, and other times, a maximum point value is awarded for each item on the rubric. Either way, rubrics provide a guideline of the teacher's expectations for the specifics of the assignment. The teacher usually discusses and/or models what is expected to fulfill each guideline, as well as provides a detailed outline of these expectations for reference.

For example, students being asked to write a research paper might be provided with a rubric. An elementary teacher may assign a total of 50 points for the entire paper. The rubric may award ten points for note taking quality, ten points for research skills, twenty points for content covered, five points for creative elements, and five points for organization and presentation. Then a certain number of points will be awarded in accordance with the students' performance. Rubrics allow students to be scored in multiple areas, rather than simply on a final product.

The bottom line is studying and preparing for any type of tests will equate to better student performance and achievement on tests. In addition, as teachers evaluate the students' work, they are able to see each student's strengths and weaknesses. This information allows teachers to differentiate instruction for each student in order to maximize their learning.

| Skill 4.7 | Demonstrates understanding of how to interpret information obtained from formal and informal assessment instruments and procedures (e.g., age/grade scores, stanines, standard error of measurement), teachers, other professionals, students with disabilities, and parents/guardians to design instruction that meets learners' current needs in the cognitive, social, emotional, ethical, and physical domains at the appropriate level of development. |

SEE also Skill 4.2 and 4.3

The degree to which the classroom teacher has control over the curriculum varies from setting to setting. Some schools have precisely defined curriculum plans and teachers are required to implement the instruction accordingly. A more common occurrence is that the textbooks become the default curriculum. A fourth-grade arithmetic book, for example, defines what must be taught in the fourth grade so that the fifth-grade teacher can continue the established sequence.

Whatever the source of limitations and requirements, the classroom teacher always has some control over the method of instructional delivery and the use of supplemental materials and procedures. The teacher is responsible for implementing the formal curricula and for providing necessary scaffolding to enhance student learning. Since the basic element of educational structure is time, the teacher must distribute the necessary learning activities over the available amount of time. The teacher can do this by: creating an overview of what material is to be presented, the total amount of time available (whether for the school year, grading period, unit, etc.), the relative importance of the components of the material, and the students' prior knowledge of portions of the material.

Interpreting Assessments

The information contained within student records, teacher observations and diagnostic tests are only as valuable as the teacher's ability to understand it. Although the student's cumulative record will contain this information, it is the responsibility of each teacher to read and interpret the information. Diagnostic test results are somewhat uniform and easy to interpret. They usually include a scoring guide that tells the teacher what the numbers actually mean. Teachers also need to realize that these number scores leave room for uncontrollable factor and are not the ultimate indicator of a child's ability or learning needs. Many factors influence these scores including the rapport the child had with the tester, how the child was feeling when the test was administered, and how the child regarded the value or importance of the test. Therefore, the teacher should regard these scores as a "ball park" figure.

When a teacher reads another teacher's observations, it is important to keep in mind that each person brings to an observation certain biases. The reader may also influence the information contained within an observation with his/her own interpretation. When using teacher observations as a basis for designing learning programs, it is necessary to be aware of these shortcomings.

Student records may provide the most assistance in guiding instruction. These records contain information that was gathered over a period of time and may show student growth and progress. They also contain information provided by several people including teachers, parents, and other educational professionals. By reading this compilation of information the teacher may get a more accurate "feel for" a student's needs. All of this information is only a stepping-stone in determining how a child learns, what a child knows, and what a child needs to know to further his/her education.

Communicating with Students

How can a teacher provide appropriate feedback so that students will be able to learn from their assessments? First, language should be helpful and constructive. Critical language does not necessarily help students learn. They may become defensive or hurt, and therefore, they may be more focused on the perceptions than the content. Language that is constructive and helpful will guide students to specific actions and recommendations that would help them improve in the future.

When teachers provide timely feedback, they increase the chance that students will reflect on their thought-processes as they originally produced the work. When feedback comes weeks after the production of an assignment, the student may not remember what it is that caused him or her to respond in a particular way.

Specific feedback is particularly important. Comments like, "This should be clearer" and "Your grammar needs to be worked on" provide information that students may already know. They may already know they have a problem with clarity. Commentary that provides very specific actions students could take to make something more clear or to improve his or her grammar is more beneficial to the student.

SEE also Skill 6.3

Communicating with Parents/Guardians

The major questions for parents in understanding student performance criterion-referenced data assessment are, "Are students learning?" and "How well are students learning?" Providing parents with a collection of student learning assessment data related to student achievement and performance is a quantifiable response to the questions.

The National Study of School Evaluation (NSSE) 1997 research on School Improvement: Focusing on Student performance adds the following additional questions for parent focus on student learning outcomes:

- What are the types of assessments of student learning that are used in the school?

- What do the results of the data assessments indicate about the current levels of student learning performance? About future predictions? What were the learning objectives and goals?
- What are the strengths and limitations in student learning and achievement?
- How prepared are students for further education or promotion to the next level of education?
- What are the trends seen in student learning in various subject areas or overall academic learning?

Providing parents with opportunities to attend workshops on data discussions with teachers and administrators creates additional opportunity for parents to ask questions and become actively involved in monitoring their child's educational progress. With state assessments, parents should look for the words "passed" or "met/exceeded standards" in interpreting the numerical data on student reports. Parents who maintain an active involvement in their students' education will attend school opportunities to promote their understanding of academic and educational achievement for students.

Communicating with Colleagues

As students leave a teacher's classroom, an accurate and updated file of information should follow them. The student permanent record is a file of the student's cumulative educational history. It contains a profile of the student's academic background as well as the student's behavioral and medical background. Other pertinent individual information contained in the permanent record includes the student's attendance, grade averages, and schools attended. Personal information such as parents' names and addresses, immunization records, child's height and weight, and narrative information about the child's progress and physical and mental well being is an important aspect of the permanent record. All information contained within the permanent record is strictly confidential and is only to be discussed with the student's parents or other involved school personnel.

The purpose of the permanent record is to provide applicable information about the student so that the student's individual educational needs can be met. If any specialized testing has been administered, the results are noted in the permanent record. Any special requirements that the student may have are indicated in the permanent record. Highly personal information, including court orders regarding custody, is filed in the permanent record as is appropriate. The importance and value of the permanent record cannot be underestimated. It offers a comprehensive knowledge of the student.

The current teacher is responsible for maintaining the student's permanent record. All substantive information in regard to testing, academic performance, the student's medical condition, and personal events are placed in the permanent record file. Updated information in regard to the student's grades, attendance, and behavior is added annually. These files are kept in a locked fireproof room or file cabinet and cannot be removed from this room unless the person removing them signs a form acknowledging full responsibility for the safe return of the complete file. Again, only the student's parents (or legal guardians), the teacher or other concerned school personnel may view the contents of the permanent record file.

The permanent record file follows the student as he/she moves through the school system with information being added and updated along the way. Anytime the student leaves a school, the permanent record is transferred with the student. The permanent record is regarded as legal documentation of a student's educational experience.

Students with Disabilities
Teachers should be aware of the concerns of parents of students with disabilities, and should be able to provide knowledge of various strategies in addressing these concerns. Teachers should know how to select, construct, and use assessment strategies and instruments for diagnosis and evaluation of students with disabilities. If needed, teachers should implement IEP goals and objectives to plan instruction for students with disabilities, and then apply these methods for monitoring progress of individuals with disabilities. Teachers should also know legal provisions, regulations, and guidelines regarding assessment (and inclusion in statewide assessments) of individuals with disabilities.

SUBAREA II   **PLANNING AND DELIVERING INSTRUCTION**

COMPETENCY 5.0   **UNDERSTANDS THE USE OF INSTRUCTIONAL PLANNING PROCESSES TO DESIGN EFFECTIVE, MEANINGFUL, INTEGRATED, AND DEVELOPMENTALLY APPROPRIATE LEARNING EXPERIENCES THAT FACILITATE ACHIEVEMENT OF INDIVIDUAL AND GROUP GOALS.**

Skill 5.1   **Identifies learning materials and experiences that are chronologically age appropriate; developmentally and functionally valid; appropriate for the discipline and curriculum goals; interdisciplinary; relevant to students' prior knowledge; responsive to students' learning styles, strengths, and needs; reflective of the principles of effective instruction; and supported by research and that have been evaluated for comprehensiveness, accuracy, and usefulness.**

Teaching was once seen as simply developing lesson plans, teaching, going home early and taking the summer off. However, the demands of a classroom involve much more than grading papers. To begin with, writing lesson plans is very complicated. Lesson plans are crucial in guiding instruction within the classroom. The lesson plan outlines the steps a teacher will implement and what forms of assessment will be used in both an instructional learning capacity. Teachers are able to both objectify and quantify learning goals and targets through the incorporating of effective performance-based assessments as well as the projected criteria for identifying when a student has learned the material presented.

All components of a lesson plan including the unit description, learning targets, learning experiences, explanation of learning rationale and assessments must be present to provide both quantifiable and qualitative data. These two data sources help the teacher to ascertain whether student learning has taken place and whether effective teaching has occurred for the students. National and state learning standards must be considered because not only will she and her students be measured by the students' scores at the end of the year, the school will also. So, not only must the teacher be knowledgeable about state and local standards, she must structure her own classes in ways that will satisfy those frameworks.

On the large scale, the teacher must think about the scope of her ambitious plans for the day, the week, the unit, the semester, the year. The teacher must also decide on the subject matter for the unit, semester, year, making certain that it is appropriate to the age of the students, relevant to their real lives, and in their realm of anticipated interest. Should politically controversial issues be introduced or avoided? S/he must make these decisions deliberatively on the basis of feedback from the students, while at the same time keeping sight of the objectives.

The teacher must be very knowledgeable about the writing of behavioral objectives which fall within the guidelines of both the state and local expectations; additionally, the objectives must be measurable so he can know for sure whether he has accomplished what he set out to do.

Once long range goals have been identified and established, it is important to ensure that all goals and objectives are also in conjunction with student ability and needs. Some objectives may be too basic for a higher level student, while others cannot be met with a student's current level of knowledge. There are many forms of evaluating student needs to ensure that all goals set are challenging yet achievable.

Teachers should check a student's cumulative file for reading level and prior subject area achievement. This provides a basis for goal setting but shouldn't be the only method used. Depending on the subject area, basic skills test, reading level evaluations, writing samples, and/or interest surveys can all be useful in determining if all goals are appropriate. Informal observation should always be used as well. Finally, it is important to take into consideration the student's level of motivation when addressing student needs.

There are a number of procedures teachers can use to address the varying need of the students. Some of the more common procedures are:

1. Vary assignments
A variety of assignments on the same content allows students to match learning styles and preferences with the assignment. If all assignments are writing assignments, for example, students who are hands-on or visual learners are at a disadvantage unrelated to the content base itself.

2. Cooperative learning
Cooperative learning activities allow students to share ideas, expertise, and insight within a non-threatening setting. The focus tends to remain on positive learning rather than on competition.

3. Structure environment

Some students need and benefit from clear structure that defines the expectation and goals of the teacher. The student clearly understands expectations and can work and plan accordingly.

4. Clearly stated assignments

Assignments should be clearly stated along with the expectation and criteria for completion. Reinforcement and practice activities should not be a guessing game for the students. The exception to this is, of course, those situations in which a discovery method is used.

5. Independent practice

Independent practice involving application and repetition is necessary for thorough learning. Students learn to be independent learners through practicing independent learning. These activities should always be within the student's abilities to perform successfully without assistance.

6. Repetition

Very little learning is successful with a single exposure. Learners generally require multiple exposures to the same information for learning to take place. However, this repetition does not have to be dull and monotonous. Varied assignments can provide repetition of content or skill practiced without repetition of specific activities. This helps keep learning fresh and exciting for the student.

Appropriate instructional strategies

No two students are alike. It follows, then, that no students *learn* alike. To apply a one dimensional instructional approach and a strict tunnel vision perspective of testing is to impose learning limits on students. All students have the right to an education, but there cannot be a singular path to that education. A teacher must acknowledge the variety of learning styles and abilities among students within a class (and, indeed, the varieties from class to class) by applying multiple instructional and assessment processes to ensure every child has appropriate opportunities to master the subject matter, demonstrate such mastery, and improve and enhance learning skills with each lesson.

It is traditionally assumed a teacher will use direct instruction in the classroom. The amount of time devoted to it will vary according by the age of the class and other factors. Lecturing can be very valuable because it is the quickest way for transferring knowledge to students and as they also learn note-taking, the students are able to organize the new information. However, having said that, there are many cautions to using very much lecture in a class of any age. In the first place, attention span even of senior high-school students is short when they are using only one sense—the sense of hearing. Teachers should limit how much lecture they use and how long the lectures last.

Most teachers find students enjoy the learning process when lecturing is limited and the students themselves become active in and responsible for their own learning. Students' attitudes and perceptions about learning are the most powerful factors influencing academic focus and success. When instructional objectives center on students' interests and are relevant to their lives, effective learning occurs.

Learners must believe that the tasks that they are being asked to perform have some value and that they have both the ability and resources to perform them. If a student believes a task is unimportant, s/he will not put much effort into it. Additionally, if a student thinks he lacks the ability or resources to successfully complete a task, even attempting the task becomes too great a risk. Not only must the teacher understand the students' abilities and interests, s/he must also help students develop positive attitudes and perceptions about learning tasks.

For information on interdisciplinary instruction, **SEE** Skill 1.6
For information on prior knowledge and district goals, **SEE** Skill 5.4

Skill 5.2   **Demonstrates understanding of how to structure instruction and design learning tasks and assignments to reflect higher-level thinking skills; stimulate student reflection on prior knowledge; link new ideas to already familiar ideas and experiences; promote students' skills in the use of technologies; and reflect an expectation for students to intellectually access, evaluate, and use information to solve problems and make decisions in all subject areas.**

Teachers should have a toolkit of instructional strategies at their disposal. Various materials and technologies should be utilized to encourage problem solving and critical thinking about subject content. Within each curriculum chosen by a district comes an expectation that students must master both benchmarks and standards of various learning skills. There is an established level of academic performance and proficiency in public schools that students are required to master in today's classrooms.

A critical thinking skill is a skill target which teachers use to help students develop and sustain learning within specific subject areas and then can be applied to other subject areas. For example, when learning to understand algebraic concepts in solving a math word problem on how much fencing material is needed to build a fence around a backyard area that is 8' x 12', a math student must understand the order of numerical expression in how to simplify algebraic expressions.

Teachers can provide instructional strategies that show students how to group the fencing measurements into an algebraic word problem that with minor addition, subtraction and multiplication can produce a simple number equal to the amount of fencing materials needed to build the fence.

Students use basic skills to understand things that are read, such as a reading passage, a math word problem, or directions for a project. However, students apply additional thinking skills to fully comprehend how what was read could be applied to their own life, how to make comparatives, or what choices could be made based on the factual information given. These higher-order thinking skills are called critical thinking skills as students think about the thinking process, and teachers are instrumental in helping students use these skills in everyday activities. Examples of these types of skills may include:

- Analyzing bills for overcharges
- Comparing shopping ads or catalogue deals
- Finding the main idea from readings
- Applying what's been learned to new situations
- Gathering information/data from a diversity of sources to plan a project
- Following a sequence of directions
- Looking for cause and effect relationships
- Comparing and contrasting information in synthesizing information

Since most teachers want their educational objectives to use higher level thinking skills, teachers need to direct students toward these higher levels on a taxonomy, such as Bloom's. Questioning is an effective tool to help build students' skills to these higher levels.

Low order questions are useful to begin the process. They insure the student is focused on the required information and understands what needs to be included in the thinking process. For example, if the objective is for students to be able to read and understand the story *Goldilocks and the Three Bears*, the teacher may wish to begin with low order questions (i.e., "What are some things Goldilocks did while in the bears home?" [Knowledge] or "Why didn't Goldilocks like the Papa Bear's chair?" [Analysis]).

Through a series of questions, the teacher can move the students toward the top of the taxonomy. (For example, "If Goldilocks had come to your house, what are some things she may have used?" [Application], "How might the story differ if Goldilocks had visited the three fishes?" [Synthesis], or "Do you think Goldilocks was good or bad? Why?" [Evaluation]). Through questioning, the teacher can control the thinking process of the class. As students become more involved in the discussion they are systematically being lead toward higher levels of thinking.

Develop a plan for progression from directed to self-directed activity

Learning progresses in stages from initial acquisition, when the student requires a lot of teacher guidance and instruction, to adaptation, where the student is able to apply what s/he has learned to new situations outside of the classroom. As students progress through the stages of learning, the teacher gradually decreases the amount of direct instruction and guidance. The teacher is slowly encouraging the student to function more independently. The ultimate goal of the learning process is to teach students how to become independent and apply their knowledge. A summary of these states and their features appears here:

State	Teacher Activity	Emphasis
Initial Acquisition	Provide rationale Guidance Demonstration Modeling Shaping Cueing	Errorless learning Backward Chaining (working from the final product backward through the steps) Forward Chaining (proceeding through the steps to a final product)
Advanced Acquisition	Feedback Error correction Specific directions	Criterion evaluation Reinforcement and reward for accuracy
Proficiency	Positive reinforcement Progress monitoring Teach self-management Increased teacher expectations	Increase speed or performance to the automatic level with accuracy Set goals Self-management
Maintenance	Withdraw direct reinforcement Retention and memory Over learning Intermittent schedule of reinforcement	Maintain high level of performance Mnemonic techniques Social and intrinsic reinforcement
Generalization	Corrective feedback	Perform skill in different times and places
Adaptation	Stress independent problem-solving	Independent problem-solving methods No direct guidance or direct instruction

Considering Student Interest

Children are not blank slates. They bring the knowledge they have already accumulated regarding their worlds and the human beings who populate them. It is a wise teacher who explores that resource and makes use of it in his own planning and management of the classroom.

Students will bring their own **preconceptions** with them about many things. These usually come from their own parents' perceptions about the world and human beings, but they are also formed by the children themselves and are unique to each child. Getting to know the students well enough to understand some of those preconceptions will make for a more successful year.

In the teaching of new skills, guided practice is an important approach to the student's development and their ability to accept and incorporate these new concepts. For example, if second graders are learning to use the computer to access certain information from a website, the teacher will use guided practice to help them develop their skills and understanding of the computer and what it offers. In this case, drills and exercises will need to be developed ahead of time.

If students are to become critical thinkers, they must also be wise explorers. The more times they are successful at solving a problem, the further along they are in developing confidence in their own abilities to think and the more likely they are to be willing to explore and claim responsibility for their own thoughts, ideas, and conclusions. An important objective for any teacher, no matter the age of her students is for students to assume responsibility for their own ideas and behaviors.

Despite a teacher's best efforts to provide important and appropriate instruction, there may be times when a teacher is required to teach a concept, skill, or topic that students may perceive as trivial and irrelevant. These tasks can be effectively presented if the teacher exhibits a sense of enthusiasm and excitement about the content. Teachers can help spark the students' interest by providing anecdotes and interesting digressions. Research indicates that as teachers become significantly more enthusiastic, students exhibit increased on-task behavior.

Skill 5.3   **Demonstrates understanding of the principles and processes for creating short- and long-term plans consistent with curriculum goals, learner diversity, and learning theory to achieve expectations for students' learning.**

The first step in planning successful instruction is having a firm grasp on the ending objectives for which the students will be held accountable. While teachers may have the best of intentions in teaching numerous, exciting topics, there are only so many days in a school year. Furthermore, the more content that is "covered" (skimmed over, so that students can be exposed to everything), the less students will have deep and lasting understandings of content. So, with that in mind, teachers may benefit from laying out all crucial standards throughout the year and aligning them in a fashion that allows for conceptual growth. Conceptual growth refers to concepts building upon one another. Certain topics simply should be taught before other topics.

Next, teachers should consider how students will be required to demonstrate proficiency of the various concepts presented. This is important, as all instruction needs to focus on making sure that students can indeed demonstrate proficiency.

Finally, as lessons and units are planned, to be most efficient with time, teachers should determine how much students already understand about the topics being taught. This will help the teacher to determine how long the concept will take to fully teach. This will allow the teacher to develop lessons that build on students' background knowledge without requiring them to repeat it. It will also help teachers manage their ability to teach all of the required standards in a one year time period.

SEE also SKILL 5.1 for lesson planning information

Skill 5.4   **Recognizes effective strategies for using information about students' individual experiences, families, cultures, and communities as a basis for connecting instruction to students' experiences and enriching instruction.**

Effective planning is a key component of effective teaching. Planning is used to select the content and the methods that will aid students in mastering, and also to set the learning objectives. Some of the key elements that must be considered when planning instruction include the following:

- Goals
- Prior Experiences
- Readiness
- Planning Instruction
- Diverse Learners
- Time Resources

See below for additional clarification for each area.

Goals

SEE Skill 5.3

Prior Experiences

Students, their needs, including developmental and readiness levels, as well as prior knowledge, must be taken into account. The teacher must be aware of the background of the individual students. Their prior experiences in the educational setting should also be taken into account. This should include their family background, previous grades, test scores, strengths, weaknesses, and how their previous teacher's viewed them. Determining student needs is complicated by the fact that nearly all classrooms include a wide variety of developmental and ability levels, as well as students with other diverse special needs.

To determine the abilities of incoming students, it may be helpful to consult their prior academic records. Letter grades assigned at previous levels of instruction as well as scores on standardized tests may be taken into account. In addition, the teacher may choose to administer pre-tests at the beginning of the school year, and perhaps also at the initial stage of each new unit of instruction. The textbooks available for classroom use may provide suitable pre-tests, tests of student progress, and post-tests.

In selecting tests and other assessment tools, the teacher should keep in mind that different kinds of tests measure different aspects of student development. The tests included in most textbooks chosen for the classroom are usually achievement tests. Few of these are the type of tests intended to measure the students' inherent ability or aptitude. Teachers will find it difficult to raise students' scores based on ability tests, but students' scores on achievement tests may be expected to improve with proper instruction and application in the area being studied.

In addition to administering tests, the teacher may assess the readiness of students for a particular level of instruction by having them demonstrate their ability to perform some relevant task. In a class that emphasizes written composition, for example, students may be asked to submit writing samples. These may be used not only to assure the placement of the students into the proper level, but as a diagnostic tool to help them understand what aspects of their composition skills may need improvement. In the like manner, students in a speech class may be asked to make an impromptu oral presentation before beginning a new level or specific level of instruction. Others may be asked to demonstrate their psychomotor skills in a physical education class, display their computational skills in a mathematics class, and so on. Whatever the chosen task, the teacher will need to select or devise an appropriate assessment scale and interpret the results with care.

Readiness

The concept of readiness is generally regarded as a developmentally based phenomenon. Various abilities, whether cognitive, affective, or psychomotor, are perceived to be dependent upon the mastery or development of certain prerequisite skills or abilities. Readiness implies that the necessary prior knowledge, experience, and prerequisites have been achieved and teaching should not proceed to the new task until first acquiring the necessary readiness foundation.

However, at each grade level, there exist readiness expectations and assumptions based on the previous year's instruction. Students who have not yet mastered those concepts are not ready to progress. Failure on the part of the teacher to address student deficiencies may lead to failure of the student to learn the new material.

Readiness for subject area learning is dependent not only on prior knowledge, but also on affective factors such as interest, motivation, and attitude. These factors are often more influential on student learning than the pre-existing cognitive base. It should be noted, then, that a concept such as "readiness to learn" is too broad to be meaningful. Readiness needs to be considered in terms of readiness to "learn science" or, even more accurately, readiness to "learn photosynthesis." Since it is not feasible for the classroom teacher to assess each student's readiness for each lesson, mastery of one lesson is generally assumed to imply readiness for the next sequential lesson.

Planning Instruction
Once the teacher has a firm handle on his students' overall readiness, the teacher will understand which concepts need to be pre-taught, what vocabulary skills are needed (i.e., before beginning a class novel or textbook chapter), and how to adjust instruction to meet the needs and interests of all the students.

Lesson plans should include a rationale that explains why a specific lesson is necessary or important. A rationale helps to justify the need for teaching content to both the student and the parent's. This enables the student to see how the topic is relevant to them and helps to motivate the student.

When organizing and sequencing objectives the teacher needs to remember that skills are building blocks. A taxonomy of educational objectives can be helpful to construct and organize objectives. Knowledge of material, for example, memorizing definitions or famous quotes, is low on the taxonomy of learning and should be worked with early in the sequence of teaching.. Eventually, objectives should be developed to include higher level thinking such as comprehension (i.e., being able to use a definition); application (i.e., being able to apply the definition to other situations); synthesis (i.e., being able to add other information); and evaluation (i.e., being able to judge the value of something).

Diverse Learners

Designing classrooms that provide optimal academic and behavioral support for a diversity of students in the classroom can be daunting for teachers. The ultimate goal for both students and teachers is creating a safe learning environment where students can construct knowledge in an engaging and positive classroom climate of learning.

The racial, cultural, and ethnic breakdown of the community that students come from should be taken into account when planning lessons that will be directly applicable to a student in respective communities. In addition, cultural, ethnic, and economic diversity are also factors that influence content decisions. The teacher must ensure that different cultural and ethnic groups are addressed in the class especially when setting curriculum themes, topics, and subjects and how they are addressed. They must ensure that the themes are not culturally or ethnically insensitive or that certain cultures or left out of the lesson who may be a dominant or insignificant part of the class.

SEE also SKILL 1.3

Time Resources
As lessons and units are planned, to be most efficient with time, teachers should determine how much students already understand and how long the concept will take to fully teach. This will allow the teacher to develop lessons that build on students' background knowledge without repeating it. It will also help teachers manage getting in so many standards in a one year time period.

The school calendar and time constraints are factors that should be taken into account during planning. There is not enough time for all the different things that teachers need to do. It is important to establish priorities, about unit content and determine which topics to include, which to emphasize, and which to leave out. When planning instruction, teachers must take into account the amount of time available to teach a particular unit of instruction. They must ensure that the lesson can be completely understood and learned in the time allotted and make room for occasions when re-teaching or teaching in another style must take place when the majority of the class does not comprehend the lesson. The availability of resources and materials is a significant aspect as this can often limit the range of possibilities for instructional activities. The Internet can be used to locate resources that can be utilized in lesson planning.

Skill 5.5 **Demonstrates knowledge of how to take the contextual considerations of instructional materials, individual students' interests, and career needs into account in planning instruction that creates an effective bridge between students' experiences and career and educational goals.**

SEE Skills 1.6 and 14.4

COMPETENCY 6.0   UNDERSTANDS THAT THERE ARE MULTIPLE PATHS TO LEARNING, AND APPLIES KNOWLEDGE OF HOW TO ADAPT INSTRUCTION IN RESPONSE TO INDIVIDUAL STRENGTHS, NEEDS, AND INTERESTS TO PROMOTE ACHIEVEMENT FOR ALL STUDENTS.

Skill 6.1   Demonstrates understanding of techniques for modifying instructional methods, curricular materials, and the environment to meet learners' needs that are appropriate to those learners' ages and skill levels.

The effective teacher will seek to connect all students to the subject matter using multiple techniques. With the goal being that each student, through their own abilities, will relate to one or more techniques and excel in the learning process. While all students need to have exposure to the same curriculum, not all students need to have the curriculum taught in the same way. Differentiation is the term used to describe the variations of curriculum and instruction that can be provided to an entire class of students.

There are three primary ways to differentiate:

- Content – The specifics of what is learned. This does not mean that whole units or concepts should be modified. However, within certain topics, specifics can be modified.
- Process – The route to learning the content. This means that not everyone has to learn the content in exactly the same method.
- Product – The result of the learning. Usually, a product is the end result or assessment of learning. For example, not all students are going to demonstrate complete learning on a quiz; likewise, not all students will demonstrate complete learning on a written paper.

There are two keys to successful differentiation:

- Knowing what is essential in the curriculum. Although certain things can be modified, other things must remain in-tact in a specific order. Disrupting central components of a curriculum can actually damage a student's ability to learn something successfully.
- Knowing the needs of the students. While this can take quite some time to figure out, it is very important that teachers pay attention to the interests, tendencies, and abilities of their students so that they understand how each of their students will best learn.

Many students will need certain concepts explained in greater depth; others may pick up on concepts rather quickly. For this reason, teachers will want to adapt the curriculum in a way that allows students with the opportunity to learn at their own pace, while also keeping the class together as a community. While this can be difficult, the more creative a teacher is with the ways in which students can demonstrate mastery, the more fun the experience will be for students and teachers. Furthermore, teachers will reach students more successfully as they will tailor lesson plans, activities, groupings, and other elements of curriculum to each student's need.

Students with Special Needs

Most special needs students have an Individual Educational Plan or a 504 Plan. These documents clearly state the students' educational objectives and learning needs as well as persons responsible for meeting these objectives. A well-written Individual Educational Plan will contain evidence that the student is receiving resources from the school and the community that will assist in meeting the physical, social and academic needs of the student.

The challenges of meeting the needs of all students in the classroom require that the teacher himself be a lifelong learner. Ongoing participation in professional staff development, attendance at local, state, and national conferences, and continuing education classes help teachers grow in many ways including an awareness of resources available for students.

Skill 6.2 Demonstrates knowledge of methods for including student development factors when making instructional decisions.

Folk wisdom says that the minute people can stand to sit and do one thing typically equals their age. While this might not have any scientific validity, most kindergarten teachers would probably agree that, yes, six minutes is about all their students can handle!

The truth of the matter is that most people, young or old, have a hard time concentrating on difficult mental tasks for too long. For children, such things as learning to read or do math are mentally taxing, and too much of one activity at one time can be detrimental. Students will not focus, and the teacher will end up having to reteach the lesson.

Generally, in younger grades, activities should change every 15-30 minutes. In older grades, activities should change every 20-40 minutes. The reason for this is not to encourage short attention spans, but rather to encourage higher levels of intellectual focus for shorter periods of time which can increase both retention and engagement.

It is important, however, for teachers in the younger grades to gradually increase the amount of time spent on reading or writing. In the younger grades, students will struggle to stay focused on a text, for example, simply because they have never been required to do such an activity. Their eyes in particular may get very tired. In writing, as well, hands and eyes will tire quickly, so gradual increases of time spent on these activities is a good idea. Over time, students will be able to handle more and more.

So, when designing and implementing lessons, it is crucial for teachers to develop multiple activities on the same content. For example, in a one hour period to cover a reading lesson, a teacher can have a whole class discussion, have students write independently, spend time reading aloud, have students read quietly, and then have students do an activity with the text. Not only will this change of activity keep students' attention, it will provide them with unique ways to think about, integrate, and learn the material.

Skill 6.3 Demonstrates understanding of how to develop and adjust plans and strategies based on students' responses and provide for different pathways based on students' needs.

Student learning is an intricate, multi-faceted process. Teachers instruct based upon their students' background knowledge. The first step teachers may take in approaching a new topic or skill is to simply ask the students what they already know and list their responses. This will provide the teacher with a beginning point from which they can build instruction. The next step will include the teacher's delivery of the topic, subject matter, or skill information. Following these steps, the teacher will always provide the necessary time and resources for student practice. Student practice is perhaps the most crucial means by which information is internalized.

There are unlimited forms of practice. Just as the teacher intricately planned his/her instructional delivery based upon student needs, the teacher will also carefully plan the practice activities necessary to enhance the learning experience. These practice activities will depend largely on the students' developmental stage and on the skill or knowledge being practiced. Although practice activities are intended to reinforce what the teacher has taught, for many students the practice—the interactive process of doing something—*is the point at which learning occurs*. Therefore, the importance of practice activities cannot be underestimated. Teachers must monitor students as they practice in order to observe difficulties that might arise as well as student proficiency. Based on the observations, teachers make during practice activities, it will be evident when additional instruction needs to occur and when the students are ready to go on to another concept or skill.

Repetitive practice can occur in many forms. Sometimes the teacher will lead the students in choral chants whereby they repeat basic skills including addition, subtraction, and multiplication facts. This activity can also be effective in memorizing spelling words and academic laws. In addition to orally repeating information, these same kinds of skills can be acquired by students repeatedly writing multiplication tables, addition or subtraction facts, or spelling words. Older students may use these types of practice in memorizing algebraic formulas, geometric theorems, and scientific laws.

Repetitive practice may also occur over time. Teachers and students may revisit skills, concepts, or knowledge throughout a school year or even over several school years as a means of internalizing important information. Repetition may come in the form of discussing, rereading, or taking information to a higher level.

Most teachers are aware that short-term retention is the first phase of long-term retention. During the time period that short-term retention is being actualized, instruction and practice are ongoing. Once it appears that a skill or concept has become internalized, the teacher plans for future follow-up activities that will foster long-term retention. Long-term retention is not the result of haphazard instruction, but rather is the result of deliberate and planned instruction. Just as assessment is ongoing, so is instruction and learning.

One of the best uses of practice time is to assign homework activities which will permit students to both reinforce learning as well as to revisit skills and concepts. This allows the teacher to use classroom time for instruction of new ideas, while giving the students opportunities and motivation to practice important skills or concepts. Sometimes, while working on homework assignments with the assistance of a parent, students will develop a broader comprehension of a concept. Also during this valuable time, students may realize valid questions that can then be addressed during class time.

The value of teacher observations cannot be underestimated. It is through the use of teacher observations that the teacher is able to informally assess the needs of the students during instruction. These observations will drive the lesson and determine the direction that future lessons will take. Teacher observations also set the pace of instruction and ascertain the flow of both student and teacher discourse. After a lesson is carefully planned, teacher observation is the single most important component of an instructional presentation.

One of the primary behaviors that teachers look for in an observation is on-task behavior. There is no doubt that student time on-task directly influences student involvement in instruction and enhances student learning. If the teacher observes that a particular student is not on-task, she will change the method of instruction accordingly. She may change from a teacher-directed approach to a more interactive approach. Questioning will increase in order to cull the participation of the students. If appropriate, the teacher will introduce manipulative materials to the lesson. In addition, teachers may switch to a cooperative group activity thereby removing the responsibility of instruction from the teacher and putting it on the students.

Teachers will also change instructional strategies based on the questions and verbal comments of the students. If the students express confusion, doubt, or are unclear in any way about the content of the lesson, the teacher will immediately take another approach in presenting the lesson. Sometimes this can be accomplished by simply rephrasing an explanation. At other times, it will be necessary for the teacher to use visual organizers or models for understanding to be clear. Effective teachers are sensitive to the reactions and responses of their students and will almost intuitively know when instruction is valid and when it is not. Teachers will constantly check for student comprehension, attention, and focus throughout the presentation of a lesson.

After the teacher has presented a skill or concept lesson, she will allow time for the students to practice the skill or concept. At this point it is essential for the teacher to circulate among the students to check for understanding. If the teacher observes that any of the students did not clearly understand the skill or concept, then she must immediately readdress the issue using another technique or approach.

SEE also skill 4.7

Using feedback to promote learning

When teachers provide feedback on a set of assignments, for example, they enhance their students' learning by teaching students how to use the feedback. For example, returning a set of papers can actually do more than provide feedback to students on their initial performance. Teachers can ask students to do additional things to work with their original products, or they can even ask students to take small sections and re-write based on the feedback. While written feedback will enhance student learning, having students do something with the feedback encourages an even deeper learning and reflection.

Experienced teachers may be reading this and thinking, "When will I ever get the time to provide so much feedback?" Although detailed and timely feedback is important—and necessary—teachers do not have to provide it all the time to increase student learning. They can also teach students how to use scoring guides and rubrics to evaluate their own work, particularly before they hand it in to be graded.

One particularly effective way of doing this is by having students examine models and samples of proficient work. Over years, teachers should collect samples, remove names and other identifying factors, and show these examples to students so that they understand what is expected of them. Often, when teachers do this, they will be surprised to see how much students gain from this in terms of their ability to assess their own performance.

Finally, teachers can help students develop plans for revising and improving upon their work, even if it is not evaluated by the teacher in the preliminary stages. For example, teachers can have students keep track of words they commonly misspell, or they can have students make personal lists of areas on which they feel they need to focus.

Skill 6.4   Demonstrates knowledge of methods for developing and/or selecting relevant instructional content, materials, resources, and strategies that respond to cultural, linguistic, gender, and learning style differences and that reflect individualized education goals and benchmarks.

In considering suitable learning materials for the classroom, the teacher must have a thorough understanding of the state-mandated competency-based curriculum. According to state requirements, certain objectives must be met in each subject taught at every designated level of instruction. It is necessary that the teacher become well acquainted with the curriculum for which he/she is assigned. The teacher must also be aware that it is unlawful to require students to study from textbooks or materials other than those approved by the State Department of Education.

Keeping in mind the state requirements concerning the objectives and materials, the teacher must determine the abilities of the incoming students assigned to his/her class or supervision. It is essential to be aware of their entry behavior—that is, their current level of achievement in the relevant areas. The next step is to take a broad overview of students who are expected to learn before they are passed on to the next grade or level of instruction. Finally, the teacher must design a course of study that will enable students to reach the necessary level of achievement, as displayed in their final assessments, or exit behaviors. Textbooks and learning materials must be chosen to fit into this context.

Once students' abilities are determined, the teacher will select the learning materials for the class. In choosing materials, teachers should also keep in mind that not only do students learn at different rates, but they bring a variety of cognitive styles to the learning process. Prior experiences influence the individual's cognitive style, or method of accepting, processing, and retaining information.

Most teachers chose to use textbooks, which are suitable to the age and developmental level of specific student populations. Textbooks reflect the values and assumptions of the society that produces them, while they also represent the knowledge and kills considered to be essential in becoming an educated adult. Finally, textbooks are useful to the school bureaucracy and the community, for they make public and accessible the private world of the classroom.

Aside from textbooks, there is a wide variety of materials available to today's teachers. Computers are now commonplace, and some schools can now afford DVDs to bring alive the content of a reference book in text, motion, and sound. Hand-held calculators eliminate the need for drill and practice in number facts, while they also support a problem solving and process to mathematics. Videocassettes (VCR's) are common and permit the use of home-produced or commercially produced tapes. Textbook publishers often provide films, recordings, and software to accompany the text, as well as maps, graphics, and colorful posters to help students visualize what is being taught. Teachers can usually scan the educational publishers' brochures that arrive at their principal's or department head's office on a frequent basis. Another way to stay current in the field is by attending workshops or conferences. Teachers will be enthusiastically welcomed on those occasions when educational publishers are asked to display their latest productions and revised editions of materials.

In addition, yesterday's libraries are today's media centers. Teachers can usually have opaque projectors delivered to the classroom to project print or pictorial images (including student work) onto a screen for classroom viewing. Some teachers have chosen to replace chalkboards with projectors that reproduce the print or images present on the plastic sheets known as transparencies, which the teacher can write on during a presentation or have machine-printed in advance. In either case, the transparency can easily be stored for later use. In an art or photography class, or any class in which it is helpful to display visual materials, slides can easily be projected onto a wall or a screen. Cameras are inexpensive enough to enable students to photograph and display their own work, as well as keep a record of their achievements in teacher files or student portfolios.

Skill 6.5 **Recognizes the principle of partial participation as it is used in the planning of instruction for all students.**

The principle of partial participation (Baumgart, 1982) states that even if a student cannot complete all steps in a task or activity, he or she can likely learn at least one step at a time, therefore maximizing his or her participation in a learning task. By encouraging a student to choose which task they can actually complete independently, each student is allowed the freedom to make active learning choices. Students can then become active partners, along with the teacher in goal setting.

Teachers should divide each uncompleted task into smaller steps enabling each student to learn skills which will allow them to complete each step independently, thus enhancing their learning involvement in the more complex task. Student participation in educational goal setting promotes active choices, which facilitates self-determination for students. Self-determined behavior is goal directed allowing students to become active partners in the learning process.

COMPETENCY 7.0   UNDERSTANDS AND APPLIES MULTIPLE APPROACHES TO INSTRUCTION AND USES THIS KNOWLEDGE TO FACILITATE LEARNING AND ENCOURAGE STUDENTS' DEVELOPMENT.

Skill 7.1   Demonstrates understanding of the principles, advantages, and limitations of a range of instructional and learning strategies (e.g., multidisciplinary instructional approaches, cooperative learning groups) and how to use these strategies to engage students in active learning opportunities that promote the development of critical-thinking, problem-solving, and performance capabilities and that help students assume responsibility for identifying and using learning resources.

SEE Skills 1.4 and 1.6

Skill 7.2   Identifies strategies for enhancing learning through the use of multiple learning activities and a wide variety of materials, including human and technological resources, that allow for variation in students' developmental levels, learning needs, learning styles, and performance modes.

Through regular evaluations, teachers can learn how to achieve learning goals for each student, often choosing alternative teaching strategies and materials to achieve different instructional purposes and to meet each student various needs. Effective teachers should also understand how to integrate technology into classroom instruction by using diverse technological tools to access and manage information.

SEE also competencies 5 and 6

Skill 7.3   Demonstrates knowledge of methods for developing a variety of clear, accurate presentations and representations of concepts, using alternative explanations at different levels of complexity to help students develop conceptual understandings, and presenting diverse perspectives to encourage critical thinking.

SEE Skill 6.3

Skill 7.4 **Demonstrates knowledge of strategies for facilitating maintenance and generalization of skills across learning environments.**

Teachers should employ multiple teaching and learning strategies to engage students in active learning opportunities that promote the development of critical thinking, problem solving, and performance capabilities.

Strategies

- Implement curriculum that demonstrates an interconnection between subject areas that will reflect life and career experiences.
- Helps students assume responsibility in using learning resources
- Understands role in the instructional process as instructor and facilitator, in relation to purposes of instruction and the needs of students
- Develops a variety of accurate representations of concepts to assist students' understanding and presents diverse perspectives to encourage critical thinking
- Uses a wide range of instructional technologies to enhance student learning

Skill 7.5 **Recognizes the variety of the teacher's role in the instructional process as instructor, facilitator, coach, or audience in relation to the content and purposes of instruction and the needs of students.**

The Teacher's Role
Teaching consists of a multitude of roles. Teachers must plan and deliver instruction in a creative and innovating way so that students find learning both fun and intriguing. The teacher must also research various learning strategies, decide which to implement in the classroom, and balance that information according to the various learning styles of the students. Teachers must facilitate all aspects of the lesson including: preparation and organization of materials, delivery of instruction, and management of student behavior and attention.

Simultaneously, the teacher must also observe for student learning, interactions, and on-task behavior while making mental or written notes regarding what is working in the lesson and how the students are receiving and utilizing the information. This will provide the teacher with immediate feedback as to whether to continue with the lesson, or if it is necessary to slow the instruction or present the lesson in another way. Teachers must also work collaboratively with other adults in the room and utilize them to maximize student learning. The teacher's job requires the teacher to establish a delicate balance among all these factors.

How the teacher handles this balance depends on the teaching style of the teacher and/or lesson. Cooperative learning will require the teacher to have organized materials ready, perhaps even with instructions for the students as well. The teacher should conduct a great deal of observations during this type of lesson. Direct instruction methods will require the teacher to have an enthusiastic, yet organized, approach to the lesson. When teaching directly to students, the teacher must take care to keep the lesson student-centered and intriguing while presenting accurate information.

The Student's Role

Like the teacher, the student has more than one role in a child-centered classroom. In collaborative settings, each student is expected to participate in class or group discussions. Through participation, students begin to realize their contributions have a place in a comprehensive discussion of a topic. Participation engages students in active learning, while increasing their self-confidence as they realize their ideas are necessary for group success.

Students also play the role of observer. As previously stated, behavioral theorists believe that through observation, a human's mind begins to make sense of the world around them as they decide to mimic or avoid certain behaviors. In a classroom, students observe many positive outcomes from behavior, as well as questioning, discussion and hands-on activities.

An important goal for students should be to become self-directed in their learning. Teachers help students obtain this goal by providing them with ample opportunities to seek out their academic interests with various types of projects and assignments. Self-directed learners gain a lot from their inquiries since the topic usually interests them, and when student's take over certain aspects of their own education, they gain a sense of empowerment and ownership over their learning. This is an important role in the classroom because the sense of ownership promotes a sense of lifelong learning in students.

COMPETENCY 8.0   UNDERSTANDS CURRICULUM DEVELOPMENT AND APPLIES KNOWLEDGE OF FACTORS AND PROCESSES IN CURRICULAR DECISION MAKING.

Skill 8.1   Demonstrates understanding of the scope and sequence of the general curriculum, including language arts and mathematics.

Curriculum development today must consider many factors including: alignment, scope, sequence, and design.

First, curriculum must be aligned to state standards, state and local assessments, and district and school goals. Curriculum alignment simply means that there is reflection in the curriculum of these elements. In other words, what students learn should reflect state requirements. Usually, this also means that what students' learn is tested on state assessments. If the district wanted all students to learn how to live in a multi-cultural society, curriculum would address that theme in a variety of ways; this would be an example of alignment to district/school goals.

Second, scope is the "horizontal" aspect of curriculum. For example, if a topic of study in a biology class is invertebrate animals, the scope would define everything that must be taught for students to adequately understand this concept. While on the other hand, sequence is the outline of what should be taught before and after a particular subject. So, for example, a sequence in math might suggest that students should learn addition and subtraction before multiplication and division. Likewise, basic math topics, like those just described, should be taught prior to decimals and fractions. A sequence would put all of these elements into an appropriate order.

Design considers the progression from the beginning of a unit of study to the end of the same unit of study. First, curriculum should be designed with the end in mind. What do you want students to know and be able to do when finished? How would they prove that they know the material or have the skill? If that information has been defined, it is much easier to design a curriculum. Too often, curricula is designed only considering forward steps in a process without concern for what students should be getting out of the curriculum.

As a teacher implements a curriculum, the teacher should be familiar with these three main components:

- The philosophy or principal aims of the curriculum—in other words, what the curriculum wants students to get out of it
- The knowledge base of the curriculum. If teachers are not deeply familiar with what they are teaching to students, they will be very ineffective at getting students to learn it
- The plan, scope, and sequence of the curriculum. What would students have learned prior? Where will they go next?

Skill 8.2   Demonstrates knowledge of general curriculum practices and materials.

SEE Skills 5.1, 5.3, 5.4, 6.1, 6.4 and 8.1

Skill 8.3   Demonstrates understanding of the central concepts of language arts (e.g., reading, writing, speaking, listening) and mathematics (e.g., numeration, geometry, measurement, statistics and probability, algebra).

<u>**Language Arts**</u>

Reading

The Alphabetic Principle is also sometimes called Graphophonemic Awareness. This term details the understanding that written words are composed of patterns of letters which represent the sounds of spoken words.

There are basically two parts to the alphabetic principle:

- An understanding that words are made up of letters and that each of these letters has a specific sound
- The correspondence between sounds and letters leads to phonological reading. This consists of reading regular and irregular words and doing advanced analysis of words.

Since the English language is dependant on the alphabet, being able to recognize and the name and sound for each of the letters is the first step for beginning readers. Relying simply on memorization for recognition of words is not feasible as a way for children to learn to recognize words. Therefore decoding is essential. The most important goal of beginning reading teachers is to teach students to be able to decode text so that they can read fluently and with understanding.

There are four basic features of the alphabetic principle:

1. Students need to be able to take spoken words apart and blend different sounds together to make new words
2. Students need to apply letter sounds to all their reading
3. Teachers need to use a systematic effective program in order to teach children to read
4. The teaching of the alphabetic principle usually begins in Kindergarten.

It is important to keep in mind that some children already know the letters and sounds before they come to school. Others may catch on to this quite quickly and still others need to have one-on-one instruction in order to learn to read. Critical skills that students need to learn are:

- Letter sound correspondence
- How to sound out words
- How to decode text to make meaning

The Structure of Language

Morphology is the study of word structure. When readers develop morphemic skills, they are developing an understanding of the patterns they see in words. For example, English speakers realize that cat, cats, and caterpillar share some similarities in structure. This understanding helps readers to recognize words at a faster and easier rate, since each word doesn't need individual decoding.

Syntax refers to the rules or patterned relationships that correctly create phrases and sentences from words. When readers develop an understanding of syntax, they begin to understand the structure of how sentences are built, and eventually the beginning of grammar.

Example: "I am going to the movies"
This statement is syntactically and grammatically correct

Example: "They am going to the movies:
This statement is syntactically correct since all the words are in their correct place, but it is grammatically incorrect with the use of the word "They" rather than "I."

Semantics refers to the meaning expressed when words are arranged in a specific way. This is where connotation and denotation of words eventually will have a role with readers.

All of these skill sets are important to eventually developing effective word recognition skills, which help emerging readers develop fluency.

Phonics

Phonological awareness refers to the ability of the reader to recognize the sound of spoken language. This recognition includes how these sounds can be blended together, segmented (divided up), and manipulated (switched around). This awareness then leads to phonics, a method for teaching children to read. It helps them "sound out words."

As opposed to phonemic awareness, the study of phonics must be done with the eyes open. It's the connection between the sounds and letters on a page. In other words, students learning phonics might see the word "bad" and sound each letter out slowly until they recognize that they just said the word.

Development of phonological skills may begin during pre-K years. Indeed by the age of 5, a child who has been exposed to rhyme can recognize a rhyme. Such a child can demonstrate phonological awareness by filling in the missing rhyming word in a familiar rhyme or rhymed picture book. You teach children phonological awareness when you teach them the sounds made by the letters, the sounds made by various combinations of letters and to recognize individual sounds in words.

Phonological awareness skills include:

- Rhyming and syllabification
- Blending sounds into words—such as pic-tur-bo-k
- Identifying the beginning or starting sounds of words and the ending or closing sounds of words
- Breaking words down into sounds-also called "segmenting" words
- Recognizing other smaller words in the big word, by removing starting sounds, "hear" to ear

Word Recognition

Knowledge of how words are built can help students with basic and more advanced decoding skills. A root word is the primary base of a word. A prefix is the affix (a morpheme that attaches to a base word) that is placed at the start of a root word, but can't make a word on its own. Examples of prefixes include re-, pre-, and un-. A suffix, also an affix, follows the root word to which it attaches and appears at the end of the word. Examples of suffixes include –s, -es, -ed, -ly, and –tion. In the word unlikely, "un" is a prefix, "like" is the root work, and "ly" is a suffix.

Word analysis (a.k.a. phonics or decoding) is the process readers use to figure out unfamiliar words based on written patterns. Word recognition is the process of automatically determining the pronunciation and some degree of the meaning of an unknown word. In other words, fluent readers recognize most written words easily and correctly, without consciously decoding or breaking them down.

Decoding

To decode means to change communication signals into messages. Reading comprehension requires that the reader learn the code within which a message is written and be able to decode it to get the message. Encoding involves changing a message into symbols. For example to encode oral language into writing (spelling) or to encode an idea into words or to encode a mathematical or physical idea into appropriate mathematical symbols.

Although effective reading comprehension requires identifying words automatically (Adams, 1990, Perfetti, 1985), children do not have to be able to identify every single word or know the exact meaning of the every word in a text to understand it. Indeed, Nagy (1988) says that, children can read and work with a high level of comprehension even if they do not fully know as many as 15 percent of the words within a given text. As children develop the ability to decode and recognize words automatically and can then extend their ability to decode multi-syllabic words.

Spelling

Spelling instruction should include words misspelled in daily writing, generalizing spelling knowledge, and mastering objectives in progressive phases of development. Developmental stages of spelling:

1) Pre-phonemic spelling—Children know that letters stand for a message, but they do not know the relationship between spelling and pronunciation.
2) Early phonemic spelling—Children are beginning to understand spelling. They usually write the beginning letter correctly, with the rest consonants or long vowels.
3) Letter-name spelling—Some words are consistently spelled correctly. The student is developing a sight vocabulary and a stable understanding of letters as representing sounds. Long vowels are usually used accurately, but silent vowels are omitted. Unknown words are spelled by the child attempting to match the name of the letter to the sound.
4) Transitional spelling—This phase is typically entered in late elementary school. Short vowel sounds are mastered and some spelling rules known. They are developing a sense of which spellings are correct and which are not.
5) Derivational spelling—This is usually reached from high school to adulthood. This is the stage where spelling rules are being mastered.

Factors that affect a reader's ability to construct meaning

If there were two words which could be synonymous with reading comprehension, as far as the balanced literacy approach is concerned, they would be "Constructing Meaning."

Cooper, Taberski, Strickland, and other key theorists and classroom teachers, conceptualize the reader as designating a specific meaning to the text using both clues in the text and his/her own prior knowledge. Comprehension for the balanced literacy theorists is a strategic process.

The reader interacts with the text, bringing his/her prior knowledge and experience to it or LACK of prior knowledge and experience to the text in order to determine adequate comprehension. Writing is interlaced with reading and is a mutually integrative and supportive parallel process. Hence the division of literacy learning by the balanced literacy folks into reading workshop and writing workshop, with the same anchor "readings: or books being used for both tasks.

Consider the sentence, "The test booklet was white with black print, but very scary looking." According to the idea of constructing meaning as the reader read this sentence, the schemata (generic information stored in the mind) of tests he or she was personally activated by the author's ideas that tests are scary. Therefore the ultimate meaning the reader derives from the page is from the reader's own responses and experiences with the ideas the author presents. The reader constructs a meaning that reflects the author's intent and also the reader's response to that intent.

It is also to be remembered that generally readings are fairly lengthy passages, comprised of paragraphs which in turn are comprised of more than one sentence. With each successive sentence, and every new paragraph, the reader refocuses. The schemata are reconsidered, and a new meaning is constructed.

The purpose of reading is to convert visual images (the letters and words) into a message. Pronouncing the words is not enough; the reader must be able to extract the meaning of the text. When people read, they utilize four sources of background information to comprehend the meaning behind the literal text (Reid, pp.166-171).

1. Word Knowledge: Information about words and letters. One's knowledge about word meanings is lexical knowledge—a sort of dictionary. Knowledge about spelling patterns and pronunciations is orthographic knowledge. Poor readers do not develop the level of automatically in using orthographic knowledge to identify words and decode unfamiliar words.

2. Syntax and Contextual Information. When children encounter unknown words in a sentence, they rely on their background knowledge to choose a word that makes sense. Errors of younger children therefore are often substitutions of words in the same syntactic class. Poor readers often fail to make use of context clues to help them identify words or activate the background knowledge that would help them with comprehension. Poor readers also process sentences word by word, instead of "chunking" phrases and clauses, resulting in a slow pace that focuses on the decoding rather than comprehension. They also have problems answering wh- (Who, what, where, when, why) questions as a result of these problems with syntax.

3. Semantic Knowledge: This includes the reader's background knowledge about a topic, which is combined with the text information as the reader tries to comprehend the material. New information is compared to the background information and incorporated into the reader's schema. Poor readers have problems with using their background knowledge, especially with passages that require inference or cause-and-effect.

4. Text Organization: Good readers are able to differentiate types of text structure, (e.g., story narrative, exposition, compare-contrast, or time sequence). They use knowledge of text to build expectations and construct a framework of ideas on which to build meaning. Poor readers may not be able to differentiate types of text and miss important ideas. They may also miss important ideas and details by concentrating on lesser or irrelevant details.

Research on reading development has yielded information on the behaviors and habits of good readers vs. poor readers. Some of the characteristics of good readers are:

- They think about the information that they will read in the text, formulate questions that they predict will be answered in the text, and confirm those predictions from the information in the text.
- When faced with unfamiliar words, they attempt to pronounce them using analogies to familiar words.
- Before reading, good readers establish a purpose for reading, select possible text structure, choose a reading strategy, and make predictions about what will be in the reading.
- As they read, good readers continually test and confirm their predictions, go back when something does not make sense, and make new predictions.

Writing

In the past teachers have assigned reports, paragraphs and essays that focused on the teacher as the audience with the purpose of explaining information; however, for students to be meaningfully engaged in their writing, they must write for a variety of reasons. Writing for different audiences and aims allows students to be more involved in their writing. If they write for the same audience and purpose, they will continue to see writing as just another assignment. Listed below are suggestions that provide students an opportunity to write in more creative and critical ways.

- Write letters to the editor, to a college, to a friend, to another student that would be sent to the intended audience.
- Write stories that would be read aloud to a group (the class, another group of students, to a group of elementary school students) or published in a literary magazine or class anthology.
- Write plays that would be performed.
- Have students discuss the parallels between the different speech styles we use and writing styles for different readers or audiences.
- Allow students to write a particular piece for different audiences.
- Expose students to writing that is on the same topic but with a different audience and have them identify the variations in sentence structure and style.
- As part of the prewriting have students identify the audience. Make sure students consider the following when analyzing the needs of their audience.

     1. Why is the audience reading my writing? Do they expect to be informed, amused or persuaded?
     2. What does my audience already know about my topic?
     3. What does the audience want or need to know? What will interest them?
     4. What type of language suits my readers?

Reminding students that it is not necessary to identify all the specifics of the audience in the initial stage of the writing process but that at some point they must make some determinations about audience is critical to the teaching process.

The Writing Process

Students gather ideas before writing. Prewriting may include clustering, listing, brainstorming, mapping, free writing, and charting. Providing many ways for a student to develop ideas on a topic will increase his/her chances for success.

Reminding students, that as they prewrite, they need to consider their audience is crucial. Prewriting strategies assist students in a variety of ways. Listed below are the most common prewriting strategies students can use to explore, plan and write on a topic. It is important to remember when teaching these strategies that not all prewriting must eventually produce a finished piece of writing. In fact, in the initial lesson of teaching prewriting strategies, it might be more effective to have students practice prewriting strategies without the pressure of having to write a finished product.

- Keep an idea book so that they can jot down ideas that come to mind
- Write in a daily journal
- Write down whatever comes to mind; this is called free writing. Students do not stop to make corrections or interrupt the flow of ideas.

A variation of this technique is focused free writing— writing on a specific topic— to prepare for an essay.

- Make a list of all ideas connected with their topic; this is called brainstorming
- Make sure students know that this technique works best when they let their mind work freely. After completing the list, students should analyze the list to see if a pattern or way to group the ideas
- Ask the questions Who? What? When? Where? When? and How? Help the writer approach a topic from several perspectives
- Create a visual map on paper to gather ideas. Cluster circles and lines to show connections between ideas. Students should try to identify the relationship that exists between their ideas. If they cannot see the relationships, have them pair up, exchange papers and have their partners look for some related ideas
- Observe details of sight, hearing, taste, touch, and taste
- Visualize by making mental images of something and write down the details in a list

After they have practiced with each of these prewriting strategies, ask them to pick out the ones they prefer and ask them to discuss how they might use the techniques to help them with future writing assignments. It is important to remember that they can use more than one prewriting strategy at a time. Also they may find that different writing situations may suggest certain techniques.

Speaking

Analyzing the speech of others is a very good technique for helping students to improve their own public speaking abilities. In most circumstances, students cannot view themselves as they give speeches and presentations. So when they get the opportunity to critique, question, and analyze others' speeches, they begin to learn what works and what doesn't work in effective public speaking. However, a very important word of warning: DO NOT have students critique each others' public speaking skills. It could be very damaging to a student to have his or her peers point out what did not work in a speech. Instead, video is a great tool teachers can use. Any appropriate source of public speaking can be used in the classroom for students to analyze and critique.

Some of the things students can analyze include the following:

- Volume: A speaker should use an appropriate volume—not too loud to be annoying, but not too soft to be inaudible.
- Pace: The rate at which words are spoken should be appropriate—not too fast to make the speech non-understandable, but not too slow so as to put listeners to sleep.
- Pronunciation: A speaker should make sure words are spoken clearly. Listeners do not have a text to go back and re-read things they didn't catch.
- Body language: While animated body language can help a speech, too much of it can be distracting. Body language should help convey the message, not detract from it.
- Word choice: The words speakers choose should be consistent with their intended purpose and the audience.
- Visual aids: Visual aids, like body language, should enhance a message. Many visual aids can be distracting, and that detracts from the message.

Overall, instead of telling students to keep the factors above in mind when presenting information orally, having them view speakers who do these things well and poorly will help them know and remember the next time they have to give a speech.

Listening

Listening is not a skill that is discussed much, except when someone clearly does not listen. The truth is that listening is a very specific skill for very specific circumstances. There are two aspects to listening that warrant attention. The first is comprehension. This is simply the student having an understanding of what someone says, the purposes behind the message, and the contexts in which it is said. The second is purpose. While someone may completely understand a message, what is the listener supposed to do with it? Just nod and smile? Go out and take action? While listening comprehension is indeed a significant skill in itself that deserves a lot of focus in the classroom (much in the same way that reading comprehension does), we will focus on purpose here. Often, when we understand the purpose of listening in various contexts, comprehension will be much easier. Furthermore, when we know the purpose of listening, we can better adjust our comprehension strategies.

First, when complex or new information is provided to us orally, the listener must analyze and interpret that information. What is the author's most important point? How do the figures of speech impact meaning? How are conclusions drawn? Often, making sense of this information can be tough when presented orally—first, because there is no place to go back and review material already stated; second, because oral language is so much less predictable than written language. However, when we focus on extracting the meaning, message, and speaker's purpose, rather than just "listen" and wait for things to make sense for us—in other words, when the listener is more "active" in his listening—there is greater success in interpreting speech.

Second, listening is often done for the purpose of enjoyment. We like to listen to stories; we enjoy poetry; we like radio dramas and theater. Listening to literature can also be a great pleasure. The problem today is that students have not learned how to extract great pleasure on a wide-spread scale from listening to literature, poetry, or language read aloud. Perhaps that is because we have not done a good enough job of showing students how listening to literature, for example, can indeed be more interesting than television or video games. In the classrooms of exceptional teachers, we will often find that students are captivated by the reading-aloud of good literature. It is refreshing and enjoyable to just sit and soak in the language, story, and poetry of literature being read aloud. Therefore, we must teach students *how* to listen and enjoy such work. We do this by making it fun and giving many possibilities and alternatives to capture the wide array of interests in each classroom.

Finally, the discussion of listening of conversations in both large and small groups. The difference here is that conversation requires more than just listening: It involves feedback and active involvement. This can be particularly challenging, as in our culture, we are trained to move conversations along, to discourage silence in a conversation, and to always have the last word. This poses significant problems for the art of listening. In a discussion, for example, when we are instead preparing our next response—rather than listening to what others are saying—we do a large disservice to the entire discussion. Students need to learn how listening carefully to others in discussions actually promotes better responses on the part of subsequent speakers. One way teachers can encourage this, in both large and small group discussions, is to expect students to respond *directly* to the previous student's comments before moving ahead with their new comments. This will encourage them to pose their new comments in light of the comments that came just before them.

Strategies for active listening

Oral speech can be very difficult to follow. Yet, aside from re-reading, many of the skills and strategies that help us in reading comprehension can help us in listening comprehension. For example, as soon as we start listening to something new, we should tap into our prior knowledge in order to attach new information to what we already know. This will not only help us understand the new information more quickly, it will also assist us in remembering the material.

We can also look for transitions between ideas. Sometimes, in oral speech, this is pretty simple when voice tone or body language changes. Of course, we don't have the luxury of looking at paragraphs in oral language, but we do have the animation that comes along with live speech. Human beings have to try very hard to be completely non-expressive in their speech. Listeners should take advantage of this and notice how the speaker changes character and voice in order to signal a transition of ideas.

Speaking of animation of voice and body language, listeners can also better comprehend the underlying intents of authors when they notice nonverbal cues. Simply looking to see expressions on the face of a speaker can do more to signal irony, for example, than trying to extract irony from actual words. And often in oral speech, unlike written text, elements like irony are not indicated by the actual words, but rather by the tone and nonverbal cues.

One good way to follow oral speech is to take notes and outline major points. Because oral speech can be more circular (as opposed to linear) than written text, it can be of great assistance to keep track of an author's message. Students can learn this strategy in many ways within the classroom: by taking notes of the teacher's oral messages, as well as other students' presentations and speeches.

Other classroom methods can help students learn good listening skills. For example, teachers can have students practice following complex directions. They can also have students orally retell stories—or retell (in writing or in oral speech) oral presentations of stories or other materials. These activities give students direct practice in the very important skills of listening. They provide students with outlets in which they can slowly improve their abilities to comprehend oral language and take decisive action based on oral speech.

Mathematics

Numeration

Rational numbers can be expressed as the ratio of two integers, $\frac{a}{b}$ where b ≠ 0

Example:

$\frac{2}{3}$, $-\frac{4}{5}$, 5 = $\frac{5}{1}$.

The rational numbers include integers, fractions and mixed numbers, terminating and repeating decimals. Every rational number can be expressed as a repeating or terminating decimal and can be shown on a number line.

Integers are positive and negative whole numbers and zero.

-6, -5, -4, -3, -2, -1, 0, 1, 2, 3, 4, 5, 6, ...

Whole numbers are natural numbers and zero.

0, 1, 2, 3, 4, 5, 6...

Natural numbers are the counting numbers.

1, 2, 3, 4, 5, 6...

Irrational numbers are real numbers that cannot be written as the ratio of two integers. These are infinite non-repeating decimals.

Examples:

$\sqrt{5}$ = 2.2360.., pi =∏ = 3.1415927...

A **fraction** is an expression of numbers in the form of x/y, where **x** is the numerator and **y** is the denominator, which cannot be zero.

Example:

$\frac{3}{7}$ 3 is the numerator; 7 is the denominator

If the fraction has common factors for the numerator and denominator, divide both by the common factor to reduce the fraction to its lowest form.

Example:

$$\frac{13}{39} = \frac{1 \times 13}{3 \times 13} = \frac{1}{3}$$ Divide by the common factor 13

A **mixed** number has an integer part and a fractional part.

Example:

$$2\frac{1}{4}, \ ^{-}5\frac{1}{6}, \ 7\frac{1}{3}$$

Percent = per 100 (written with the symbol %). Thus 10% $= \dfrac{10}{100} = \dfrac{1}{10}$.

Decimals = deci = part of ten. To find the decimal equivalent of a fraction, use the denominator to divide the numerator as shown in the following example.

Example:

Find the decimal equivalent of $\dfrac{7}{10}$.

Since 10 cannot divide into 7 evenly

Properties of real numbers

Proper Properties are rules that apply for addition, subtraction, multiplication, or division of real numbers. These properties are:

Commutative: You can change the order of the terms or factors as
follows.

For addition:
$$a + b = b + a$$

For multiplication:
$$ab = ba$$

Since addition is the inverse operation of subtraction and multiplication is the inverse operation of division, no separate laws are needed for subtraction and division.

Example:
$$5 + {}^{-}8 = {}^{-}8 + 5 = {}^{-}3$$

Example:
$${}^{-}2 \times 6 = 6 \times {}^{-}2 = {}^{-}12$$

Associative: You can regroup the terms as you like.

For addition:
$$a + (b + c) = (a + b) + c$$

For multiplication:
$$a(bc) = (ab)c$$

This rule does not apply for division and subtraction.

<u>Example</u>:
$$(\bar{}2 + 7) + 5 = \bar{}2 + (7 + 5)$$
$$5 + 5 = \bar{}2 + 12 = 10$$

<u>Example</u>:
$$(3 \times \bar{}7) \times 5 = 3 \times (\bar{}7 \times 5)$$
$$\bar{}21 \times 5 = 3 \times \bar{}35 = \bar{}105$$

Identity: Finding a number so that when added to a term it results in that number (additive identity); finding a number such that when multiplied by a term it results in that number (multiplicative identity).

For addition:
$$a + 0 = a \qquad \text{(zero is additive identity)}$$

For multiplication:
$$a \cdot 1 = a \qquad \text{(one is multiplicative)}$$

<u>Example</u>:
$$17 + 0 = 17$$

<u>Example</u>:
$$\bar{}34 \times 1 = \bar{}34$$

The product of any number and one is that number.

Inverse: Finding a number such that when added to the number it results in zero; or when multiplied by the number results in 1.

For addition:
$$a + (-a) = 0$$

For multiplication:
$$a \cdot (1/a) = 1$$

(-a) is the additive inverse of a; (1/a), also called the reciprocal, is the multiplicative inverse of a.

Example:
$$25 + {}^{-}25 = 0$$

Example:
$$5 \times \tfrac{1}{5} = 1$$

The product of any number and its reciprocal is one.

Distributive: This technique allows us to operate on terms within parentheses without first performing operations within the parentheses. This is especially helpful when terms within the parentheses cannot be combined.
$$a\,(b + c) = ab + ac$$

Example:
$$6 \times ({}^{-}4 + 9) = (6 \times {}^{-}4) + (6 \times 9)$$
$$6 \times 5 = {}^{-}24 + 54 = 30$$

To multiply a sum by a number, multiply each addend by the number, then add the products.

The order of real numbers

Symbol for inequality: In the symbol '>' (greater than) or '<' (less than), the big open side of the symbol always faces the larger of the two numbers and the point of the symbol always faces the smaller number.

<u>Example</u>:

Compare 15 and 20 on the number line.

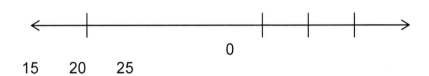

15   20   25

Since 20 is further away from the zero than 15 is, then 20 is greater than 15, or $20 > 15$.

<u>Example</u>:

Compare $\dfrac{3}{7}$ and $\dfrac{5}{10}$.

To compare fractions, they should have the same least common denominator (LCD). The LCD in this example is 70.

$$\frac{3}{7} = \frac{3 \times 10}{7 \times 10} = \frac{30}{70} \qquad\qquad \frac{5}{10} = \frac{5 \times 7}{10 \times 7} = \frac{35}{70}$$

Since the denominators are equal, compare only the numerators.

$30 < 35$, so:

The base ten number system

A number in standard form is represented by a number of digits separated by a decimal point. Each digit to the left of the decimal point increases progressively in powers of ten. Each digit to the right of the decimal point decreases progressively in powers of ten.

<u>Example</u>:

12345.6789   occupies the following powers of ten positions:

10^4	10^3	10^2	10^1	10^0
0	10^{-1}	10^{-2}	10^{-3}	10^{-4}
1	2	3	4	5
6	7	8	9	

Names of power-of-ten positions:

10^0 = ones (note that any non-zero base raised to power zero is 1).

10^1 = tens (number 1 and 1 zero or 10)

10^2 = hundred (number 1 and 2 zeros or 100)

10^3 = thousand (number 1 and 3 zeros or 1000)

10^4 = ten thousand (number 1 and 4 zeros or 10000)

$10^{-1} = \dfrac{1}{10^1} = \dfrac{1}{10}$ = tenths (1st digit after decimal point or 0.1)

$10^{-2} = \dfrac{1}{10^2} = \dfrac{1}{100}$ = hundredth (2nd digit after decimal point or 0.01)

$10^{-3} = \dfrac{1}{10^3} = \dfrac{1}{1000}$ = thousandth (3rd digit after decimal point or 0.001)

$10^{-4} = \dfrac{1}{10^4} = \dfrac{1}{10000}$ = ten thousandth (4th digit after decimal point or 0.0001)

Example:

Write 73169.00537 in expanded form.

- We start by listing all the powers of ten positions.
- $10^4 \quad 10^3 \qquad 10^2 \qquad 10^1 \qquad 10^0$.
  $\qquad\quad 10^{-1} \; 10^{-2} \quad 10^{-3} \qquad 10^{-4} \qquad 10^{-5}$
- Multiply each digit by its power of ten. Add all the results.
- Thus 73169.00537 = $(7 \times 10^4) + (3 \times 10^3) + (1 \times 10^2) + (6 \times 10^1)$

$+(9 \times 10^0) + (0 \times 10^{-1}) + (0 \times 10^{-2}) + (5 \times 10^{-3})$

$+(3 \times 10^{-4}) + (7 \times 10^{-5})$

Example:

Determine the place value associated with the underlined digit in 3.16$\underline{9}$5.

10^0	.	10^{-1}	10^{-2}	10^{-3}	10^{-4}
3	.	1	6	9	5

- The place value for the digit 9 is 10^{-3} or $\dfrac{1}{1000}$.

Example:
   Find the number that is represented by

- $(7 \times 10^3) + (5 \times 10^0) + (3 \times 10^{-3})$.
- $= 7000 + 5 + 0.003$
- $= 7005.003$

Example:
   Write 21×10^3 in standard form.
        $= 21 \times 1000 = 21,000$

Example:
   Write 739×10^{-4} in standard form.

To convert a fraction to a decimal, simply divide the numerator (top) by the denominator (bottom). Use long division if necessary.

If a decimal has a fixed number of digits, the decimal is said to be *terminating*. To write such a decimal as a fraction, first determine what place value the farthest right digit is in, for example: tenths, hundredths, thousandths, ten thousandths, hundred thousands, etc. Then drop the decimal and place the string of digits over the number given by the place value.

If a decimal continues forever by repeating a string of digits, the decimal is said to be *repeating*. To write a repeating decimal as a fraction, follow these steps.

a. Let $x =$ the repeating decimal
   (ex. $x = .716716716...$)
b. Multiply x by the multiple of ten that will move the decimal just to the right of the repeating block of digits.
   (ex. $1000x = 716.716716...$)
c. Subtract the first equation from the second.
   (ex. $1000x - x = 716.716.716... - .716716...$)
d. Simplify and solve this equation. The repeating block of digits will subtract out.
   (ex. $999x = 716$ so $x = {}^{716}\!/_{999}$)
e. The solution will be the fraction for the repeating decimal.

COMMON EQUIVALENTS

- $\frac{1}{2} = 0.5 = 50\%$
- $\frac{1}{3} = 0.33\frac{1}{3} = 33\frac{1}{3}\%$
- $\frac{1}{4} = 0.25 = 25\%$
- $\frac{1}{5} = 0.2 = 20\%$
- $\frac{1}{6} = 0.16\frac{2}{3} = 16\frac{2}{3}\%$
- $\frac{1}{8} = 0.12\frac{1}{2} = 12\frac{1}{2}\%$
- $\frac{1}{10} = 0.1 = 10\%$
- $\frac{2}{3} = 0.66\frac{2}{3} = 66\frac{2}{3}\%$
- $\frac{5}{6} = 0.83\frac{1}{3} = 83\frac{1}{3}\%$
- $\frac{3}{8} = 0.37\frac{1}{2} = 37\frac{1}{2}\%$
- $\frac{5}{8} = 0.62\frac{1}{2} = 62\frac{1}{2}\%$
- $\frac{7}{8} = 0.87\frac{1}{2} = 87\frac{1}{2}\%$
- $1 = 1.0 = 100\%$

Prime numbers are numbers that can only be factored into 1 and the number itself. When factoring into prime factors, all the factors must be numbers that cannot be factored again (without using 1). Initially numbers can be factored into any 2 factors. Check each resulting factor to see if it can be factored again. Continue factoring until all remaining factors are prime. This is the list of prime factors. Regardless of what way the original number was factored, the final list of prime factors will always be the same.

Example: Factor 30 into prime factors.

Factor 30 into any 2 factors.
$5 \cdot 6$ Now factor the 6.
$5 \cdot 2 \cdot 3$ These are all prime factors.

Factor 30 into any 2 factors.
$3 \cdot 10$ Now factor the 10.
$3 \cdot 2 \cdot 5$
These are the same prime factors even though the original factors were different.

Example: Factor 240 into prime factors.

Factor 240 into any 2 factors.
24 · 10   Now factor both 24 and 10.
4 · 6 · 2 · 5   Now factor both 4 and 6.
2 · 2 · 2 · 3 · 2 · 5   These are prime factors.

This can also be written as $2^4 · 3 · 5$.

Geometry
The **lateral** area is the area of the faces excluding the bases.

The **surface area** is the total area of all the faces, including the bases.

The **volume** is the number of cubic units in a solid. This is the amount of space a figure holds.

Right prism

V = Bh   (where B = area of the base of the prism and h = the height of the prism)

Rectangular right prism

S = 2(lw + hw + lh) (where l = length, w = width and h = height)
V = lwh

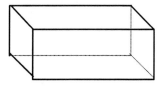

B   h

Example: Find the height of a box whose volume is 120 cubic meters and the area of the base is 30 square meters.

V = Bh
120 = 30h
h = 4 meters

Regular pyramid

V = 1/3Bh

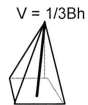

h

Right circular cylinder

$S = 2\Pi r(r + h)$ (where r is the radius of the base)
$V = \Pi r^2 h$

r

h

Right circular cone

$V = \frac{1}{3}Bh$

r

h

Measurement

"When you can measure what you are speaking about and express it in numbers, you know something about it; but when you cannot measure it, when you cannot express it in numbers, your knowledge is of a meager and unsatisfactory kind."

Lord Kelvin

Non-standard units are sometimes used when standard instruments might not be available. For example, students might measure the length of a room by their arm-spans. An inch originated as the length of three barley grains placed end to end. Seeds or stones might be used for measuring weight. In fact, our current "carat," used for measuring precious gems, was derived from carob seeds. In ancient times, baskets, jars and bowls were used to measure capacity.

To estimate measurement of familiar objects, it is first necessary to determine the units to be used.

Examples:

Length
1.	The coastline of Florida	miles or kilometers
2.	The width of a ribbon	inches or millimeters
3.	The thickness of a book	inches or centimeters
4.	The length of a football field	yards or meters
5.	The depth of water in a pool	feet or meters

Weight or mass
1.	A bag of sugar	pounds or grams
2.	A school bus	tons or kilograms
3.	A dime	ounces or grams

Capacity
1.	Paint to paint a bedroom	gallons or liters
2.	Glass of milk	cups or liters
3.	Bottle of soda	quarts or liters
4.	Medicine for child	ounces or milliliters

Statistics & Probability

Mean, median and mode are three measures of central tendency. The **mean** is the average of the data items. The **median** is found by putting the data items in order from smallest to largest and selecting the item in the middle (or the average of the two items in the middle). The **mode** is the most frequently occurring item.

Range is a measure of variability. It is found by subtracting the smallest value from the largest value.

Example:
Find the mean, median, mode and range of the test score listed below:

85	77	65
92	90	54
88	85	70
75	80	69
85	88	60
72	74	95

Mean (X) = sum of all scores ÷ number of scores
= 78

Median = put numbers in order from smallest to largest. Pick middle number.
54, 60, 65, 69, 70, 72, 74, 75, 77, 80, 85, 85, 88, 88, 90, 92, 95

If there are two numbers in the middle, the median is an average of the two middle numbers.

Therefore, median is average of two numbers in the middle or 78.5

Mode = most frequent number
= 85

Range = largest number minus the smallest number
= 95 – 54
= 41

Algebra
The function or relationship between two quantities may be analyzed to determine how one quantity depends on the other. For example, the function below shows a relationship between y and x:

$y=2x+1$

The relationship between two or more variables can be analyzed using a table, graph, written description or symbolic rule. The function, y=2x+1, is written as a symbolic rule. The same relationship is also shown in the table below:

x	0	2	3	6	9
y	1	5	7	13	19

A relationship could be written in words by saying the value of y is equal to two times the value of x, plus one. This relationship could be shown on a graph by plotting given points such as the ones shown in the above table.

Another way to describe a function is as a process in which one or more numbers are input into an imaginary machine that produces another number as the output. If 5 is input, (x), into a machine with a process of x +1, the output, (y), will equal 6.

In real situations, relationships can be described mathematically. The function, y=x+1, can be used to describe the idea that people age one year on their birthday. To describe the relationship in which a person's monthly medical costs are 6 times a person's age, we could write y=6x. The monthly cost of medical care could be predicted using this function. A 20 year-old person would spend $120 per month (120=20*6). An 80 year-old person would spend $480 per month (480=80*6). Therefore, one could analyze the relationship to say: as you get older, medical costs increase $6.00 each year.

Skill 8.4   Demonstrates knowledge of the Illinois Learning Standards, curriculum development, content, learning theory, and student development and how to incorporate this knowledge in planning instruction.

The Illinois Learning Standards (ILS) defines what all students in the Illinois public schools should know and be able to accomplish within the seven core areas as a result of their elementary and secondary schooling. The ILS contains 30 goals, 98 standards and over 1,000 benchmarks.

The standards framework is divided into seven learning areas:

- English Language Arts
- Mathematics
- Science
- Social Science
- Physical Development and Health
- Fine Arts
- Foreign Languages (advisory standards)

The Applications of Learning section includes five cross-disciplinary abilities:

- Solving Problems
- Communicating
- Using Technology
- Working on Teams
- Making Connections.

Charts of Goals, Standards and Learning Benchmarks that define the essential knowledge and skills are identified for each of the seven learning areas.

SEE also Skill 8.2

Skill 8.5   **Recognizes effective methods for developing a curriculum that reflects the principles of scope and sequence and demonstrates an interconnection among subject areas that reflects life and career expectations.**

SEE Skills 8.1 and 1.6

COMPETENCY 9.0   UNDERSTANDS HOW TO STRUCTURE AND MANAGE A LEARNING ENVIRONMENT THAT ENCOURAGES POSITIVE SOCIAL INTERACTION AND ENGAGEMENT IN LEARNING; PROMOTES COOPERATIVE, PURPOSEFUL, AND RESPONSIBLE BEHAVIOR; AND FACILITATES STUDENTS' ACHIEVEMENT OF EDUCATIONAL GOALS.

Skill 9.1   **Demonstrates understanding of basic principles and theories of classroom management and strategies and methods for creating a learning community in which students assume responsibility for themselves and one another, participate in decision making, work collaboratively and independently, use appropriate technology, and engage in purposeful learning activities.**

SEE skill 2.3 for information related to classroom management

Utilizing Peers

Flexible grouping, pair shares, small groups, base groups, etc. These are all terms used to describe the ways in which students can learn in community-like settings. Much research has shown that students are highly successful learners when learning with peers. This is primarily due to the social interaction that helps to stimulate ideas in natural contexts. Furthermore, students learning in group settings have additional opportunities to learn material successfully:

By talking about concepts, students have to put ideas into words. By putting ideas into words, students will remember the ideas better, and by articulating the ideas, they will begin to make better sense of those ideas.

Students get to test ideas out in comfortable settings. In whole-group settings, students may be fearful to share ideas with the whole class. However, without the sharing of thoughts, students never get the chance to really think through more complex ideas. Small groups are safer places to do this. Help is immediately available. Students can get assistance from those right next to them in a social, natural setting. When students help other students learn, they commit ideas to memory for themselves.

Often, teachers consider grouping students by ability level. While this can be productive some of the time, it is often best to mix and match students for various lesson purposes. Sometimes, it is important to have similar levels together; other times, it is good to have different levels together. It is always important to change groups often.

Grouping does not have to be highly structured or scientific all the time. Sometimes, it is helpful just to have students turn to their neighbors and discuss an idea.

Whatever the method, it is important that students not just sit and listen to the teacher; rather, the more that students can interact and discuss knowledge, the more opportunity they will have to really understand it.

Group-Oriented Contingencies in Behavior Management
This strategy uses the power of the peer group to reinforce appropriate behavior. In one variation, *dependent group-oriented contingencies*, the rewards of consequences for the entire group depend upon the performance of a few members. Example: Susan's class receives a candy reward if she does not have a crying outburst for two days. *Interdependent group-oriented* contingencies mean that each member of the group must achieve a specified level of performance in order for the group to get the reward. Example: The entire class earns one period of free time if everyone passes the science test with at least 80%.

Other Strategies for Behavior Management

1. **Counseling Techniques**-These techniques include life-space interview, reality therapy, and active listening.

2. **Consequences**-Consequences should be as close as possible to the outside world, especially for adolescents.

3. **Student Participation**-Students, especially older students, should participate as much as possible in the planning, goal setting, and evaluation of their behavior management plans.

4. **Contingency Plans**-Because adolescents frequently have a number of reinforcers outside of school, the teacher should try to incorporate contingencies for school behavior at home, since parents can control important reinforcers such as movies, going out with friends, car privileges, etc

5. **Consistency**-Consistency, especially with adolescents, reduces the occurrence of power struggles and teaches them that predictable consequences follow for their choice of actions.

Initially, the target behavior may increase or worsen when the student realizes that the behavior no longer is being reinforced. However, if the behavior management plan is properly administered, the teacher should begin to see results. Behavior management plan evaluation is a continuous process, since changes in behavior require changes in the target behavior, looking for outside variables that may account for behavior change, or changes in reinforcement schedules and menus is important.

It has already been established that appropriate verbal techniques include: a soft non-threatening voice, void of undue roughness, anger, or impatience regardless of whether the teacher is instructing, providing student alert, or giving a behavior reprimand.

Verbal techniques, which may be effective in modifying student behavior, include: simply stating the student's name, explaining briefly and succinctly what the student is doing that is inappropriate, and what the student should be doing.

Verbal techniques for reinforcing behavior include both encouragement and praise delivered by the teacher. In addition, for verbal techniques to positively effect student behavior and learning, the teacher must give clear, concise directives while implying her warmth toward the students.

Other factors that contribute to enhanced student learning have to do with body language. The teacher needs to make eye contact with individual students, smile and nod approvingly, move closer to the students, give gentle pats on the shoulder, arm or head, and bend over so that the teacher is face to face with the children. Some of these same techniques can be applied as a means of desisting student misbehaviors. Rather than smiling, the teacher may need to make eye contact first and then nod disapprovingly. Again a gentle tap on the shoulder or arm can be used to get a student's attention in an attempt to stop deviancy.

It is also helpful for the teacher to display prominently the classroom rules. This will serve as a visual reminder of the students' expected behaviors. In a study of classroom management procedures, it was established that the combination of conspicuously displayed rules, frequent verbal references to the rules, and appropriate consequences for appropriate behaviors led to increased levels of on-task behavior.

Skill 9.2   Demonstrates knowledge of strategies for individual behavior management; crisis prevention and intervention; conflict resolution; appropriate, non-aversive, least-intrusive procedures for managing spontaneous behavioral problems; and procedures to help individuals develop self-awareness, self-control, self-reliance, self-esteem, and self-determination and manage their own behavior.

Behavior Management Plan Strategies for Increasing Desired Behaviors

1. **Prompt**-A prompt is a visual or verbal cue that assists the child through the behavior shaping process. In some cases, the teacher may use a physical prompt such as guiding a child's hand. Visual cues include signs or other visual aids. Verbal cues include talking a child through the steps of a task. The gradual removal of the prompt as the child masters the target behavior is called fading.

2. **Modeling**-In order for modeling to be effective, the child must first be at a cognitive and developmental level to imitate the model. Teachers are behavior models in the classroom, but peers are powerful models as well, especially in adolescence. A child who does not perceive a model as acceptable will not likely copy the model's behavior. This is why teachers should be careful to reinforce appropriate behavior and not fall into the trap of attending to inappropriate behaviors. Children who see that the students who misbehave get the teacher's constant attention will most likely begin to model those students' behaviors.

3. **Contingency Contracting**-Also known as the Premack Principle or "Grandma's Law", this technique is based on the concept that a preferred behavior that frequently occurs can be used to increase a less preferred behavior with a low rate of occurrence. In short, performance of X results in the opportunity to do Y, such as getting 10 minutes of free time for completing the math assignment with 85% accuracy.

Contingency contracts are a process that continues after formal schooling and into the world of work and adult living. Contracts can be individualized, developed with input of the child, and accent positive behaviors. Contingencies can also be simple verbal contracts, such as the teacher telling a child that he or she may earn a treat or special activity for completion of a specific academic activity. Contingency contracts can be simple daily contracts or more formal, written contracts.

Written contracts last for longer periods of time, and must be clear, specific, and fair. Payoffs should be deliverable immediately after the student completes the terms of the contract. An advantage of a written contract is that the child can see and re-affirm the terms of the contract. By being actively involved in the development of the contract with the teacher and/or parent, the child assumes responsibility for fulfilling his share of the deal. Contracts can be renewed and renegotiated as the student progresses toward the target behavior goal.

4. **Token Economy**-A token economy mirrors our money system in that the students earn tokens ("money") which are of little value in themselves, but can be traded for tangible or activity rewards, just as currency can be spent for merchandise. Using stamps, stickers, stars, or point cards instead of items like poker chips decrease the likelihood of theft, loss, and noise in the classroom.

Tips for a token economy:

- Keep the system simple to understand and administer
- Develop a reward "menu" which is deliverable and varied
- Decide on the target behaviors
- Explain the system completely and in positive terms before beginning the economy
- Periodically review the rules
- Price the rewards and costs fairly, and post the menu where it will be easily read
- Gradually fade to a variable schedule of reinforcement

Behavior Management Plan Strategies for Decreasing Undesirable Behaviors

1. Extinction-Reinforcement is withheld for an unacceptable behavior. A common example is ignoring the student who calls out without raising his hand and recognizing the student who is raising his hand to speak. This would not be a suitable strategy for serious misbehaviors where others are in danger of being hurt.

2. Differential Reinforcement of Incompatible Behaviors (DRI)-In this method, the teacher reinforces an acceptable behavior that is not compatible with the target behavior. A child cannot be out of her seat and in her seat at the same time, so the teacher would reinforce the time when the child is in her seat.

3. Differential Reinforcement of Alternative Behaviors (DRA)-Student is reinforced for producing a behavior that is an alternative to the undesired target behavior, such as talking with a classmate instead of arguing.

4. Differential Reinforcement of Other Behaviors (DRO)-Reinforcement is provided for producing any appropriate behaviors except for the target behavior during a specified time interval. This technique works well with stereotypic, disruptive, or self-injurious behaviors.

5. Satiation or Negative Practice-This technique involves reinforcing the inappropriate behavior on a fixed reinforcement schedule until the student discontinues the behavior. The reinforcement must be consistently applied until the student does not want to do it. Behaviors suitable for satiation would be chronic "borrowing" of school supplies, getting up to go to the wastebasket or pencil sharpener, or asking for the time. An example would be giving a student a pencil to sharpen at frequent intervals throughout the day so that the act of getting up to sharpen a pencil no longer has any appeal.

6. Verbal Reprimands-Reprimands are best delivered privately, especially for secondary students, who may be provoked into more misbehavior if they are embarrassed in front of their peers. Verbal reprimands also may be a source of attention and reinforcement with some students.

Punishment as a " Deterrent" to Misbehavior

Punishment should **not** be the first strategy in behavior management plans because it tends to suppress behavior, not eliminate it. Punishment focuses on the negative rather than positive behaviors. There is also the chance that the child will comply out of fear, stress, or tension rather than a genuine behavior change. Furthermore, there is the chance that punishment may be misused to the point where it is no longer effective. Forms or punishment include:

- **Adding an aversive event** -(i.e., detention, lunchroom cleanup, extra assignments)

- **Subtracting something that the child likes**- (i.e., recess)

- **Response Cost**-In token economies, response cost results in loss of points or token. Response-cost or loss of privileges is preferred to adding aversives, but for long-term changes in behavior, punishment is less effective than other forms of decreasing misbehavior, such as extinction and ignoring.

-

- **Time-Out**-Time-out means removing a child from the reinforcing situation to a setting that is not reinforcing. Time out may be **observational** (i.e., sitting at the end of the basketball court for five minutes or putting one's head down at the desk). The point is to have the child observe the others engaging in the appropriate behavior. **Exclusion time-out** involves placing a visual barrier between the student and the rest of the class. This could be a divider between the desks and the time-out area, or removing the child to another room. **Seclusion time-out** necessitates a special time-out room that adheres to mandated standards, as well as a log of the children who are taken to time out, the reasons, and the time spent there.

In order to be effective, time-out must be consistently applied, and the child must know why he is being sent to the time out area and for how long. The teacher briefly explains the reason for time-out, directs the child to the area, and refrains from long explanations, arguments, or debates. The time-out area should be as neutral as possible, away from busy areas, and easily observed by the monitor, but not from the rest of the class. The duration of time-out should vary with the age of the child, and timed so the child knows when the end of time-out has arrived.

Time-out as part of a behavior management plan needs to be periodically evaluated for its effectiveness. By analyzing records of time-out (as required and directed by the school district), the teacher can see if the technique is working. If a student regularly goes to time-out at a certain time, the student may be avoiding a frustrating situation or a difficult academic subject. Seclusion time out may be effective for children who tend to be group-oriented, acting-out, or aggressive. Isolation from the group is not rewarding for them. Shy, solitary, or withdrawn children may actually prefer to be in time-out and increase the target behavior in order to go to time-out.

- **Overcorrection**-Overcorrection is more effective with severe and profoundly handicapped students. The student is required to repeat an appropriate behavior for a specified number of times when the inappropriate behavior is exhibited.

- **Suspension**-Suspension is the punishment of last resort. In addition to restrictions on suspension for students with disabilities, suspension translates into a "vacation" from school for many students with behavioral problems. Furthermore, suspension does not relieve the teacher from the responsibility of exploring alternatives that may be effective with the child. An alternative to out-of-school suspension is in-school suspension, where the student is placed in a special area to do his or her class work for a specified time and with minimal privileges. Extended suspensions (i.e., for drugs, weapons, or assault) or offenses punishable by expulsion result in a change of placement, which calls for special meetings to discuss alternative placement and/or services.

Classroom Management and Technology
Personal, professional time management is as significant for a teacher's effectiveness, today, as classroom management. As new educational programs, services and techniques are continually introduced, demands upon the teacher's time (in and out of the classroom) are increased. Using the available technology to perform (or aid in the performance) of administrative tasks, increasingly becomes a necessity for the modern teacher.

The technology itself will continue to change and, presumably, improve the processes we use to access and manipulate a variety of functional tools for the classroom and for administrative use, and the teacher should stay informed about these changes and the availability to access new or enhanced technologies through his or her school system. But more significant to the teacher than the types of technology available are the uses for these tools:

1) Expeditious access to varieties of data
2) The ability to manipulate large quantities of data
3) The ability to expeditiously store and retrieve large quantities of data
4) The ability to acquire and share information, on a local, network or global scope

Whether the teacher accesses administrative tools via a stand-alone computer, through a local area network, or a terminal networked into a system maintained by the school district, there are numerous application programs now being produced which allow the teacher to expedite processing and share files.

Common applications for which teachers use this technology are:

- Capturing, maintaining and reporting attendance
- Developing, producing, updating and storing lesson plans and integrating data modules, visual materials, presentation materials, etc., within the lesson plan, specifically, and into the total curriculum, generally.
- Producing and storing test and evaluation materials; linking modules where applicable
- Maintaining, storing and reporting student grades and evaluations
- Facilitating communication with administration, peers (within and beyond the school system) and parents
- Developing an integrated curriculum
- Accessing professional development applications
- Researching and acquiring new applications, as well as non-computer related instructional media and activities, for use in the classroom, for lesson planning and curriculum development

Whether tied into a school network or not, the teacher will find a portable/home computer to be an asset in planning, grading, communicating and preparing a variety of materials for professional and classroom use. Individual teachers as well as teacher organizations are online and available to the teaching community through numerous websites. Today, a teacher with a problem, a question or an idea to share has virtual access to thousands of peers and mentors.

Personal, professional time management is as significant for a teacher's effectiveness, today, as classroom management. As new educational programs, services and techniques are continually introduced, demands upon the teacher's time (in and out of the classroom) are increased. Using the available technology to perform (or aid in the performance) of administrative tasks, increasingly becomes a necessity for the modern teacher.

Educational Technology Professor Bernie Poole concludes that every teacher, today should be proficient with at least the basic productivity tools available on all computers: word processor, spreadsheet, database, presentation software. He adds that a teacher, today, who is not adept at utilizing Web search engines, will also be restricted in his or her productivity.

Skill 9.3 **Recognizes the characteristics of environments, including materials, equipment, and spatial arrangements, that facilitate all students' development, learning, motivation, engagement in productive work, positive behavior, and social relationships.**

The physical setting of the classroom contributes a great deal toward the propensity for students to learn. An adequate, well-built, and well-equipped classroom will invite students to learn. This has been called "invitational learning." Among the important factors to consider in the physical setting of the classroom are the following:

- o Adequate physical space
- o Repair status
- o Lighting adequacy
- o Adequate entry/exit access (including handicap accessibility)
- o Ventilation/climate control
- o Coloration

A classroom must have adequate physical space so students can conduct themselves comfortably. Some students are distracted by windows, pencil sharpeners, doors, etc. Some students prefer the front, middle, or back rows.

The teacher has the responsibility to report any items of classroom disrepair to maintenance staff. Broken windows, falling plaster, exposed sharp surfaces, leaks in ceiling or walls, and other items of disrepair present hazards to students.

Another factor which must be considered is adequate lighting. Report any inadequacies in classroom illumination. Florescent lights placed at acute angles often burn out faster. A healthy supply of spare tubes is a sound investment.

Local fire and safety codes dictate entry and exit standards. In addition, all corridors and classrooms should be wheelchair accessible for students and others who use them. Older schools may not have this accessibility.

Another consideration is adequate ventilation and climate control. Some classrooms in some states use air conditioning extensively. Sometimes it is so cold as to be considered a distraction. Specialty classes such as science require specialized hoods for ventilation. Physical Education classes have the added responsibility for shower areas and specialized environments that must be heated such as pool or athletic training rooms.

Classrooms with warmer subdued colors contribute to students' concentration on task items. Neutral hues for coloration of walls, ceiling, and carpet or tile are generally used in classrooms so distraction due to classroom coloration may be minimized.

In the modern classroom, there is a great deal of furniture, equipment, supplies, appliances, and learning aids to help the teacher teach and students learn. The classroom should be provided with furnishings that fit the purpose of the classroom. The kindergarten classroom may have a reading center, a playhouse, a puzzle table, student work desks/tables, a sandbox, and any other relevant learning/interest areas.

Whatever the arrangement of furniture and equipment may be the teacher must provide for adequate traffic flow. Rows of desks must have adequate space between them for students to move and for the teacher to circulate. All areas must be open to line-of-sight supervision by the teacher.

In all cases, proper care must be taken to ensure student safety. Furniture and equipment should be situated safely at all times. No equipment, materials, boxes, etc. should be placed where there is danger of falling. Doors must have entry and exit accessibility at all times.

The major emergency responses include two categories for student movement: tornado warning response; and building evacuation, which includes most other emergencies (fire, bomb threat, etc.). For tornadoes, the prescribed response is to evacuate all students and personnel to the first floor of multi-story buildings, and to place students along walls away from windows. All persons, including the teacher, should then crouch on the floor and cover their heads with their hands. These are standard procedures for severe weather, particularly tornadoes.

Most other emergency situations require evacuation of the school building. Teachers should be thoroughly familiar with evacuation routes established for each classroom in which they teach. Teachers should accompany and supervise students throughout the evacuation procedure, and check to see that all students under their supervision are accounted for.

Teachers should then continue to supervise students until the building may be reoccupied (upon proper school or community authority), or until other procedures are followed for students to officially leave the school area and cease to be the supervisory responsibility of the school. Elementary students evacuated to another school can wear nametags and parents or guardians should sign them out at a central location.

SEE also Skill 10.3

Skill 9.4 **Demonstrates knowledge of methods for organizing, allocating, and managing time, routines, transitions, materials, and physical space to provide active and equitable engagement of students in productive tasks; maximizing the amount of class time spent in learning; and facilitating appropriate behaviors, development, and learning for students with diverse learning characteristics.**

Instructional momentum requires an organized system for material placement and distribution. Inability to find an overhead transparency, a necessary chart page, or the handout worksheet for the day not only stops the momentum, but is very irritating to students. Disorganization of materials frustrates both teacher and students. Effective teachers deal with daily classroom procedures efficiently and quickly because then students will spend the majority of class time engaged in academic tasks, which will likely result in higher achievement.

In the lower grades an organized system uses a "classroom helper" for effective distribution and collection of books, equipment, supplies, etc. At higher grade levels, the teacher is concerned with materials such as textbooks, written instructional aids, worksheets, computer programs, etc., which must be produced, maintained, distributed, and collected for future use. One important consideration is the production of sufficient copies of duplicated materials to satisfy classroom needs. Another is the efficient distribution of worksheets and other materials. The teacher may decide to hand out materials as students are in their learning sites (desks, etc.), or to have distribution materials at a clearly specified place (or small number of places) in the classroom. In any case, there should be firmly established procedures, completely understood by student for receiving classroom materials.

An effective teacher will also consider the needs and abilities of her students when developing routines or a daily schedule. For routines, a teacher might motivate a low-achieving student with a coveted task (such as taking down the attendance sheet or a recommendation for Safety Patrol) in order to increase confidence in that child. This increased confidence could lead to an increased interest in school and improved learning. Likewise, a teacher should also consider the needs of his or her students when developing the aspects of the daily schedule. For instance, if faced with a "hard to calm down" group, a teacher might schedule quiet reading time after recess. Being aware of their students trends and characteristics in developing a classroom routine can significantly impact student learning.

Handling Transitions
Effective teachers use class time efficiently. This results in higher student subject engagement and will likely result in more subject matter retention. One way teachers use class time efficiently is through a smooth transition from one activity to another; this is also known as "management transition."

Management transition is defined as "teacher shifts from one activity to another in a systemic, academically oriented way" (Florida Performance Measurement System, Domain III). One factor that contributes to efficient management transition is the teacher's management of instructional material. Effective teachers gather their materials during the planning stage of instruction. Doing this, a teacher avoids flipping through things and looking for the items necessary for the current lesson. Momentum is lost and student concentration is broken when this occurs.

Additionally, teachers who keep students informed of the sequencing of instructional activities maintain systematic transitions because the students are prepared to move on to the next activity. For example, the teacher says, "When we finish with this guided practice together, we will turn to page twenty-three and each student will do the exercises. I will then circulate throughout the classroom helping on an individual basis. Okay, let's begin." Following an example, such as this, will lead to systematic smooth transitions between activities because the students will be turning to page twenty-three when the class finishes the practice without a break in concentration.

Another method that leads to smooth transitions is to move students in groups and clusters rather than one by one. This is called *group fragmentation*. For example, if some students do seat work while other students gather for a reading group, the teacher moves the students in pre-determined groups. Instead of calling the individual names of the reading group, which would be time consuming and laborious, the teacher simply says, "Will the blue reading group please assemble at the reading station. The red and yellow groups will quietly do the vocabulary assignment I am now passing out." As a result of this activity, the classroom is ready to move on in a matter of seconds rather than minutes.

Additionally, the teacher may employ academic transition signals, defined as "teacher utterance that indicate[s] movement of the lesson from one topic or activity to another by indicating where the lesson is and where it is going," (Florida Performance Measurement System, Domain III). For example, the teacher may say, "That completes our description of clouds, now we will examine weather fronts." Like the sequencing of instructional materials, this keeps the student informed on what is coming next so the students will move to the next activity with little or no break in concentration.

Therefore, effective teachers manage transitions from one activity to another in a systematically oriented way through efficient management of instructional matter, sequencing of instructional activities, moving students in groups and by employing academic transition signals. Through an efficient use of class time, achievement is increased because students spend more class time engaged in on-task behavior.

Transition refers to changes in class activities that involve movement. Examples are:

- Breaking up from large group instruction into small groups for learning centers and small-group instructions
- Classroom to lunch, to the playground, or to elective classes
- Finishing reading at the end of one period and getting ready for math the next period
- Emergency situations such as fire drills

Successful transitions are achieved by using proactive strategies. Early in the year, the teacher pinpoints the transition periods in the day and anticipates possible behavior problems, such as students habitually returning late from lunch. After identifying possible problems with the environment or the schedule, the teacher plans proactive strategies to minimize or eliminate those problems.

Proactive planning also gives the teacher the advantage of being prepared, addressing behaviors before they become problems, and incorporating strategies into the classroom management plan right away. Transition plans can be developed for each type of transition and the expected behaviors for each situation taught directly to the students.

Skill 9.5 **Recognizes effective methods for coordinating, training, monitoring, directing the activities of, evaluating, and providing feedback to paraeducators, volunteers, and/or peer tutors and facilitating the integration of related services into the instructional program.**

Teachers should demonstrate the ability to co-teach and co-plan in collaboration with paraeducators, volunteers, and other professionals. By initializing collaboration with others, this creates effective learning situations where student learning is optimized.

Methods

- Works with colleagues to develop an effective learning climate within the school
- Coordinates and/or collaborates in directing activities of a classroom paraeducator, volunteer, or peer tutor.
- Participates in collaborative decision-making and problem solving with other professionals to achieve student success
- Collaborates with the student and family in meeting instructional goals and charting progress of students

COMPETENCY 10.0   UNDERSTANDS BEST PRACTICES RELATED TO MOTIVATION AND BEHAVIOR TO CREATE LEARNING ENVIRONMENTS THAT ENCOURAGE POSITIVE SOCIAL INTERACTION, SELF MOTIVATION, AND ACTIVE ENGAGEMENT IN LEARNING.

Skill 10.1   Demonstrates understanding of how individuals influence groups and how groups function in society.

Groups are formally or informally organized associations of individuals who share one or more common characteristics, interests or demands.

In order to define a group, each member must have a self-definition as a group member. It is especially important that other group members also identify and accept the individual as belonging to the group. Normative expectations, (rules) often influence each individual member's behavior and these combined actions influence the entire group.

Different cultural groups and diversity of groups support different points of view and complement each other's information. Extra effort may be needed to create a cohesive group of members who arrive with diverse backgrounds and experiences. In modern, complex societies, members perform very different tasks, meaning that a strong interdependence develops between them. Complex societies are groups that function together to sustain the whole society. Socialization and communication within these groups are the avenues in which individuals pass along their values systems, interests, and beliefs.

Skill 10.2   Analyzes factors that influence motivation and engagement and help students become self-motivated.

Teachers can enhance student motivation by planning and directing interactive, "hands-on" learning experiences. Research substantiates that cooperative group projects decrease student behavior problems and increase student on-task behavior. Students who are directly involved with learning activities are more motivated to complete a task to the best of their ability.

Students generally do not realize their own abilities and frequently lack self-confidence. Teachers can instill positive self-concepts in children and thereby enhance their innate abilities by providing certain types of feedback. Such feedback includes attributing students' successes to their effort and specifying what the student did that produced the success. Qualitative comments influence attitudes more than quantitative feedback such as grades.

Teachers must avoid teaching tasks that fit their own interests and goals and design activities that address the students' concerns. In order to do this, it is necessary to find out about students and to have a sense of their interests and goals. Teachers can do this by conducting student surveys and simply by questioning and listening to students. Once this information is obtained the teacher can link students' interests with classroom tasks.

Teachers are learning the value of giving assignments that meet the individual abilities and needs of students. After instruction, discussion, questioning, and practice have been provided, rather than assigning one task to all students—teachers are asking students to generate tasks that will show their knowledge of the information presented. Students are given choices and thereby have the opportunity to demonstrate more effectively the skills, concepts, or topics that they as individuals have learned. It has been established that student choice increases student originality, intrinsic motivation, and higher mental processes.

SEE Skill 12.5

Skill 10.3 **Demonstrates knowledge of strategies for engaging students in and monitoring individual and group learning activities that help them develop the motivation to achieve.**

Classroom climate is a significant influence on successful student learning. Interactions among and relationships between students are an important factor of a positive classroom climate. In past classroom practices, it was common for students to be grouped according to ability. This practice is sometimes referred to as tracking or homogenous grouping. For example, students who found math challenging would be in the "low" math group, average math students would be in the "grade-level" math group, and excelling math learners would make up the "advanced" group.

This type of grouping can lead to problems with students' self-concept and motivation in class. Students who found themselves in the low group would feel ashamed or stupid. The label associated with these students is that they were difficult, incapable and/or dim learners. At the same time, students in the advanced group may feel superior and boast their successes in front of other students, as well as stressed over the feeling to perform. In summary, this type of grouping typically leads to a combination of feelings including resentment, stress, inferiority, and failure; feelings that do not enhance learning.

It's not that teachers can never group students by ability. Used once in a while, this method does allow students to work at a comfortable level. However, teachers often find that heterogeneous grouping (grouping by mixed abilities) allows all students to feel success without the negative effects of homogenous groups. In mixed groups, students can learn from more advanced students, while advanced students can still be provided with opportunities to excel in an activity.

Cooperative learning is an excellent setting for heterogeneous groups as students work together to solve problems or complete activities while benefiting from all learning abilities. In this setting, all students feel they are successful in their learning, and feelings of confidence, friendship, and achievement are experienced.

When students are interested in the lesson their interest and motivation for learning increases. Teachers should provide opportunities so students may work toward becoming self-directed, and therefore, self-motivated, learners.

Success-Oriented Activities

Skill knowledge, strategy use, motivation, and personal interests are all factors that influence individual student success. Success-oriented activities are tasks that are selected to meet the individual needs and interests of the student. During the time a student is learning a new skill, tasks should be selected so that the student will be able to earn a high percentage of correct answers during the teacher questioning and seatwork portions of the lesson. Later, the teacher should also include work that challenges students to apply what they have learned and stimulate their thinking.

In the success-oriented classroom, mistakes are viewed as a natural part of the learning process. The teacher can also show that adults make mistakes by correcting errors without getting unduly upset. The students feel safe to try new things because they know that they have a supportive environment and can correct their mistakes.

Activities that promote student success:

- Are based on useful, relevant content that is clearly specified, and organized for easy learning
- Allow sufficient time to learn the skill and is selected for high rate of success
- Allow students the opportunity to work independently, self-monitor, and set goals
- Provide for frequent monitoring and corrective feedback
- Include collaboration in group activities or peer teaching

Students with learning problems often attribute their successes to luck or ease of the task. Their failures are often blamed on their supposed lack of ability, difficulty of the task, or the fault of someone else. Successful activities, attribution retraining, and learning strategies can help these students to discover that they can become independent learners. When the teacher communicates the expectation that the students can be successful learners and chooses activities that will help them be successful, achievement is increased.

SEE also Skill 9.1

Skill 10.4   Identifies and evaluates appropriate reinforcers to enhance learning and motivation.

Extrinsic motivation is motivation that comes from the expectation of rewards or punishments. The rewards and punishments can be varied. For example, in social situations, most human beings are extrinsically motivated to behave in common, socially-accepted ways. The punishment for NOT doing so might be embarrassment or ridicule. The reward for doing so might be the acceptance of peers. In the classroom, rewards might be grades, candy, or special privileges. Punishments might be phone calls to parents, detention, suspension, or poor grades.

Intrinsic motivation is motivation that comes from within. For example, while some children only read if given extrinsic rewards (e.g., winning an award for the most pages read), other children read because they enjoy it.

There are benefits and drawbacks of both methods of motivation. Well, in reality, it should be noted that in an ideal world, all motivation would be intrinsic. But this is not the case. Consider having to clean your apartment, dorm room, or house. We might appreciate the "reward" of a clean living space at the end of the activity, but most of us do not particularly enjoy the process of cleaning, and we only put up with it so that we get the end result.

In learning, we of course want all students to be intrinsically motivated. We would want students to not care about grades or prizes as much as we might want them to do their work, listen attentively, and read just because they want to learn. And while all teachers should work tirelessly to ensure that they develop intrinsic motivation as much as possible within their students, everyone knows that for certain students and subjects, extrinsic motivators must be used.

What extrinsic motivators are useful in the classroom? Well, to start, if things like candy and prizes are always used to get students to pay attention in class, soon, they will expect these things and possibly not pay attention in their absence. Likewise, if punishment is always used as a motivator, students may be more consumed with fear than having the frame of mind that is most conducive to learning.

So, while grades can consume many students, having benchmarks and standards are indeed useful for many teachers. Punishments, if they are reasonable and if students know what to expect (with consistent application), can be useful in making sure students behave appropriately. The best punishments, though, are ones in which a whole school has decided will be consistently used from classroom to classroom and grade level to grade level.

In general, teachers must walk a careful line with motivation. They must utilize extrinsic motivators when all possible intrinsic motivators have failed to work.

Effects of Motivational Strategies

As a rule, teachers should strive to encourage intrinsic motivation for students' learning. To do so lessens the need to use extrinsic motivators, such as frivolous rewards and harsh punishments.

The best way to encourage intrinsic motivation is to engage students in the learning. Engagement happens most when students work with material that is of greatest interest to them and if they feel there is a useful application for such material. For example, teachers will notice intrinsic motivation in reading when students have found books that they relate to. When teachers believe that certain students just will not read, often (though not always), those students have not found books that they like. Considering there are hundreds of thousands of books out there, most likely, each student can find at least one book they are initially interested in.

The extrinsic motivator of grades can be a particularly large challenge for well-meaning high school teachers who have college-bound students. Such students may not care much about the learning as they do about the grades, so that their college applications look more competitive. Unfortunately, across the country, this has resulted in very troubling behavior. Plagiarism and cheating have been noticed in high schools everywhere. While teachers may want to encourage students to learn for the sake of the learning itself, they must contend with students who have been trained to "win at all costs." Teachers can therefore use many strategies—NOT to eradicate the very act of cheating, for example—but to encourage students to explore topics that are of interest to them or to create more meaningful, authentic assessments. Authentic assessments are those in which students have to use new learning in a real-world, deeply meaningful way.

Finally, it must be noted that punishment as an extrinsic motivator, while necessary at some times, often creates greater problems in the future. Students who feel like they are constantly punished into better behavior or to do better academically lose interest in pleasing teachers, acting appropriately, or learning. It is always better, whenever possible, for teachers to work at engaging students first, and then punishing if all options have been exhausted.

Skill 10.5   Demonstrates knowledge of effective methods for collaborating with parents and educators in the use of specific academic or behavior management strategies and counseling techniques.

Research proves that the more families are involved in a child's educational experience, the more that child will succeed academically. The problem is that often teachers assume that involvement in education simply means that the parents show up to help at school events or participate in parental activities on campus. With this belief, many teachers devise clever strategies to increase parental involvement at school. However, just because a parent shows up to school and assists with an activity does not mean that the child will learn more. Many parents work all day long and cannot assist in the school. Teachers, therefore, have to think of different ways to encourage parental and family involvement in the educational process.

Quite often, teachers have great success within involving families by just informing families of what is going on in the classroom. Newsletters are particularly effective at this. Parents love to know what is going on in the classroom, and this way, they'll feel included. In newsletters, for example, teachers can provide suggestions on how parents can help with the educational goals of the school. For example, teachers can recommend that parents read with their children for twenty minutes per day. To add effectiveness to that, teachers can also provide suggestions on what to do when their children come across difficult words or when they ask a question about comprehension. This gives parents practical strategies to use with their children.

Parents often equate phone calls from teachers with news about misbehaviors of their children. Teachers can change that tone by calling parents with good news. Or they can send positive notes home with students. By doing this, when negative phone calls need to be made, teachers will have greater success.

Teachers can also provide very specific suggestions to individual parents. For example, let's say a student needs additional assistance in a particular subject. The teacher can provide tips to parents to encourage and increase deeper understandings in the subject outside of class.

When it is necessary to communicate (whether by phone, letter, or in person) with a parent regarding a concern about a student, the teacher should allow herself a "cooling off" period before making contact with the parent. It is important that the teacher remain professional and objective. The purpose for contacting the parent is to elicit support and additional information that may have a bearing on the student's behavior or performance. The teacher should be careful to not demean the child and not to appear antagonistic or confrontational. Be aware that the parent is likely to be quite uncomfortable with the bad news and will respond best if you take a cooperative, problem solving approach to the issue. It is also a nice courtesy to notify parents of positive occurrences with their children. The teacher's communication with parents should not be limited to negative items.

Parent conferences

The parent-teacher conference is generally for one of three purposes. First, the teacher may wish to share information with the parents concerning the performance and behavior of the child. Second, the teacher may be interested in obtaining information from the parents about the child. Such information may help answer questions or concerns that the teacher has. A third purpose may be to request parent support or involvement in specific activities or requirements. In many situations, more than one of the purposes may be involved.

Planning the conference

When a conference is scheduled, whether at the request of the teacher or parent, the teacher should allow sufficient time to prepare thoroughly. Collect all relevant information, samples of student work, records of behavior, and other items needed to help the parent understand the circumstances. It is also a good idea to compile a list of questions or concerns you wish to address. Arrange the time and location of the conference to provide privacy and to avoid interruptions.

Conducting the conference

Begin the conference by putting the parents as ease. Take the time to establish a comfortable mood, but do not waste time with unnecessary small talk. Begin your discussion with positive comments about the student. Identify strengths and desirable attributes, but do not exaggerate.

The teacher should address issues or areas of concern, being sure to focus on observable behaviors and concrete results or information. It is important to not make judgmental statements about parent or child. Sharing specific work samples, anecdotal records of behavior, etc., which demonstrate clearly the concerns is important as well. The teacher should be a good listener by hearing the parent's comments and explanations. Such background information can be invaluable in understanding the needs and motivations of the child.

Finally, end the conference with an agreed plan of action between parents and teacher (and, when appropriate, the child). Bring the conference to a close politely but firmly and thank the parents for their involvement.

After the conference

A day or two after the conference, it is a good idea to send a follow-up note to the parents. In this note, briefly and concisely reiterate the plan or step agreed to in the conference. Be polite and professional; avoid the temptation to be too informal or chatty. If the issue is a long-term one such as behavior or on-going work performance of the student, make periodic follow-up contacts to keep the parents informed of the progress.

COMPETENCY 11.0   UNDERSTANDS STRATEGIES FOR ENHANCING STUDENTS' SOCIAL SKILLS DEVELOPMENT.

Skill 11.1   Demonstrates knowledge of effective methods and strategies for teaching social skills development to all students.

Teaching social skills can be rather difficult because social competence requires a repertoire of skills in a number of areas. The socially competent person must be able to get along with family and friends, function in a work environment, take care of personal needs, solve problems in daily living, and identify sources of help. A class of students with emotional disabilities may present several deficits in a few areas or a few deficits in many areas. Therefore, the teacher must begin with an assessment of the skill deficits and prioritize the ones to teach first.

Type of Assessment	Description
Direct Observation	Observe student in various settings with a checklist
Role Play	Teacher observes students in structured scenarios
Teacher Ratings	Teacher rates student with a checklist or formal assessment instrument
Sociometric Measures: Peer Nomination	Student names specific classmates who meet a stated criterion (i.e., playmate). Score is the number of times a child is nominated.
Peer Rating	Students rank all their classmates on a Likert-type scale (e.g., 1-3 or 1-5 scale) on stated criterion. Individual score is the average of the total ratings of their classmates.
Paired-Comparison	Student is presented with paired classmate combinations and asked to choose who is most or least liked in the pair.
Context Observation	Student is observed to determine if the skill deficit is present in one setting, but not others
Comparison with other student	Student's social skill behavior is compared to two other students in the same situation to determine if there is a deficit, or if the behavior is not really a problem.

Social skills instruction can include teaching conversation skills, assertiveness, play and peer interaction, problem solving and coping skills, self-help, task-related behaviors, self-concept related skills (i.e., expressing feelings, accepting consequences), and job related skills.

One advantage of schooling organizations for students is to facilitate social skills and social development. While teachers cannot take the largest role for developing such traits as honesty, fairness, and concern for others, they are extremely important in the process. The first recommendation is to be a very good role model. As we all know, actions do indeed speak louder than words.

Second, teachers need to communicate expectations and be firm about them. When teachers ignore certain "infractions" and make a big deal about others, they demonstrate to students that it isn't about manners and social skills, but rather discipline and favoritism. All students need to feel safe, cared about, and secure with their classmates. Teachers are the best people to ensure that students understand how to be generous, caring, considerate, and sociable individuals.

Skill 11.2   Demonstrates understanding of strategies for preparing individuals to live harmoniously and productively in a multiethnic, multicultural, and multinational world.

In personalized learning communities, relationships and connections between students, staff, parents and community members promote lifelong learning for all students. School communities that promote an inclusion of diversity in the classroom, community, curriculum and connections enable students to maximize their academic capabilities and educational opportunities. Setting school climates that are inclusive of the multicultural demographic student population create positive and proactive mission and vision themes that align student and staff expectations.

The following factors enable students and staff to emphasize and integrate diversity in student learning:

- Inclusion of multicultural themes in curriculum and assessments
- Creation of a learning environment that promotes multicultural research, learning, collaboration, and social construction of knowledge and application
- Providing learning tasks that emphasize student cognitive, critical thinking and problem-solving skills
- Learning tasks that personalize the cultural aspects of diversity and celebrate diversity in the subject matter and student projects
- Promotion of intercultural positive social peer interrelationships and connections

Teachers communicate diversity in instructional practices and experiential learning activities that create curiosity in students who want to understand the interrelationship of cultural experiences. Students become self-directed in discovering the global world in and outside the classroom. Teachers understand that when diversity becomes an integral part of the classroom environment, students become global thinkers and doers.

In the intercultural communication model, students are able to learn how different cultures engage in both verbal and nonverbal modes of communicating meaning. Students who become multilingual in understanding the stereotypes that have defined other cultures are able to create new bonding experiences that will typify a more integrated global culture. Students who understand how to effectively communicate with diverse cultural groups are able to maximize their own learning experiences by being able to transmit both verbally and non-verbally cues and expectations in project collaborations or in performance based activities.

The learning curve for teachers in intercultural understanding is exponential, in that they are able to engage all learners in the academic process and learning engagement. Teaching students how to incorporate learning techniques from a cultural aspect enriches the cognitive expansion experience since students are able to expand their cultural knowledge bases.

Teachers must demonstrate respect for cultural diversity and individual differences by planning learning activities that are sensitive to issues of class, gender, race, ethnicity, family composition, age, and special needs. Teachers should look at the special characteristics of students within cultural contexts, using developmental and pedagogical knowledge to continuously refine teaching practices.

The teacher should treat students fairly, acknowledging the individual differences that make one student different from another and taking these differences into account. Teachers should modify their instruction based on observation and knowledge of their students' interests, abilities, skills, knowledge, family circumstances, and peer relationships. Teachers must take into account the impact of context and culture on behavior. They should enhance student's self esteem, motivation, character, and their respect for individual, cultural, religious and racial differences.

Teacher's should appreciate individual variation within each area of development, show respect for the diverse talents of all learners, and remain committed to helping them develop self-confidence and competence.

Teacher's should appreciate the cultural dimensions of communication, and respond appropriately, and attempt to develop culturally sensitive communication between students.

Skill 11.3   Recognizes effective strategies for helping students work cooperatively and productively in groups.

Cooperative learning situations, as practiced in today's classrooms, grew out of searches conducted by several groups in the early 1970's. Cooperative learning situations can range from very formal applications such as STAD (Student Teams-Achievement Divisions) and CIRC (Cooperative Integrated Reading and Composition) to less formal groupings known variously as "group investigation," "learning together," "discovery groups." Cooperative learning as a general term is now firmly recognized and established as a teaching and learning technique in American schools.

Since cooperative learning techniques are so widely diffused in the schools, it is necessary to orient students in the skills cooperative learning groups use to operate smoothly, and thereby enhance learning. Students who cannot interact constructively with other students will not be able to take advantage of the learning opportunities provided by the cooperative learning situations and will furthermore deprive their fellow students of the opportunity for cooperative learning.

These skills form the hierarchy of cooperation in which students first learn to work together as a group, so they may then proceed to levels at which they may engage in simulated conflict situations. This cooperative setting allows different points of view to be constructively entertained.

To teach cooperative skills, the teacher should:

- Ensure that students see the need for the skill
- Ensure that students understand what the skill is and when it should be used
- Set up practice situations and encourage mastery of the skill
- Ensure that students have the time and the needed procedures for discussing (and receiving feedback on)how well they are using the skill
- Ensure that students persevere in practicing the skill until the skill seems a natural action

A further goal of cooperative learning techniques is to establish and/or enhance mutual respect for other students. Cooperative learning can promote positive social goals when used effectively as a teaching/learning tool. When the teacher promotes interaction of students among ethnic and/or social groups, students tend to respond positively by forming friendships and having enhanced respect for other sociological groups. Thus, the teacher who effectively manages cooperative learning groups has not only promoted cognitive learning, but has also promoted desirable behaviors in terms of mutual respect for all students.

Skill 11.4   Demonstrates knowledge of methods for designing, implementing, and evaluating instructional programs that enhance an individual's social participation in family, school, and community activities.

Academic skills do not exist in a vacuum. All skills we teach students should relate to real-world activities, thought processes, and expectations. Considering how skills can be incorporated into family and community activities can be a fun, innovative method for encouraging relevancy in academics. For example, instead of simply having students write research reports utilizing library materials, students can be encouraged to go out into the community after school hours and interview or survey people.

In terms of designing, implementing, and evaluating instructional programs to enhance social participation, often, schools and teachers consider utilizing service-learning projects. Service-learning projects offer students the opportunity to learn through doing things in the community. For example, students can visit nursing homes and read stories to the elderly. They can participate in a litter clean-up activity. The possibilities are endless. And each possibility can be tied to instructional objectives. For example, students can write stories and read them to the elderly at nursing homes. They can learn about environmental factors in conjunction with litter clean-up projects.

Evaluating programs entails setting outcomes. Measuring whether or not outcomes have been met requires collecting data from a variety of sources. In terms of litter clean-up, data might come from students, community members, assessments, and observation.

In general, academia becomes more meaningful and relevant to students when it involves social, real-world phenomena. Having the students get out into the community and interact with other people allows them to experience learning through multiple venues. All of these are great ways to make learning more fun, meaningful and important to students.

COMPETENCY 12.0 **UNDERSTANDS HOW TO COMMUNICATE EFFECTIVELY TO PROMOTE ACTIVE INQUIRY, LEARNING, COLLABORATION, AND POSITIVE INTERACTION IN THE CLASSROOM; FOSTER A CLIMATE OF TRUST AND SUPPORT; AND FACILITATE ACHIEVEMENT OF STUDENT GOALS.**

Skill 12.1 **Recognizes methods for establishing and communicating expectations for students' learning.**

Albert Einstein, the highly noted German physicist on the theory of relativity, once wrote, "The general level of world information is high but usually based, influenced by national prejudices serving to make us citizens of our nation but not of our world." In order for students to learn, teachers must facilitate learning in the classroom and provide continued motivation to learn and synthesize knowledge as national citizens and world learners.

Teacher responsibility in today's classroom includes establishing a learning conducive environment that is both positive and proactive where class values and rules are determined by the student community and visibly posted in the classroom. Collaborative learning defines student roles and academic outcomes by creating multiple learning perspectives and integration of cultural and ethnic inclusion in the learning process. Helping students to develop cognitive learning skills that include both local and global problem-solving of academic and interpersonal skills will provide students with safe interactive learning environments to process and acquire skills that will create world-wide learners.

The focus on student performance begins with a vision and mission that supports the direction of NCLB (No Child Left Behind) where all educational directives are focused on improving academic achievement and success for all students. The next goal for teachers and school communities is to develop an action plan, which incorporates the following:

- Clearly defined goals and objects for student learning and school improvement
- Clear alignment of goals and objectives
- Developing clear timelines and accountability for goal implementation steps
- Constructing an effective evaluation plan for assessing data around student performance and established objectives for student learning outcomes.
- Defining a plan B in case plan A falls short of meeting the goals and objectives for student achievement and school improvement.

The priorities for school communities should continue to be consistent with the desired results of their action plans. Analyzing teacher instructional practices and curriculum adoptions will provide data for evaluating the effectiveness of student learning and access to academic goals and objectives.

Skill 12.2   Identifies realistic expectations for student behavior in various settings.

SEE Skill 9.1 and 9.2

Skill 12.3   Identifies ways to enhance a reinforcer's effectiveness in instruction.

A teacher's enthusiasm can significantly impact a student's desire to learn. If the teacher is droning on about a topic with little personal interest, how are the students expected to enjoy the lesson and learn?

Not only does the teacher need to be enthusiastic while teaching, he or she needs to model his or her own enthusiasm for gaining knowledge. For example, the teacher should be reading during silent reading time. Or, if a question is asked that the teacher does not know the answer, the teacher should get excited about finding out the right answer while modeling how to do so with the students.

The effective teacher communicates non-verbally with students by using positive body language, expressing warmth, concern, acceptance, and enthusiasm. Effective teachers augment their instructional presentations by using positive non-verbal communication such as smiles, open body posture, movement, and eye contact with students. The energy and enthusiasm of the effective teacher can be amplified through positive body language.

Skill 12.4   Demonstrates understanding of strategies for maintaining proper classroom decorum

A classroom is a community of learning, and when students learn to respect themselves and the members around them, learning is maximized. A positive environment, where open, discussion-oriented, non-threatening communication among all students can occur, is a critical factor in creating an effective learning culture. The teacher must take the lead and model appropriate actions and speech, and intervene quickly when a student makes a misstep and offends (often inadvertently) another.

Teachers should create a classroom climate that encourages extensive participation from the students. Collaborations and discussions are enhanced when students like and respect each other, and therefore, each student's learning can benefit. This is increases when students engage in full participation. When everyone's thoughts, perspectives, and ideas are offered, the class can consider each idea carefully in their discussion. The more students who participate, the more learning is gained through a more thorough examination of the topic.

To create this environment, teachers must first model how to welcome and consider all points of view for the students. The teacher should then positively affirm and reinforce students for offering their ideas in front of the other students. Even if somewhat amiss, the teacher should receive the idea while perhaps offering a modification or corrected statement (for more factual pieces of information). The idea is for students to feel confident and safe in being able to express their thoughts or ideas. Only then will students be able to engage in independent discussions that consider and respect everyone's statements.

Classroom Interactions
Student-student and teacher-student interactions play a significant role in a positive classroom climate. When interactions among classroom members are encouraging, learning becomes a more natural and genuine process. Cold or routine interactions discourage questioning, critical thinking and useful discussion. Teachers should make every effort to be available to their students, as well as provide natural, collaborative opportunities for students in order to strengthen classroom interactions. Reflection, observations and asking for feedback regarding one's classroom interactions (perhaps during a yearly observation) will help teachers to analyze the effectiveness of their classroom's interactions.

SEE also skill 3.5

Skill 12.5 **Demonstrates understanding of teachers' attitudes and behaviors that can positively or negatively influence the behavior of all students.**

Teachers need to be aware that much of what they say and do can be motivating and may have a positive effect on students' achievement. Studies have been conducted to determine the impact of teacher behavior on student performance. Surprisingly, a teacher's voice can really make an impression on students. Teachers' voices have several dimensions—volume, pitch, rate, etc. A recent study on the effects of speech rate indicates that, although both boys and girls prefer to listen at the rate of about 200 words per minute, boys preferring slower rates overall than girls. This same study indicates that a slower rate of speech directly affects processing ability and comprehension.

Other speech factors such as communication of ideas, communication of emotion, distinctness/pronunciation, quality variation and phrasing, correlate with teaching criterion scores. These scores show that "good" teachers ("good" meaning teachers who positively impact and motivate students) use more variety in speech than do "less effective" teachers.

A teacher's speech skills can be strong motivating elements. A teacher's body language has an even greater effect on student achievement and the ability to set and focus on goals. Teacher smiles provide support and give feedback about the teacher's affective state. A deadpan expression can actually be a detriment to the student's progress. Teacher frowns are perceived by students to mean displeasure, disapproval, and even anger. Studies also show that teacher posture and movement are indicators of the teacher's enthusiasm and energy, which emphatically influence student learning, attitudes, motivation, and focus on goals. Teachers have a greater efficacy on student motivation than any person other than parents.

Children believe that their teacher has "eyes in the back of his/her head." The with-it teacher is truly aware of what the students are doing and sends this message to the students through her behavior. When a deviancy occurs in the classroom, the effective teacher knows which student(s) caused the deviancy and swiftly stops the behavior before the deviant conduct spreads to other students or becomes more serious.

The effective teacher demonstrates awareness of what the entire class is doing and is in control of the behavior of all students even when the teacher is working with only a small group of children. In an attempt to prevent student misbehaviors the teacher makes clear, concise statements about what is happening in the classroom directing attention to content and the students' accountability for their work rather than focusing the class on the misbehavior. It is also effective for the teacher to make a positive statement about the appropriate behavior that is observed.

The teacher must be careful to control the voice, both the volume and the tone. Research indicates that soft reprimands are more effective in controlling disruptive behavior than loud reprimands and that when soft reprimands are used fewer are needed.

The teacher who can attend to a task situation and an extraneous situation simultaneously without becoming immersed in either one is said to have "with-it-ness." This ability is absolutely imperative for teacher effectiveness and success. It can be a difficult task to address deviant behavior while sustaining academic flow, but this is a skill that teachers need to develop early in their careers and one that will become second nature, intuitive, instinctive.

Verbal techniques, which may be effective in modifying student behavior and setting the classroom tone, include simply stating the student's name, explaining briefly and succinctly what the student is doing that is inappropriate and what the student should be doing. Verbal techniques for reinforcing behavior include both encouragement and praise delivered by the teacher. In addition, for verbal techniques to positively effect student behavior and learning, the teacher must give clear, concise directives while implying her warmth toward the students.

SUBAREA IV. COLLABORATION, COMMUNICATION, AND PROFESSIONALISM

COMPETENCY 13.0 **UNDERSTANDS HOW TO ESTABLISH AND MAINTAIN COLLABORATIVE RELATIONSHIPS WITH OTHER MEMBERS OF THE LEARNING COMMUNITY TO ENHANCE LEARNING FOR ALL STUDENTS.**

Skill 13.1 **Demonstrates understanding of the processes and skills necessary to initiate collaboration with others (e.g., individual students, parents/guardians, families, school and community personnel) and create situations in which collaboration will enhance students' learning in a culturally responsive program.**

Part of being an effective teacher is to not only have students to grow educationally, but to allow oneself to also continue to grow as a teacher. Working with other members of the school community—peers, supervisors, and other staff—will give the teacher the necessary grounding needed to increase skills and knowledge sets. Identifying possible mentors, teachers should choose fellow teachers who are respected and whom should be emulated. Searching out other teachers who have had an amount of success in the area needing growth is another step. Asking them questions and for advice on brushing up lesson plans or techniques for delivery of instruction can be helpful. Talk to the supervisor or the principal when you are having difficulties, or when you want to learn more about a topic. They may know of development training seminars, books, journals, or other resources that might be available. Teachers should remember that they are part of a team of professionals, and that their personal success is part of a greater success that everyone hopes to achieve.

Collaboration with professional colleagues

The teacher is the manager of his classroom. This can seem a lonely business sometimes, especially when he has a particularly troubling student or troubled group of students. Fortunately, he is not alone. He has colleagues who are usually more than willing to step in and help out. Sharing ownership of the classroom with other teachers who may be dealing with the same students makes this job tenable. If teachers are sharing the same student, they can, together, develop a strategy for dealing with that student. The same is true of parents. That relationship must not be adversarial unless there is no other way to handle the student and the situation.

In communications with other teachers, administration, and parents, respectful, reciprocal communication solves many problems. This is especially true if the teacher truly respects the opinions and ideas of others involved in the life of the students. The teacher may be the classroom expert, but parents may be the experts in what is going on with their child.

Bringing them into the decision-making process in dealing with their child may lead to solutions and success beyond what the teacher could envision alond. The teacher may be the principal in the life of the child for a few hours each day five days a week nine months of the year, but the parents' role in the life of the child is constant. A sense of partnership between parents and teacher is vital and useful. When decisions are made regarding the management of the time of the child in the classroom, they should be shared decisions.
SEE Skill 10.5 for more information on conferences.

Connecting School to the Outside World

SEE Skill 14.4

Skill 13.2   **Recognizes the benefits of participating in collaborative decision making and problem solving with other professionals to create an effective learning climate within the school and to achieve success for students.**

As a teacher, you share the goal of educating the children with not only other teachers but a wide-ranging staff of local and state administrators. Therefore, collaboration and cooperation can only help you achieve that goal.

To make sure the students in the classroom are getting the most out of the teaching efforts, evaluating and updating lesson plans regularly and asking for suggestions and tips from other teachers can go a long way in providing new ideas and keeping lessons fresh and fun—for the teacher as well as for the students.

Joining a professional organization can also help by putting the teacher in touch with other educators they wouldn't otherwise meet outside of their own school, district, or system. (For example, a math teacher might benefit from joining the National Council for Teachers of Mathematics.) Again, being in touch with other teachers may provide new insights into alternate methods of teaching.

Each state's education department also has resources on core curriculum and learning standards. Keeping up-to-date with these will help ensure that students meet the educational goals set by the state and federal governments.

SEE also Skill 13.1

Skill 13.3   **Identifies the skills involved in co-teaching and co-planning with other educators and members of the larger school community.**

SEE Skill 13.1

Skill 13.4 **Demonstrates knowledge of strategies for communicating and collaborating effectively with parents/guardians and other members of the community from diverse home and community situations, encouraging and supporting families' participation in their children's programs, and developing cooperative partnerships to promote students' learning and well-being.**

SEE Skill 13.1

COMPETENCY 14.0   UNDERSTANDS HOW TO ESTABLISH AND MAINTAIN POSITIVE SCHOOL-HOME AND SCHOOL COMMUNITY RELATIONSHIPS AND HOW TO USE THESE RELATIONSHIPS TO SUPPORT STUDENTS' LEARNING AND DEVELOPMENT.

Skill 14.1   Demonstrates knowledge of family systems theory and dynamics and diversity in family structures and beliefs.

When considering the family as part of the educational process, it is imperative to consider multiple factors. Understanding how families work together, the dynamics which make up families, and the diversity within families we service in the school systems.

Family Systems Theory developed and popularized by Murray Bowen, M.D. uses the psychological and psychiatric information gained about human behavior to help people work through problems in their life. The focus differs from traditional psychological therapy in that Family Systems Theory works with people to think of their problems in broader terms as related to the entire family system, across multiple generations. It is a problem solving approach used to improve the relationships people have in their lives by shifting away from blaming others and into accepting the responsibility for their own actions. There are eight factors discussed in Family Systems Theory; they include:

- Triangles
- Differentiation of Self
- Nuclear Family Emotional System
- Multigenerational Transmission Process
- Emotional Cutoff
- Sibling Position
- Family Projection Process
- Societal Emotional Process

The mobile nature of society today provides a broader mixture of cultures around the country. Students moving from school to school may experience different curriculums and different school cultural factors. As educators expect the students to adapt, they must also remember that the schools themselves must also consider the student's individual cultural influences.

Cultural relationships, mores and values are a continual part of what we must consider when educating students. It is important to keep in mind that in certain cultures individual differences may be thought of very differently than perhaps the current school views them. Many cultures have different views on education and the implications of various factors which may affect schooling, such as disabilities.

Additionally, acculturation is not something that occurs overnight. It takes years for students to become acculturated. Students who move from a foreign country and do not speak English can take up to seven years to become proficient in English. This is not a disability, but in fact the natural progression of language acquisition. It can be similar for other aspects of culture. When considering students who are not succeeding in school, the teacher must take into consideration these types of cultural factors. There are a number of acculturation surveys that can be used to help guide the teacher in examining the role of culture in the academic performance of the student.

Community agencies can often help schools to bridge these cultural gaps. Reaching out to families by including appropriate translators/translations, encouraging parents to share their heritage and traditions with the school and other students, and respecting that differences of what is acceptable do exist will help all involved parties. Beyond language, it is important to respect and provide accommodations for other cultural factors. Holidays may be significantly different for certain ethnicities. Another area may even include the food served in the cafeteria, if the culture requires that foods be Kosher or a vegetarian option may need to be offered.

Skill 14.2   Demonstrates understanding of the benefits, barriers, and techniques involved in parent/family relationships.

Schools today must continually respond and interact with the parents and family of the students they service. These relationships are essential in building a firm academic basis upon which all future learning throughout life will be based. Family support encourages a life-long value to education and learning. It also provides support in areas of behavior and social skill development for the students involved. Additionally, there is a great body of research demonstrating the higher test scores, better emotional development and overall improved life of students for whom family is an active participant in the educational process. In the elementary grades having fathers come in and participate by reading to the class or eating lunch with their children can provide tremendous benefits.

There are many different factors which can provide barriers to the learning in students. It is important schools understand these situations and develop appropriate strategies to provide support for the family and student.

A family in crisis (caused by economic difficulties, divorce, substance abuse, physical abuse, etc.) creates a negative environment which may profoundly impact all aspects of a student's life, and particularly his or her ability to function academically. The situation may require professional intervention. It is often the classroom teacher who will recognize a family in crisis situation and instigate an intervention by reporting on this to school or civil authorities.

This disruption in what we consider a normal childhood can make it difficult or impossible for a student to cope in the regular classroom environment. Professional assessment is most often necessary to determine an effective means of meeting the child's needs, behaviorally, emotionally, physically and socially.

There are many different places a classroom teacher can turn to find support to help a student and family who may be struggling. The teacher can turn to the administrator, guidance counselor, school psychologist, or other community agencies to begin to find support. All schools also have a pre-referral team of experts within the school system who are available to meet and discuss issues specific to a student and help support the classroom teacher develop strategies to provide the necessary support.

Administrators can pull this team of intervention specialists together who can meet regularly to address the needs of the students in the school setting. This team of specialists will usually include: special educators, reading specialists, literacy coaches, math coaches, guidance counselors etc.

Additionally, classroom teachers often deal with numerous outside of the school setting agencies, due to the needs of the students they serve. Becoming familiar with support services available to students and helping parents sort through the maze of paperwork usually required to receive these services, helps not only the student and family but in the end provides additional assistance to the school. It is important to keep a file of counseling agencies, local pediatricians, local psychologists, social services, and mental health services available. This becomes a place for the educator to turn when asked by parents. It is important, however, to simply report the names as possible contacts.

Some possible long term effects of situational problems which go unrecognized and unaltered or unresolved may include:

- Impairment of cognitive development: A mind that is stressed by the child's need to cope with situations he or she can not fully comprehend, let-alone resolve, is unlikely to develop the capacity to think abstractly, synthesize and evaluate information and solve complex problems.
- Restriction in the Affective Domain: Inability to concentrate, focus on classroom activities, the teachers instructions; lack of interest or participation in activities or discussions; inconsistent behavior; inability to express himself or herself coherently; inconsistent behavior.
- Psychomotor Skills: Normal functioning within the physical domain can also be reduced through a reaction to emotional stress and/or intellectual bewilderment.

No one can predict the effects familial relationships will have on the school work of students. The same can be said for cultural issues left unresolved. It is also important to understand, the school system cannot solve all of the outside issues which may be affecting the learning of a student. There will always be some factors outside of the school's control. What is most important is to be empathetic, compassionate, and provide the most appropriate support available to educate the student. In some cases, school may be the most structured and safest place for a student; keeping this in mind when delivering instruction will not only make you a better teacher, but will ensure your students learn more information.

Skill 14.3   Recognizes effective strategies for developing relationships with parents/guardians to acquire an understanding of the students' lives outside of the school in a professional manner that is fair and equitable.

It is now generally accepted that when parents are involved in their students' academic lives, students perform better. There are many strategies available in order to enlist the support of parents. Furthermore, when teachers access that support, they often have new and more authentic views of who their students are and what they can do to assist their students academically.

One common strategy is for teachers to ask parents to tell them about their own children. Often, during parent-teacher conferences, teachers talk and parents listen. This does not help the teacher to learn more about the child, nor does it make the parent feel welcome. By asking the parents to explain who their children are teachers can learn more about what their students are like outside of the classroom, which in turn, may provide very useful information to teachers about how their students think, behave, and operate.

Another common strategy is to call home regularly with good news. Often, parents only hear negative news from schools. When teachers call home with positive news, they begin to trust the school and the teacher more often, and they learn to appreciate the hard work of teaching even more. Doing this also encourages parents to talk with their children more about academic work.

Activities, such as book nights, can get parents involved in the life of the classroom. Parents who work cannot always assist in the classroom, so providing them unique opportunities to learn and grow academically with their children in the context of school can be very powerful, as well as convenient.

In all, there are dozens of strategies. Whatever strategy a teacher uses, it is important to recognize that parents want to be a part of their children's academic lives; however, often, they do not know how. Teachers can fill that gap with positive, encouraging strategies.

Skill 14.4   Identifies community resources that enhance students' learning and provide opportunities for students to explore career opportunities.

The community is a vital link to increasing learning experiences for students. Community resources can supplement the minimized and marginal educational resources of school communities. With state and federal educational funding becoming increasingly subject to legislative budget cuts, school communities welcome the financial support that community resources can provide in terms of discounted prices on high end supplies (e.g. computers, printers, and technology supplies), along with providing free notebooks, backpacks and student supplies for low income students who may have difficulty obtaining the basic supplies for school.

Community stores can provide cash rebates and teacher discounts for educators in struggling school districts and compromised school communities. Both professionally and personally, communities can enrich the student learning experiences by including the following support strategies:

- Provide programs that support student learning outcomes and future educational goals
- Create mentoring opportunities that provide adult role models in various industries to students interested in studying in that industry
- Provide financial support for school communities to help low-income or homeless students begin the school year with the basic supplies
- Develop paid internships with local university students to provide tutorial services for identified students in school communities who are having academic and social difficulties processing various subject areas.
- Providing parent-teen-community forums to create public voice of change in communities
- Offer parents without computer or Internet connection stipends to purchase technology to create equitable opportunities for students to do research and complete requirements.
- Stop in classrooms and ask teachers and students what's needed to promote academic progress and growth.

Community resources are vital in providing the additional support to students, school communities and families struggling to remain engaged in declining educational institutions competing for federal funding and limited district funding. The commitment that a community shows to its educational communities is a valuable investment in the future. Community resources that are able to provide additional funding for tutors in marginalized classrooms or help schools reduce classrooms of students needing additional remedial instruction directly impact educational equity and facilitation of teaching and learning for both teachers and students.

Skill 14.5   Demonstrates understanding of school- and work-based learning environments and the need for collaboration with business organizations in the community.

The bridge to effective learning for students begins with a collaborative approach by all stakeholders that support the educational needs of students. Underestimating the power and integral role of the community institutions in impacting the current and future goals of students can carry high stakes for students beyond the high school years who are competing for college access, student internships, and entry level jobs in the community.

Researchers have shown that school involvement and connections with community institutions have greater retention rates of students graduating and seeking higher education experiences. The current disconnect and autonomy that has become commonplace in today's society must be reevaluated in terms of promoting tomorrow's citizens.

When community institutions provide students and teachers with meaningful connections and input, the commitment is apparent in terms of volunteering, loyalty and professional promotion. Providing students with placements in leadership positions such as the ASB (Associated Student Body); the PTSA (Parent Teacher Student Association); School Boards; neighborhood sub-committees addressing political or social issues; or government boards that impact and influence school communities creates an avenue for students to explore ethical, participatory, collaborative, transformational leadership that can be applied to all areas of a student's educational and personal life.

Community liaisons provide students with opportunities to experience accountability and responsibility. They also allow students to learn about life and how organizations work with effective communication and the ability of teams to work together to accomplish goals and objectives. Teaching students skills of inclusion, social and environmental responsibility and creating public forums that represent student voice and vote foster student interest and access in developing and reflecting on individual opinions and understanding the dynamics of the world around them.

When a student sees that the various support systems are in place and consistently working as a team to effectively provide resources and avenues of academic promotion and accountability, students have no fear of taking risks to grow by becoming a teen voice on a local committee about "Teen Violence" or volunteering in a local hospice for young children with terminal diseases. The linkages of community institutions provide role-models of a world in which the student will soon become an integral and vital member, so being a part of that world as a student makes the transition easier as a young adult.

COMPETENCY 15.0 UNDERSTANDS HOW TO USE PROFESSIONAL DEVELOPMENT OPPORTUNITIES, RELATIONSHIPS WITH OTHER EDUCATION PROFESSIONALS, AND PERSONAL REFLECTION TO ENHANCE TEACHING EFFECTIVENESS AND PROFESSIONAL GROWTH.

Skill 15.1 Demonstrates understanding of the unique characteristics of education as a profession, the continuum of lifelong professional development, and the importance of creating a professional development plan that includes activities to remain current regarding research-validated practices.

Teaching is an amazing profession that offers an incredible amount of professional growth opportunities, as well as internal rewards that money simply cannot buy. Teaching is also a profession characterized by much political debate. Hundreds of thousands of Americans have been or are teachers, and it is useful to understand the context of teaching in American society.

In the past, teaching was generally viewed as a non-professional position. Now that schools are larger and districts are more centralized, teaching has become a highly professionalized career. Throughout the country, most teachers must take graduate coursework in order to teach. Additionally, teaching is a profession marked by the need for extensive professional development, as new theories and methods are continually being developed.

Historically, teaching, as many other professions, has resisted life-long professional development. The old view was that once the professional has earned a degree, there is little else to learn outside of the actual context of the work itself. This view has indeed changed; now, most districts and states require extensive professional development so that teachers can stay well informed about the innovations in the field.

While no one plan will fit all needs, it is generally recommended that teachers consider learning new strategies in-depth and practicing them for considerable amounts of time. Rather than learning a variety of strategies at superficial levels, when teachers go into depth on something, they are able to practice it, learn from mistakes, and spend considerable time theorizing possible improvements.

Many strategies have been proven to work, based on rigorous scientific research. There are also, of course, many strategies that have not been proven to work. It is important that teachers keep up-to-date on the profession by reading professional journals, attending conferences, and paying attention to the newest information available.

Skill 15.2 **Demonstrates understanding of the role of reflection on one's practice as an integral part of professional growth and improvement of instruction; central concepts and methods of inquiry that provide for a variety of self assessment and problem-solving strategies for reflecting on practice; methods for using classroom observation, information about students, pedagogical knowledge, and research as sources for active reflection, evaluation, and revision of practice; and strategies for assessing one's own needs for knowledge and skills related to teaching a diverse population of students and seeking assistance and resources.**

The very nature of the teaching profession—the yearly cycle of doing the same thing over and over again—creates the tendency to fossilize, to quit growing, to become complacent. The teachers who are truly successful are those who have built into their own approach against that tendency. They see themselves as constant learners. They believe that learning never ends. They are careful never to teach their classes the same as they did the last time. They build in a tendency to reflect on what is happening to their students under their care or what happened this year as compared to last year. What worked the best? What didn't work so well? What can be changed to improve success rates? What about continuing education? Should they go for another degree or should they enroll in more classes?

There are several avenues a teacher might take in order to assess his or her own teaching strengths and weaknesses. Having several students who are unable to understand a concept might be an early indicator of the need for a self-evaluation. In such a case, a teacher might want to go over his or her lesson plans to make sure the topic is being covered thoroughly and in a clear fashion. Brainstorming other ways to tackle the content might also help. Speaking to other teachers, asking how they teach a certain skill, might give new insight to one's own teaching tactics.

Any good teacher will understand that he or she needs to self-evaluate and adjust his or her lessons periodically. Signing up for professional courses or workshops can also help a teacher assess his or her abilities by opening one's eyes to new ways of teaching.

Skill 15.3 **Identifies major areas of research on the learning process and resources that are available for professional development; opportunities for seeking and sharing collaboratively a variety of instructional resources with colleagues; and strategies for accessing, evaluating, and using information to improve learning and teaching.**

Professional development opportunities for teacher performance improvement or enhancement in instructional practices are essential for creating comprehensive learning communities. In order to promote the vision, mission and action plans of school communities, teachers must be given the toolkits to maximize instructional performances. The development of student-centered learning communities that foster the academic capacities and learning synthesis for all students should be the fundamental goal of professional development for teachers.

The level of professional development may include traditional district workshops that enhance instructional expectations for teachers or the more complicated multiple day workshops given by national and state educational organizations. Most workshops on the national and state level provide clock hours that can be used to renew certifications for teachers every five years. Typically, 150 clock hours is the standard certification number needed to provide a five year certification renewal, so teachers must attend and complete paperwork for a diversity of workshops that range from 1-50 clock hours according to the timeframe of the workshops.

Most districts and schools provide in-service professional development opportunities for teachers during the school year dealing with district objectives/expectations and relevant workshops or classes that can enhance the teaching practices for teachers. Clock hours are provided with each class or workshop and the type of professional development being offered to teachers determines clock hours. Each year, schools are required to report the number of workshops, along with the participants attending the workshops to the superintendent's office for filing. Teachers collecting clock hour forms are required to file the forms to maintain certification eligibility and job eligibility.

The research by the National Association of Secondary Principals,' "Breaking Ranks II: Strategies for Leading High School Reform" created the following multiple listing of educational practices needed for expanding the professional development opportunities for teachers:

- Interdisciplinary instruction between subject areas
- Identification of individual learning styles to maximize student academic performance
- Training teachers in understanding and applying multiple assessment formats and implementations in curriculum and instruction
- Looking at multiple methods of classroom management strategies
- Providing teachers with national, federal, state and district curriculum expectations and performance outcomes
- Identifying the school communities' action plan of student learning objectives and teacher instructional practices
- Helping teachers understand how to use data to impact student learning goals and objectives
- Teaching teachers on how to disaggregate student data in improving instruction and curriculum implementation for student academic equity and access
- Develop leadership opportunities for teachers to become school and district trainers to promote effective learning communities for student achievement and success

In promoting professional development opportunities for teachers that enhance student achievement, the bottom line is that teachers must be given the time to complete workshops at no or minimal costs. School and district budgets must include financial resources to support and encourage teachers to engage in mandatory and optional professional development opportunities that create a "win-win" learning experience for students.

Whether a teacher is using criterion-referenced, norm-referenced or performance-based data to inform and impact student learning and achievement, the more important objective is ensuring that teachers know how to effectively use the data to improve and reflect upon existing teaching instructions. The goal of identifying ways for teachers to use the school data is simple, "Is the teacher's instructional practice improving student learning goals and academic success?"

School data can include demographic profiling, cultural and ethic academic trends, state and/or national assessments, portfolios, academic subject pre-post assessment and weekly assessments, projects, and disciplinary reports. By looking at trends and discrepancies in school data, teachers can ascertain whether they are meeting the goals and objectives of the state, national, and federal mandates for school improvement reform and curriculum implementation.

Assessments can be used to motivate students to learn and shape the learning environment to provide learning stimulation that optimizes student access to learning. Butler and McMunn (2006) have shown that "factors that help motivate students to learn are:

1. Involving students in their own assessment,
2. Matching assessment strategies to student learning
3. Consider thinking styles and using assessments to adjust the classroom environment in order to enhance student motivation to learn."

Teachers can shape the way students learn by creating engaging learning opportunities that promote student achievement.

Skill 15.4   Recognizes the benefits of participating in professional collaboration, dialogue, mentoring relationships, and continuous learning to solve problems, generate new ideas, share experiences, and seek and give feedback and of contributing knowledge and expertise about teaching and learning to the profession.

According to Walther-Thomas et al (2000), "Collaboration for Inclusive Education," ongoing professional development that provides teachers with opportunities to create effective instructional practice is vital and necessary, "A comprehensive approach to professional development is perhaps the most critical dimension of sustained support for successful program implementation." The inclusive approach incorporates learning programs that include all stakeholders in defining and developing high quality programs for students. Figure 1 below shows how an integrated approach of stakeholders can provide the optimal learning opportunity for all students.

Figure 1-Integrated Approach to Learning

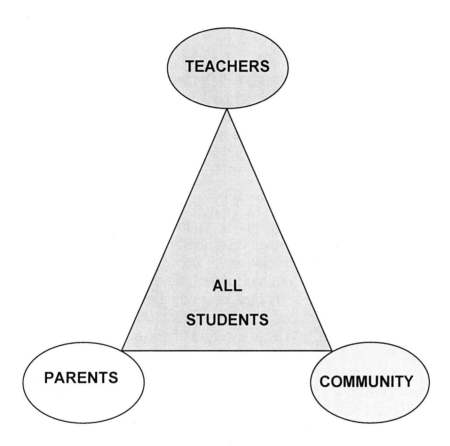

In the integrated approach to learning, teachers, parents, and community support become the integral apexes to student learning. The focus and central core of the school community is triangular as a representation of how effective collaboration can work in creating success for student learners. The goal of student learning and achievement now become the heart of the school community. The direction of teacher professional development in constructing effective instruction is clearly articulated in a greater understanding of facilitating learning strategies that develop skills and education equity for students.

Teachers need diversity in their instructional toolkits, which can provide students with clear instruction, mentoring, inquiry, challenge, performance-based assessment, and journal reflections on their learning processes. For teachers, having a collaborative approach to instruction fosters for students a deeper appreciation of learning, subject matter and knowledge acquisition. Implementing a consistent approach to learning from all stakeholders will create equitable educational opportunities for all learners.

Research has shown that educators who collaborate become more diversified and effective in implementation of curriculum and assessment of effective instructional practices. The ability to gain additional insight into how students learn and modalities of differing learning styles can increase a teacher's capacity to develop proactive instruction methods. Teachers who team-teach or have daily networking opportunities can create a portfolio of curriculum articulation and inclusion for students.

People in business are always encouraged to network in order to further their careers. The same can be said for teaching. If English teachers get together and discuss what is going on in their classrooms, those discussions make the whole much stronger than the parts. Even if there are not formal opportunities for such networking, it is wise for schools or even individual teachers to develop them and seek them out.

Mentors

Novice teachers can benefit greatly from access to effective mentors. Mentoring gives new teachers access to the expertise of their colleagues through their accumulated instructional and problem-solving knowledge and experience. A mentor's role is to guide the new teacher through the day-to-day reality of teaching in the classroom and to serve as a sounding board, a confidant, and a resource for good teaching practices. Further, an effective mentoring program boosts teacher retention rates, and both mentors and mentees often report increased job satisfaction.

Skill 15.5 **Recognizes the benefits of participating in courses and other professional development activities to enhance teaching and learning; initiating and developing educational projects and programs; actively participating in or leading such activities as curriculum development, staff development, and student organizations; and serving on curriculum committees and policy design and development committees to develop single-subject and cross-subject teaching goals and objectives.**

Schools are communities of learners. Gone are the days when we consider teachers to be the people with all the knowledge and students to be the people who have limited amounts of knowledge. Today, schools attempt to be "professional learning communities" where teachers, parents, administrators, and specialists work together to learn about new and exciting methods of instruction and better ways of addressing student needs. For a school to be considered a professional learning community, teachers need to see their environment not just as the classroom, but as the entire school. Many school administrators do depend on teachers working together to make decisions. Not because they need extra people to make decisions, but because they believe that when teachers are invested in their schools, teachers will work more productively to make their schools powerful places of learning for all students.

Collaboration is a powerful tool on which to build a professional learning community. When teachers work together on lesson and unit planning, they learn new techniques, test ideas on each other, and develop stronger instructional methods. Many researchers say that collaborating can be more powerful in instructional practice than attending professional development. This is because people learn in a more natural setting and can get assistance from those who give them the new ideas.

When teachers get involved in the operations of the school, by serving on committees, volunteering for projects, and participating in problem solving and decision making, they influence the direction of the school in terms of the needs the teachers see for the school. As teachers are the ones dealing with students on a daily basis, they see what needs to be done to assist the school in providing the best educational opportunities for their students. By being so involved, they will bring new ideas and effective strategies to help the whole school develop into an extremely effective organization.

Skill 15.6   Demonstrates understanding of the importance of active participation and leadership in professional organizations, and makes use of resources and activities offered by professional and trade organizations, including those that benefit individuals with disabilities and their families, to improve teaching and learning.

Teaching is more commonly viewed not just as a career involving isolated teachers working alone in their classrooms; now, teachers are being viewed as professionals who take leadership roles in their departments, grade levels, schools, districts, and regions. Additionally, many take leadership roles in national and local professional organizations.

The importance of being involved in leadership roles cannot be understated. First, teachers who are more involved learn more; and more knowledgeable teachers are more effective in the classroom. Second, being involved in a variety of aspects promotes a greater sense of motivation and excitement about the profession and the work. Third, teachers who are involved enhance the profession overall, particularly the reputation of the profession.

Many organizations publish journals and host conferences that provide valuable innovative information regarding teaching. Additionally, they often promote unique and highly effective practices in a variety of ways.

It is particularly important to learn from organizations that help teachers learn more about and become more comfortable with changing demographics in their schools. As schools change so must teachers change. Organizations can provide useful information—and often, strong support—to teachers as they keep up to date on pertinent information.

COMPETENCY 16.0   UNDERSTANDS THE PROFESSIONAL ROLES, EXPECTATIONS, AND RESPONSIBILITIES OF ILLINOIS EDUCATORS.

Skill 16.1   Demonstrates understanding of schools as organizations within the larger community context, school policies and procedures, and how school systems are organized and operate.

The entire state system of education works to support each school, each classroom, and each teacher. The general structure, including the federal, U.S. Department of Education system, is described in the proceeding paragraphs.

At the top is the U.S. Department of Education. The Secretary of this department is appointed by the President of the United States. While significant amounts of money get distributed from this department for various projects and needs, its primary role, at least in this day and age, is to enforce No Child Left Behind.

Under the U.S. Department of Education are various research and "service" centers. Scattered around the country, these centers conduct research in education and distribute it to school systems around the country. Often, the research is posted online. See http://ies.ed.gov/ncee/edlabs/ for more information.

The next level is the state level. The state is the primary controller for public education. Each state has a set of laws and requirements for public education. All public schools in the state must follow these laws. In addition, the state sets standards for student learning and mandates and oversees achievement testing.

Under the state are local service centers. Usually, these are operated by counties or localities. These service centers provide professional development to teachers and administrators, provide additional student services, and set instructional tones for all districts within the region.

Under these centers are the school districts themselves. Districts are set up to run the day-to-day operations of schools. They deal with the hiring of teachers, the management of bus and food services, the facilities of schools, and many more things.

Under the districts are the schools. So while a teacher may work at a particular school, the teacher is really an employee of the district.

So, what does this all mean for teachers? First, when there is a simple advice question, teachers should go to their colleagues in their own school. However, for professional development, teachers may want to contact their local service centers. For large-scale research, the teacher may want to investigate which federal research laboratory is closest to the district. Having multiple layers of support available is extremely beneficial to teachers looking for the best, most pertinent instructional information.

A district superintendent is the chief officer of the school district over which he or she supervises. The superintendent's job is to implement the policies set by the Board of Regents and to advocate for his district when necessary.

A school principal is head of the individual school. He or she is under the supervision of the superintendent. The principal handles disciplinary actions for students in the school and may also discipline teachers for minor infractions. For major violations, the principal will consult with the superintendent, who may in turn go to the Board of Regents.

Unions such as the Illinois Education Association or the Illinois Federation of Teachers allow teachers to work together and develop professionally. These organizations also help keep teachers up-to-date on current educational standards and developments. Unions in particular often work to make sure teachers receive fair wages and that when a teacher is facing charges for an alleged crime, s/he receives adequate legal counsel. Unions tend to be active in lobbying the legislature on behalf of the teaching community.

Parent organizations, such as the PTO or PTA, allow parents to have access to their children's schools, and it also provides them a voice in school-based decisions. These organizations also allow parents and teachers to work together on behalf of the students.

Skill 16.2   Recognizes the importance of serving as a role model and advocate for all students

As an individual who spends a great deal of time with his or her students, the teacher is one who truly understands what students and schools need. It is important for teachers to vocalize concerns, issue and/or problems regarding their students, class, school and district.

To speak coherently and intellectually regarding any of these educational domains, teachers must maintain the highest professional standards for themselves. To do so, teachers must utilize the practices of this book and their state's educational resources, including professional development, collaboration with peers, continuing higher education, professional organizations, community resources and other resources to stay current in the profession of teaching.

Skill 16.3   Identifies strategies for promoting and maintaining a high level of integrity in the practice of the profession.

SEE Skill 16.4

Skill 16.4   Demonstrates knowledge of codes of professional conduct, legal directives, rules and regulations, and school policy and procedures; respecting the boundaries of professional responsibilities; and exercising objective professional judgment when working with students, colleagues, and families.

One of the first things that a teacher learns is how to obtain resources and help for his/her students. All schools have guidelines for receiving this assistance especially since the implementation of the Americans with Disabilities Act. The first step in securing help is for the teacher to approach the school's administration or exceptional education department for direction in attaining special services or resources for qualifying students. Many schools have a committee designated for addressing these needs such as a Child Study Team or Core Team. These teams are made up of regular and special education teachers, school psychologists, guidance counselors, and administrators. The particular student's classroom teacher usually has to complete some initial paper work and will need to complete some behavioral observations.

The teacher will take this information to the appropriate committee for discussion and consideration. The committee will recommend the next step to be taken. Often subsequent steps include a complete psychological evaluation along with certain physical examinations such as vision and hearing screening and a complete medical examination by a doctor.

The referral of students for this process is usually relatively simple for the classroom teacher and requires little more than some initial paper work and discussion. The services and resources the student receives as a result of the process typically prove to be invaluable to the student with behavioral disorders.

At times, the teacher must go beyond the school system to meet the needs of some students. An awareness of special services and resources and how to obtain them is essential to all teachers and their students. When the school system is unable to address the needs of a student, the teacher often must take the initiative and contact agencies within the community. Frequently there is no special policy for finding resources. It is simply up to the individual teacher to be creative and resourceful and to find whatever help is available to meet the student's needs. Meeting the needs of all students is certainly a team effort that is most often spearheaded by the classroom teacher.

Family involvement

Under the IDEA, parent/guardian involvement in the development of the student's IEP is required and absolutely essential for the advocacy of the disabled student's educational needs. IEPs must be tailored to meet the student's needs, and no one knows those needs better than the parent/guardian and other significant family members. Optimal conditions for a disabled student's education exist when teachers, school administrators, special education professionals and parents/guardians work together to design and execute the IEP.

Due process

Under the IDEA, Congress provides safeguards for students against schools' actions, including the right to sue in court, and encourages states to develop hearing and mediation systems to resolve disputes. No student or their parents/guardians can be denied due process because of disability.

Inclusion, mainstreaming, and least restrictive environment

Inclusion, mainstreaming and least restrictive environment are interrelated policies under the IDEA, with varying degrees of statutory imperatives.

- Inclusion is the right of students with disabilities to be placed in the regular classroom.
- Least restrictive environment is the mandate that children be educated to the maximum extent appropriate with their non-disabled peers
- Mainstreaming is a policy where disabled students can be placed in the regular classroom, as long as such placement does not interfere with the student's educational plan.

Abuse Situations

The child who is undergoing the abuse is the one whose needs must be served first. A suspected case gone unreported may destroy a child's life, and their subsequent life as a functional adult. It is the duty of any citizen who suspects abuse and neglect to make a report, and it is especially important and required for state licensed and certified persons to make a report. All reports can be kept confidential if required, but it is best to disclose your identity in case more information is required of you. This is a personal matter that has no impact on qualifications for license or certification. Failure to make a report when abuse or neglect is suspected is punishable by revocation of certification and license, a fine, and criminal charges.

It is the right of any accused individual to have counsel and make a defense, as in any matter of law. The procedure for reporting makes clear the rights of the accused, who stands before the court innocent until proven guilty, with the right to representation, redress and appeal, as in all matters of United States law. The State is cautious about receiving spurious reports, but investigates any that seem real enough. Some breaches of standards of decency are not reportable offenses, such as possession of pornography that is not hidden from children.

There is no time given as an acceptable or safe period of time to wait before reporting, so hesitation to report may be a cause for action against you. Do not wait once your suspicion is firm. All you need to have is a reasonable suspicion, not actual proof, which is the job for the investigators.

Maintaining Permanent Records

SEE skill 4.7 for information on permanent records

Skill 16.5 Demonstrates knowledge of the effects of teacher attitudes and behaviors, including personal and cultural perspectives and biases that affect one's teaching and interactions with others, on all students; and demonstrate respect for individual students and their families, regardless of race, culture, religion, gender, sexual orientation, socioeconomic background, and/or varying abilities.

Teachers today will deal with an increasingly diverse group of cultures in their classrooms. And while this is an exciting prospect for most teachers, it creates new challenges in dealing with a variety of family expectations for school and teachers.

First, teachers must show respect to all parents and families. They need to set the tone that suggests that their mission is to develop students into the best people possible. Then they need to realize that various cultures have different views of how children should be educated.

Second, teachers will have better success when they talk personally about their children. Even though teachers may have many students, when they share personal things about each child, parents will feel more confident that their child will be "in the right hands."

Third, it is very important that teachers act like they are partners in the children's education and development. Parents know their children best, and it is important to get feedback, information, and advice from them.

Finally, teachers will need to be patient with difficult families, realizing that certain methods of criticism (including verbal attacks, etc.) are unacceptable. Such circumstances would require the teacher to get assistance from an administrator. This situation, however, is very unusual, and most teachers will find that when they really attempt to be friendly and personal with parents, the parents will reciprocate and assist in the educational program.

A teacher does not want to lose his or her position over a difference of opinion. This is one reason it is key to remain level-headed when dealing with an argumentative person, be it a parent, student, or peer. Passions—and tempers—tend to run high when people have very definite ideas and feelings about policies. For example, there has been much debate and argument about "zero tolerance" policies which gives strict punishment at the first offense, no matter how small that offense might be. (A "zero tolerance" drug policy, for example, might expel a student if he or she is found with aspirin or ibuprofen.) Remind an argumentative parent that you did not write the policy they are contesting, but that as a teacher you are bound to uphold that policy. Have the school principal and superintendent advocate on your behalf in this situation. Parents, students, and even other teachers have avenues they can use to affect change in policy, but that avenue does not go directly through you. They should lodge complaints to the appropriate venue, petition the school board or State Education Department for changes.

It is usually best to have witnesses to any discussion when there is a difference of opinion so that subsequent recounts do not become "he said, she said" or hearsay. Bringing up such topics during a meeting may be appropriate so that there is a record of the discussion in the minutes. In order to get a fair analysis of whether a teacher's response to an attack by a parent, educator, or student was appropriate, witnesses to that attack will be a key factor.

Skill 16.6   Recognizes signs of emotional distress, child abuse, and neglect and follow procedures for reporting known or suspected abuse or neglect to appropriate authorities

Helping students to develop healthy self-images and self-worth are integral to the learning and development experiences. Learning for students who are experiencing negative self-image and peer isolation is not necessarily the top priority, when students are feeling bullied or negated in the school community. When a student is attending school from a homeless shelter or is lost in the middle of a parent's divorce or feeling a need to conform to fit into a certain student group, the student is being compromised and may be unable to effectively navigate the educational process or engage in the required academic expectations towards graduation or promotion to the next grade level or subject core level.

Most schools will offer health classes that address teen issues around sexuality, self-image, peer pressure, nutrition, wellness, gang activity, drug engagement and a variety of other relevant teen experiences. Students are required to take a health class as a core class requirement and graduation requirement, so the incentive from the district and school's standpoint is that students are exposed to issues that directly affect them. The fact that one health class is not enough to effectively appreciate the multiplicity of issues that could create a psychological or physiological trauma for a teenager is lost in today's era of school budgets and financial issues that provide the minimum educational experience for students, but lose the student in the process.

Some schools have contracted with outside agencies to develop collaborative partnerships to bring in after school tutorial classes; gender and cultural specific groupings where students can deal authentically with integration of cultural and ethic experiences and lifestyles. Drug intervention programs and speakers on gang issues have created dynamic opportunities for school communities to bring these issues to the forefront and alleviate fears that are rampant in schools that are afraid to "Say No to Drugs and Gangs." Both students and teachers must be taught about the world of teenagers and understand the social, psychological and learning implications that underscore the process of academic acquisition for society's most vulnerable citizens.

Unfortunately, many students come from past or previous exposure to dangerous situations. Child abuse may perpetuate itself in a phenomenon known as chronic shock. The system becomes geared up to handle the extra flow of hormones and electrical impulses accompanying the "fight or flight" syndrome each time the abuse happens, creating a shift in the biology of the brain and allied systems. Essentially, the victim becomes allergic (hypersensitized) to stress of the kind that prevailed during the period of abuse. Recent research indicates such a shift is reflected in brain chemistry and structural changes and may last a lifetime.

The abused child differs from the neglected one. While the neglected child suffers from under-stimulation, the abused one suffers from over-stimulation. The neglected child will be withdrawn, quiet, unanticipating, sedate almost, while the abused child may be angry, energetic, rebellious, aggressive, and hard to control. In each case, the environment of abuse or neglect shapes the behavior of the child away from home. Often, out of reflex, the child will flinch when seeming to anticipate a blow, or be unable to accept or understand healthy attention directed to him. The teacher merely needs to watch the child's reaction to a sudden loud noise, another child's aggression, or the response when offered some companionship by another child, or test their own feelings to sense what the child's feelings and experiences may be.

The affective range of the abused and/or neglected child varies from very limited and expressionless to angry, to a distracted effect that is characterized by inattentiveness and poor concentration. Some are tearful, some angry and hitting, and some are just sedentary. In most cases, the effect displayed will not be appropriate to the situation at hand. They have just too much to think about in their mind. Their sense of powerlessness is too strong, and they are unable to tell the terrible tale. Often, they may block it out or become obsessed by it.

The obvious thing the teacher sees are marks from the hand, fist, belt, coat hangers, kitchen utensils, extension cord, and any other imaginable implement for striking and inflicting pain on a child. Now, the suspicion has to be backed up with hard evidence. Unusual marks in geometric shapes may indicate the presence of an implement for spanking such as a spoon, home-made paddle, extension cord, or coat hanger. Marks on the arms and legs may indicate being whipped there. Always be suspicious about bruising.

Bruises on the neck and face are usually not the result of a trip and fall, but have a lot to do with intentional hitting, and even choking. Noting the size and shapes of bruises and using some simple imagination may reveal the source of the injury. Notice whether the bruise has reddened areas, indicating ruptured capillaries, or is uniformly colored but shaded toward the perimeter. The rupture of capillaries indicates a strong hit while the shaded bruise indicates a softer compression. The job of the educator who discovers this is just to have a reasonable suspicion that abuse is going on, but it helps to have some specific indicators and firm evidence, not only for the sake of the child, but also in the rare event that your report is questioned. Take note of the size of the injury. Compare it to something such as a quarter or an orange, etc.

The neglected child may appear malnourished, may gorge at lunch, yet still be thin and underweight. Quiet and shy, he's typically shabby looking, and doesn't seem to care about his appearance. Poor nutrition at home may result in him having more than his share of colds and it is of utmost importance to guarantee that his immunizations are current, as they probably have been overlooked. He is not usually a very social child, may isolate, and not respond to invitations to join in. Many children display this trait, but a persistence in social anxiety with a sad effect will indicate that something is happening at home to be concerned about.

In cases of sexual abuse the most blatant warning sign is the sexualization of the child. They become interested in matters of sexuality way before their development stage would predict. They are sexual. They may be seen to quietly masturbate in school at pre-pubertal ages, and may even act out sexually with other children of their own age. The child who suddenly begins to engage in promiscuous sexual behavior is likely to have been molested.

Sexual abuse of children is widespread and takes many forms. Kissing episodes by a parent, when out of normal context, are just as damaging as more overt forms of contact, as is the sexualized leer or stare by a perverted parent or elder. Because of the complexity of dealing with sexual abuse, situations must be dealt with extreme care. Never attempt an exhaustive interview of a student who admits to being sexually abused, or abused in any way, but wait for the trained professional who knows the methodology to help out. The outcome of an interview can make or break a prosecution.

COMPETENCY 17.0   UNDERSTANDS PROCESSES AND THEORIES OF COMMUNICATION.

Skill 17.1   **Demonstrates knowledge of communication theory, language development, and the role of language in learning as well as communication modes and patterns of individuals with varying abilities.**

Communication
While teachers should never consider that all student learning is based on teacher's communication to students, much valuable information does occur in the transmission of words between teacher and student. The problem, however, is in dealing with the various types of learning difficulties that students have, as well as all the other environmental factors and learning preferences.

First, various disabilities, including hearing loss, Attention Deficit Hyperactivity Disorder, as well as others, can severely impact a student's ability to successfully listen and comprehend what the teacher may be saying. In such cases, teachers should communicate with Special Education and other resource teachers about procedures and practices to follow. But teachers can also place these students in specific classroom locations, give them "partners" who can assist, and periodically walk near them to find out how they are doing.

Environmental factors can inhibit a teacher's communication to students. Often, air conditioners and other room or building noises can impact students' understanding of course content. Students also have various preferences in how they best understand. Some need a lot of teacher explanation and assistance, and others need very little. While a teacher can never judge how much students understand simply by looking at their expressions, the teacher may get a pretty good idea if the students are in need of a change of communication style, activity, or if they simply need further review.

Language Development
One of the most important things to know about the differences between L1 (first language) and L2 (second language) acquisition is that people usually will master L1, but they will almost never be fully proficient in L2. However, if children can be trained in L2 before about the age of seven, their chances at full mastery will be much higher.

Children learn language with little effort, which is why they can be babbling at one year and speaking with complete, complex ideas just a few years later. It is important to know that language is innate, meaning that our brains are ready to learn a language from birth. Yet a lot of language learning is behavioral, meaning that children imitate adults' speech.

L2 acquisition is much harder for adults. Multiple theories of L2 acquisition have come developed. One of the more notable ones come from Jim Cummins. Cummins argues that there are two types of language that usually need to be acquired by students learning English as a second language: Basic Interpersonal Communication Skills (BICS) and Cognitive Academic Language Proficiency (CALP).

BICS is general, everyday language used to communicate simple thoughts, whereas CALP is the more complex, academic language used in school. It is harder for students to acquire CALP, and many teachers mistakenly assume that students can learn complex academic concepts in English if they have already mastered BICS. The truth is that CALP takes much longer to master, and in some cases, particularly with little exposure in certain subjects, it may never be mastered.

Another set of theories is based on Stephen Krashen's research in L2 acquisition. Most people understand his theories based on five principles:

1. The acquisition-learning hypothesis: This states that there is a difference between learning a language and acquiring it. Children "acquire" a first language easily—it's natural. But adults often have to "learn" a language through coursework, studying, and memorizing. One can acquire a second language, but often it requires more deliberate and natural interaction within that language.
2. The monitor hypothesis: This is when the learned language "monitors" the acquired language. In other words, this is when a person's "grammar check" kicks in and keeps awkward, incorrect language out of a person's L2 communication.
3. The natural order hypothesis: This suggests that the learning of grammatical structures is predictable and follows a "natural order."
4. The input hypothesis: Some people call this "comprehensible input." This means that a language learner will learn best when the instruction or conversation is just above the learner's ability. That way, the learner has the foundation to understand most of the language, but still will have to figure out, often in context, what that extra more difficult element means.
5. The affective filter hypothesis: This suggests that people will learn a second language when they are relaxed, have high levels of motivation, and have a decent level of self-confidence.

Teaching students who are learning English as a second language poses some unique challenges, particularly in a standards-based environment. The key is realizing that no matter how little English a student knows, the teacher should teach with the student's developmental level in mind. This means that instruction should not be "dumbed-down" for ESOL students. Different approaches should be used, however, to ensure that these students (a) get multiple opportunities to learn and practice English and (b) still learn content.

Many ESOL approaches are based on social learning methods. By being placed in mixed level groups or by being paired with a student of another ability level, students will get a chance to practice English in a natural, non-threatening environment. Students should not be pushed in these groups to use complex language or to experiment with words that are too difficult. They should simply get a chance to practice with simple words and phrases.

In teacher-directed instructional situations, visual aids, such as pictures, objects, and video are particularly effective at helping students make connections between words and items they are already familiar with

ESOL students may need additional accommodations with assessments, assignments, and projects. For example, teachers may find that written tests provide little to no information about a student's understanding of the content. Therefore, an oral test may be better suited for ESOL students. When students are somewhat comfortable and capable with written tests, a shortened test may actually be preferable; take note that they will need extra time to translate.

Second Language Acquisition

SEE Skill 17.5

Skill 17.2 Demonstrates understanding of how cultural and gender differences affect communication

The effective teacher uses advanced communication skills such as clarification, reflection, perception, and summarization as a means to facilitate communication. Teachers who are effective communicators are also good listeners. Teacher behaviors such as eye contact, focusing on student body language, clarifying students' statements, and using "I" messages are effective listeners. The ability to communicate with students, listen effectively, identify relevant and non-relevant information, and summarize students' messages facilitates establishing and maintaining an optimum classroom learning environment.

The Performance Measurement System: Domains defines body language as teachers' facial or other body behavior that express interest, excitement, joy, and positive personal relations, or boredom, sadness, dissatisfaction, or negative personal relations, or else, no clear message at all.

Skill 17.3   Demonstrates understanding of the social, intellectual, and political implications of language use and how they influence meaning.

Many people naively believe that language is neutral—that it simply is symbolic of ideas and objects. The truth is, though, that all language has deeper social, intellectual, and political implications. Consider, for example, the differences between *connotation* and *denotation*. Denotation is the dictionary definition of a word, while connotation is the assumed meaning of a word in a general population. So, while the term "organize" has very specific dictionary definitions, when people use the word "organize" in relationship to labor, the connotation of the word refers to labor unions.

In addition to the differences between connotative and denotative meanings of words, language can be thought of as having local "flair" or dialect. Sometimes, dialect goes beyond location and has implications for social and economic class, race, and gender. In such cases, the use of certain words, phrases, or sentence structures may inspire racist or classist beliefs among outsiders. Currently, debates about "Ebonics," an African-American dialect of English, center on whether or not the dialect is a legitimate form of English.

In general, all language can be construed in particular ways. Teachers must realize that as they assist their students in becoming critical readers, writers, and speakers, language carries with it various assumptions. Therefore, careful language use is necessary, while acceptance of various dialects is also important for a caring, democratic society.

Skill 17.4   Demonstrate understanding of the needs for literacy development in general and in specific disciplines or at specific grade levels.

In 2000, the National Reading Panel released its now well-known report on teaching children to read. In a way, this report slightly put to rest the debate between phonics and whole-language. It argued, essentially, that word-letter recognition was as important as was understanding of what the text means. The report's "Big 5" critical areas of reading instruction are as follows:

Phonemic Awareness
The acknowledgement of sounds and words, for example, a child's realization that some words rhyme is one of the skills that fall under this category. Onset and rhyme are skills that might help students learn that the sound of the first letter "b" in the word "bad" can be changed with the sound "d" to make it "dad." The key in phonemic awareness is that when you teach it to children, it can be taught with the students' eyes closed. In other words, it's all about sounds, not about ascribing written letters to sounds.

Phonics

As opposed to phonemic awareness, the study of phonics must be done with the eyes open. It's the connection between the sounds and letters on a page. In other words, students learning phonics might see the word "bad" and sound each letter out slowly until they recognize that they just said the word.

Fluency

When students practice fluency, they practice reading connected pieces of text. In other words, instead of looking at a word as just a word, they might read a sentence straight through. The point of fluency is for the student to comprehend what she is reading. She would need to be able to "fluently" piece words in a sentence together quickly. If a student is NOT fluent in reading, he or she would sound each letter or word out slowly and pay more attention to the phonics of each word. A fluent reader, on the other hand, might read a sentence out loud using appropriate intonations.

The best way to test for fluency is to have a student read something out loud, preferably a few sentences in a row—or more. Sure, most students just learning to read will probably not be very fluent right away; but with practice, they will increase their fluency. Even though fluency is not the same as comprehension, it is said that fluency is a good predictor of comprehension. Think about it: If you're focusing too much on sounding out each word, you're not going to be paying attention to the meaning.

Comprehension

Comprehension simply means that the reader can ascribe meaning to text. Even though students may be good with phonics, and even know what many words on a page mean, some of them are not able to demonstrate comprehension because they do not have the strategies that would help them to comprehend. For example, students should know that stories often have structures (beginning, middle, and end). They should also know that when they are reading something and it does not make sense, they will need to employ "fix-up" strategies where they go back into the text they just read and look for clues. Teachers can use many strategies to teach comprehension, including questioning, asking students to paraphrase or summarize, utilizing graphic organizers, and focusing on mental images.

Vocabulary

Students will be better at comprehension if they have a stronger working vocabulary. Research has shown that students learn more vocabulary when it is presented in context, rather than in vocabulary lists, for example. Furthermore, the more students get to use particular words in context, the more they will (a) remember each word, and (b) utilize it in the comprehension of sentences that contain the words.

Skill 17.5   Demonstrates understanding of the effects of second-language acquisition on communication patterns.

The most important concept to remember regarding the difference between learning a first language and a second one is that if the learner is approximately age seven or older, learning a second language will occur very differently in the learner's brain than it will had the learner been younger.

The reason for this is that there is a language-learning function that exists in young children that appears to go away as they mature. Learning a language prior to age seven is almost guaranteed, with relatively little effort. The mind is like a sponge, and it soaks up language very readily. Some theorists, including the famous linguist Noam Chomsky, argue that the brain has a "universal grammar" and that only vocabulary and very particular grammatical structures, related to specific languages, need to be introduced in order for a child to learn a language. What this really means is that, in essence, there are slots into which language gets filled in a child's mind. This is definitely not the case with learning a second language after about seven years old.

Learning a second language as a pre-adolescent, adolescent, or adult requires quite a bit of translation from the first language to the second. Vocabulary and grammar particulars are memorized, not necessarily internalized (at least, as readily as a first language). In fact, many (though not all) people who are immersed in a second language never fully function as fluent in the language. They may appear to be totally fluent, but often there will be small traits that are hard to pick up and internalize.

It is fairly clear that learning a second language successfully does require fluency in the first language. This is because, as stated above, the second language is translated from the first in the learner's mind. First language literacy is also a crucial factor in second language learning, particularly second language literacy.

When helping second language learners make the "cross-over" in language fluency or literacy from first language to second language, it is important to help them identify strategies they use in the first language and apply those to the second language. It is also important to note similarities and differences in phonetic principals in the two languages. Sometimes it is helpful to encourage students to translate; other times, it is helpful for them to practice production in the target language. In either case, teachers must realize that learning a second language is a slow and complicated process.

Stages and patterns of second-language acquisition

There is wide agreement that there are generally five stages of second language development. The first stage is "pre-production." While these students may actually understand what someone says to them (for the most part), they have a much harder time talking back in the target language. Teachers must realize that if a student cannot "produce" the target language, it does not mean that they aren't learning. Most likely, they are. They are taking it in, and their brains are trying to figure out what to do with all the new language.

The second phase is early production. This is where the student can actually start to produce the target language. It is quite limited, and teachers most likely should not expect students to produce eloquent speeches during this time.

The third phase is emergent speech or speech emergence. Longer, more complex sentences are used, particularly in speech—and in social situations. But remember that students aren't fully fluent in this stage, and they cannot handle complex academic language tasks.

The fourth phase is intermediate fluency. This is where more complex language is produced. Grammatical errors are common.

The fifth stage is advanced fluency. While students may appear to be completely fluent, though, they will still need academic and language support from teachers.

Many people say that there are prescribed amounts of time by which students should reach each stage. However, keep in mind that it depends on the level at which students are exposed to the language. For example, students who get opportunities to practice with the target language outside of school may have greater ease in reaching the fifth stage quicker. In general, though, it does take years to reach the fifth stage, and students should never be expected to have complete mastery within one school year.

Factors that affect second-language acquisition

There are many factors that impact someone's ability to pick up a second or third language. Age is one common factor. It is said that after a certain age (usually seven), learning a second language becomes dramatically harder. But there are also many social factors, such as anxiety, that influence language learning. Often, informal, social settings are more conducive to second language learning. Motivation is another factor, obviously. A final important factor, particularly for teachers, is the strategies one uses to learn a language. For example, memorizing words out of context is not as effective as using words strategically for a real-life purpose.

NOTE: See www.everythingesl.net or
http://www.nwrel.org/request/2003may/overview.html for more information.

COMPETENCY 18.0   UNDERSTANDS STRATEGIES FOR USING COMMUNICATION EFFECTIVELY IN INSTRUCTION.

Skill 18.1   Demonstrates knowledge of accurate, effective communication methods for conveying ideas and information, asking questions, and responding to students.

The most important component in probing for student understanding is trust. Only if students trust their teacher will the communications process yield such things as the level of understanding a student has attained on any topic. If that component is in place, then creative questioning, which requires planning ahead, can sometimes reveal what the teacher needs to know. So can writing exercises that focus not on correctness but on a recording of the student's thoughts on a topic. Sometime assuring the student that only the teacher will see what is written is helpful in freeing students to reveal their own thoughts. When a new unit is introduced, including vocabulary lessons related to the unit can help students find the words they need to talk or write about the topic.

If a teacher can help students to take responsibility for their own ideas and thoughts, much has been accomplished. They will only reach that level in a non-judgmental environment. An environment that doesn't permit criticism of the ideas of others and that accepts any topic for discussion that is in the realm of appropriateness. Success in problem solving boosts students' confidence and makes them more willing to take risks, and the teacher must provide those opportunities for success.

Skill 18.2   Identifies effective strategies for communicating with and challenging students in a supportive manner, and provide students with constructive feedback.

Teachers who couple diversity in instructional practices with engaging and challenging curriculum and the latest advances in technology can create the ultimate learning environment for creative thinking and continuous learning for students. Teachers who are innovative and creative in instructional practices are able to model and foster creative thinking in their students. Encouraging students to maintain journals or portfolios of their valued work from projects and/or assignments will allow students to make conscious choices on including a diversity of their creative endeavors in a filing format that can be treasured throughout the educational journey.

When teachers are very deliberate about the questions they use with their students, amazing things in the classroom can happen. Most of us remember questions at the end of the chapter in the textbook, or we remember quiz or test questions. While these things potentially have value, they are complete useless if the questions are not crafted well, the purposes for the questions are not defined, and the methods by which students will "answer" the questions are not engaging.

Keep in mind that good questioning does not always imply that there are correct answers (by the way, yes/no questions in the classroom do not provide much in the way of stimulation and thought). Good questioning usually implies that teachers are encouraging deep reflection and active thinking in students. In general, we can say that through questioning, we want students to take risks, solve problems, recall facts, and demonstrate understanding.

When we say that we want students to take risks, we mean that we want them to "try out" various answers and possibilities. By answering a "risk-taking" question, students experiment with their academic voices.

Problem solving questions provoke thought and encourage students to think of questions as entries into problems, not indicators that correct answers are always available in the world.

Even though factual recall questions should not be over-used, it is important to teach students how to comprehend reading, speech, film, or other media. It is also important that students remember certain facts—and questioning can bring on small levels of stress that potentially trigger memory. However, realize that stress may be very upsetting for some students, and such questions, particularly in public settings, may be inappropriate.

Finally, by questioning students, we see how much they know. All types of questioning can be done in a variety of formats. For example, we can question students out loud with a whole class. Teachers should refrain from calling on students too often, but occasionally it is an effective technique. Wait time is particularly important: When asking a question, a teacher should not assume that nobody will answer it if a couple seconds have elapsed. Often wait time encourages some students to answer, or it allows all students time to think about the question. Questioning can also take place in small groups or on paper.

Skill 18.3 Recognizes a variety of communication modes and tools that can be used to communicate effectively with a diverse student population and enrich learning opportunities.

The use of media in lesson presentation has become an instructional staple. In order to address the many learning styles that are present within a classroom, the teacher must incorporate the use of media. In today's society where children have been stimulated and entertained by television, teachers must rely on this and other media to secure the interest of students.

A wide variety of media is available in most schools including overhead projectors, tape recorders, and videos. Other low technology media are important motivators in helping students maintain academic focus such as posters, graphs, matrices and charts. Not only are these visuals valuable as motivators, they are also organizers and assist the students in understanding and retaining information.

The implementation of media into instruction offers both the students and the teacher variety. There is "something for everybody". Teachers can be on the cutting edge and address all learning styles and all learners will be stimulated by something within the structure and presentation of the lesson.

Many sophisticated high technology media are now available and are being actuated on lesson presentations throughout our schools. Computers connected to televisions or LCD panels allow teachers to present information in all content areas including technology. Laser disc players connected to either computer monitors or televisions allow students to view a voluminous amount of visual material. Media is an integral tool in delivering instruction and is applied by both teachers and students. Media can never replace teachers but it can offer teachers alternative teaching strategies that students will respond to in a positive and enlightened manner.

Students learn more when they decide what they will learn because the desire to learn is already present. Not only should students be encouraged to decide what they will learn, they should also be given the opportunity to decide what methods they will use to learn. Frequently students have ideas as to how to acquire information and knowledge and how to demonstrate their understanding of newly acquired knowledge.

More and more students are generating the tasks that will aid them in learning and in assessing what they have learned. Teachers are also capitalizing upon the talents of students to enhance instruction. Research indicates that many times students learn best from other students. It is natural for teachers to tap this valuable resource and to encourage students to share their expertise. Teachers are no longer the only or even the most effective deliverers of information. Students can help one another by working together in cooperative groups, by engaging in peer tutoring activities, or by giving presentations to the entire group.

Some of the most influential motivating resources that can stimulate learning are student products. The process of creating a product can be exhilarating to the student engaged in the learning activity. The actual creation of the finished product can be a strong motivator to other students due to the excitement of the student who created the product. Enthusiasm and excitement are contagious. Nothing is more rewarding to a teacher than to observe students who are excited about learning and who become absorbed in the process.

Teacher-student interactions with regard to communication issues
Communication between teachers and students is important, sometimes complex, and always necessary. First, even when secondary teachers, for example, have over 100 students that they see each day, any communication from teacher to each individual student is prized. What this means is that students in especially large public schools sometimes feel lost and not cared about by teachers. When teachers go that extra mile to let students know they care and that they notice them, students feel welcome, important, and less "alone."

However, teacher-student interaction can often be complex. For example, on a busy day, teachers may accidentally say something to a student or to their classes that may get misinterpreted by students. Of particular concern is any message that conveys to students that they are not capable, trustworthy, not smart enough, or important enough. We've all heard stories from people who say that they were told by a teacher that they would not amount to much. People carry negative sentiments about such comments through their entire lives. And in many cases, their teachers may not have even realized what they had said. The point is this: Teachers must speak carefully and considerately so to ensure that their words are appropriate for all students.

It is particularly important in many circumstances that teachers listen carefully to what students are saying to them. Often, teachers may disregard cries for help. Whenever students talk to teachers, teachers must think specifically about potential messages of concern that students are trying to get across. However, do not constantly worry about this; often, students simply want an adult to talk with about random issues and observations. Teachers do quite often serve in the capacity of loving parent to many students who do not get much attention at home. Realize that students sometimes just want an adult friend to talk with about their lives.

One important consideration, though, is ensuring that all interaction between teachers and students is appropriate. It is never a good idea to be in a classroom alone with one student. Typically, when such cases occur, it is a good idea to open the door. This ensures that miscommunication about intent of student or teacher messages do not occur.

In all, teachers in K-12 settings are more than providers of educational content. They serve in a strong social capacity for the healthy social and emotional development of all their students.

Skill 18.4   Demonstrates knowledge of effective listening, conflict resolution, and group-facilitation skills.

Effective teachers use good communication skills. For example, teachers can clarify students' meanings, summarize speakers' statements, ask probing questions, and encourage dialogue between students. Teachers who are clear communicators realize that students come to the classroom with a variety of things on their minds. In fact, good teachers realize that when they speak, students are not always listening. Those teachers also admit that it is okay when students tune out here and there—it's a natural thing for any human being to do, particularly when faced with the extreme mental stimulation of school. But those teachers also use concise, effective language in ways that help students understand important messages. They don't speak more than necessary, and they use consistent rules and procedures for successful classroom operation.

Teachers who are effective communicators are also good listeners. Good listening is evidenced through eye contact, a focus on body language, and clarification of speaker statements. Listening is important in that it allows students to see that their needs are cared about and that their opinions are valued.

Effective conflict management skills include the ability to help various parties see each others' viewpoints. Additionally, having strong conflict management skills entails good listening and the ability to re-phrase peoples' concerns. A teacher who can easily resolve conflicts between two students, for example, is interested primarily in helping the two students understand how to manage their own conflicts in the future. The point of resolving conflicts between students should not be to quickly get rid of the conflict; rather, caring, ethical teachers must help students learn how to do this on their own so that when they are out in the world, they can behave democratically, civilly, and politely.

Finally, group facilitation skills are important for classroom activities, as well as for supervising student, parent, or faculty meetings. Teachers are often put in charge of meetings, and having the skills to effectively run those meetings is crucial. It is important to first have a clear agenda and objectives. In addition, it is crucial to allow people to speak equally (this includes toning down those who want to talk too much). It also includes the ability to keep a group on track, focused on the objectives of the group's meeting.

Skill 18.5   Demonstrates understanding of how to analyze an audience to determine culturally appropriate communication strategies and to share ideas effectively in both written and oral formats with students and their families, other faculty and administrators, and the community and business in general.

Each audience is different. Audiences come with different purposes, backgrounds, understandings, and sizes. Every time a speaker, for example, goes in front of an audience, that speaker must analyze the audience to understand what it expects, how it interprets messages, and the beliefs it carries. First, though, it is important not to generalize. For example, while it may seem culturally sensitive to make references to the culture that is most represented by an audience, a speaker cannot assume that (a) every person representing a particular race has ties to its predominant culture and (b) that the audience is made up entirely of people within that culture. Furthermore, such comments may come across as insensitive, awkward, or incorrect.

It is generally a good idea to focus on (a) communicating important ideas clearly and (b) connecting to the audience in the most appropriate, considerate, careful ways. Connecting to culturally diverse audiences does not mean that the speaker pretends to be someone else. Rather, it is demonstrating the understanding if some of the basic, fundamental beliefs, positions, and traits of certain groups. It is acknowledging that represented cultures are important and valued.

In terms of written communication, clear, concise, non-biased communication is essential. Whether the audience is parents, community members, or fellow faculty, written communication must be carefully constructed for a few reasons. First, it is crucial that ideas are expressed simply. Too much wordy language can over-burden a reader and cause great miscommunication. Writing that contains spelling and grammatical errors gives an unprofessional impression. While writing that has biased words or ideas is insensitive and may turn readers off.

Skill 18.6   Demonstrates knowledge of how to use diverse instructional strategies and assessments that include an appropriate balance of direct instruction, discussion, activity, and written and oral work.

Generally speaking, concepts can be taught in two manners: deductively or inductively. In a deductive manner, the teacher gives a definition along with one or two examples and one or two non-examples. As a means of checking understanding, the teacher will ask the students to give additional examples or non-examples and perhaps to repeat the definition. In an inductive manner, the students will derive the definition from examples and non-examples provided by the teacher. The students will test these examples and non-examples to ascertain if they possess the attributes that meet the criteria of the definition.

Research indicates that when students gain knowledge through instruction that includes a combination of giving definitions, examples, non-examples, and by identifying attributes, they are more likely to grasp complicated concepts than by other instructional methods. Several studies have been carried out to determine the effectiveness of giving examples as well as the difference in effectiveness of various types of examples. It was found conclusively that the most effective method of concept presentation included giving a definition along with examples and non-examples and also providing an explanation of the examples and non-examples. These same studies indicate that boring examples were just as effective as interesting examples in promoting learning.

Learning is further enhanced when critical attributes are listed along with a definition, examples, and non-examples. Classifying attributes is an effective strategy for both very young students and older students. According to Piaget's pre-operational phase of development, children learn concepts informally through experiences with objects just as they naturally acquire language. One of the most effective learning experiences with objects is learning to classify objects by a single obvious feature or attribute. Children classify objects typically, often without any prompting or directions. This natural inclination to classify objects carries over to classifying attributes of a particular concept and contributes to the student's understanding of concepts.

It is not always guaranteed that once a teacher instructs a concept, that students have automatically retained the information. It is often the case that students may need to see or hear information in more than one manner (kinesthetically, spatially, and visually) before it is truly internalized. Teachers can accomplish this by presented information to benefit various learning styles (or multiple intelligences), as well as utilizing technologies (i.e., overhead projectors, related video clips, music, Power Point presentations, etc) or other additional resources to supplement student learning and retention.

COMPETENCY 19.0   UNDERSTANDS STRATEGIES FOR PROVIDING EFFECTIVE LANGUAGE ARTS INSTRUCTION TO STUDENTS.

Skill 19.1   Demonstrates knowledge of methods for creating varied formal and informal opportunities for all students to use effective written, verbal, nonverbal, and visual communication using appropriate materials.

Teachers can use a variety of instructional-organizational techniques to encourage informal and formal venues for writing, visual communication, and oral communication. A few are detailed below:

Writing Workshops are venues in which students can work on written pieces that interest them in particular. For example, while one student works on poetry, another can be working on a non-fiction piece. Workshops allow time for students to collaborate, peer edit, and obtain teacher assistance. They also allow for students to creatively engage in a wide variety of unique writing styles.

Multi-Media Presentations consist of montages of music, video, pictures, and text, usually created through various software programs on computers. Multi-media presentations allow students to creatively explore and present ideas from various academic content areas. They also permit students to interpret content area material through contemporary means, such as popular music.

Classroom Publications consist of venues for students to present written or artistic materials they produce. Often, teachers can guide their students as they produce "newspapers" of student work. Posting work on bulletin boards is a traditional method of sharing student work, as well.

Oral Presentations are student-designed presentations that can be delivered to a whole class or a small portion of the class. Often, these presentations are formal, in that they have received careful attention and preparation from students. However, informal presentations can be given by students, as well. Informal opportunities allow students to get practice with speaking and presenting "on the cuff."

There are many other ideas out there, however, this list should provide new teachers with a good foundation of the many ways in which formal and informal written or spoken text can be prepared and delivered in a classroom.

Skill 19.2 **Demonstrates understanding of effective literacy techniques that activate prior student knowledge and build schema to enhance comprehension of text, and that make reading purposeful and meaningful.**

The point of comprehension instruction is not necessarily to focus just on the text(s) students are using at the very moment of instruction, but rather to help them learn the strategies that they can use independently with any other text.

Some of the most common methods of teaching instruction are as follows:

Summarization: This is where, either in writing or verbally, students go over the main point of the text, along with strategically chosen details that highlight the main point. This is not the same as *paraphrasing*, which is saying the same thing in different words. Teaching students how to summarize is very important as it will help them look for the most critical areas in a text, and in non-fiction. For example, it will help them distinguish between main arguments and examples. In fiction, it helps students to learn how to focus on the main characters and events and distinguish those from the lesser characters and events.

Question answering: While this tends to be over-used in many classrooms, it is still a valid method of teaching students to comprehend. As the name implies, students answer questions regarding a text, either out loud, in small groups, or individually on paper. The best questions are those that cause students to have to think about the text (rather than just find an answer within the text).

Question generating: This is the opposite of question answering, although students can then be asked to answer their own questions or the questions of peer students. In general, we want students to constantly question texts as they read. This is important because it causes students to become more critical readers. To teach students to generate questions helps them to learn the types of questions they can ask, and it gets them thinking about how best to be critical of texts.

Graphic organizers: Graphic organizers are graphical representations of content within a text. For example, Venn Diagrams can be used to highlight the difference between two characters in a novel or two similar political concepts in a Social Studies textbook. A teacher can use flow-charts with students to talk about the steps in a process (for example, the steps of setting up a science experiment or the chronological events of a story). Semantic organizers are similar in that they graphically display information. The difference, usually, is that semantic organizers focus on words or concepts. For example, a word web can help students make sense of a word by mapping from the central word all the similar and related concepts to that word.

Text structure: Often in non-fiction, particularly in textbooks, and sometimes in fiction, text structures will give important clues to readers about what to look for to find the information they require. Often, students do not know how to make sense of all the types of headings in a textbook and do not realize that, for example, the side-bar story about a character in history is not the main text on a particular page in the history textbook. Teaching students how to interpret text structures gives them tools in which to tackle other similar texts.

Monitoring comprehension: Students need to be aware of their comprehension, or lack of it, in particular texts. So, it is important to teach students what to do when suddenly text stops making sense. For example, students can go back and re-read the description of a character. Or, they can go back to the table of contents or the first paragraph of a chapter to see where they are headed.

Textual marking: This is where students interact with the text as they read. For example, armed with Post-it Notes, students can insert questions or comments regarding specific sentences or paragraphs within the text. This helps students to focus on the importance of the small things, particularly when they are reading larger works (such as novels in high school). It also gives students a reference point on which to go back into the text when they need to review something.

Discussion: Small group or whole-class discussion stimulates thoughts about texts and gives students a larger picture of the impact of those texts. For example, teachers can strategically encourage students to discuss related concepts to the text. This helps students learn to consider texts within larger societal and social concepts, or teachers can encourage students to provide personal opinions in discussion. By listening to various students' opinions, this will help all students in a class to see the wide range of possible interpretations and thoughts regarding one text.

Many people mistakenly believe that the terms "research-based," "research-validated," or "evidence-based" relate mainly to specific programs, such as early reading textbook programs. While research does validate that some of these programs are effective, much research has been conducted regarding the effectiveness of particular instructional strategies.

In reading, many of these strategies have been documented in the report from the National Reading Panel (2000). However, just because a strategy has not been validated as effective by research does not necessarily mean that it is not effective with certain students in certain situations. The number of strategies out there far outweighs researchers' ability to test their effectiveness. Some of the strategies listed above have been validated by rigorous research, while others have been shown consistently to help improve students' reading abilities in localized situations. There simply is not enough space to list all the strategies out there that have been proven effective; just know that the above strategies are very commonly cited ones that work in a variety of situations.

Skill 19.3   **Demonstrates knowledge of strategies for conducting effective classroom discussions by managing groups, asking questions, eliciting and probing responses, and summarizing**

SEE Skill 19.2

Skill 19.4   **Identifies a variety of resources that can be used to enhance students' learning from reading, writing, and oral communication.**

The resources for assisting students in improving and learning from reading, writing, and oral communication are varied. Let's consider that there are two broad categories of resources: those that the teacher can use and those that the student can use. Each will be discussed separately.

Teacher resources for assisting students in learning from reading, writing, and oral communication include websites, books, teacher journals, and professional development opportunities. All these resources require that teachers do some investigation and research. However, the myriad of websites and books out there, for example, have terrific ideas for student learning from reading and writing. Typically, teachers can expect to find whole lesson plans. However, often, teachers will be able to find activities that differentiate lessons or provide students with enrichment activities to add on to already in-progress lessons.

Student resources include books that model specific genres of writing, encyclopedic materials (online, in book form, and on CD ROM), trade materials (non-fiction books on a variety of academic topics, and reference materials books, journals, and websites that help students craft written and oral pieces in more professional ways.

The trick for finding and using the wide variety of materials out there is to be patient and focused. There are so many resources out there, and of course, few are truly excellent. So, a critical eye is also very important.

Skill 19.5   **Demonstrates knowledge of methods for helping students understand a variety of modes of writing (e.g., persuasive, descriptive, expository, narrative).**

Writing about literature is a very tough task. It demands that students have fully comprehended the text. It demands that they understand unstated elements of the text, such as character motives. It demands that they dig deep into their personal experiences to help make connections to the author's intentions. Finally, it also demands that they consider other works of literature to help explain literary conventions, issues, and other complex components of literature.

Of course, when you incorporate writing into the mix just presented above, you make the task even more difficult. Imagine just for a moment that you, the teacher, have given students the assignment of writing about a novel or story they have just read. Your students must face a blank piece of paper and make sense of a complex piece of literature. They must explain literary conventions, characters, settings, and plot. Most will sit and stare at the blank piece of paper, nervous about how to even begin.

What are some ways to help students get beyond that fear of writing about literature? First, utilizing graphic organizers helps students make visual sense of various literary elements. This often helps them organize their writing. Sometimes, outlining major points is also helpful.

Even more helpful is to give students a more authentic task than simply writing about literature in an abstract sense. Although writing about literature analytically may be the end goal in mind, teachers can help students get there by giving them very specific writing tasks. For example, teachers can ask students to write a newspaper story explaining an event in the story. Or they can have students write a letter from one character to another. Once students feel comfortable with these tasks, teachers can move them beyond by having them incorporate knowledge of more than one book—or they can have them involve their own personal experiences into writing about literature. Eventually, with enough practice, students will be more facile with writing about literature that an analysis writing task will not be so strenuous. The key, though, is building students up to the task by having them experiment with writing about the literature in fun, authentic, natural ways.

SEE skill 8.3 also

Skill 19.6   **Demonstrates understanding of the process of second-language acquisition and strategies to support the learning of students whose first language is not English.**

SEE Skill 17.5

COMPETENCY 20.0   UNDERSTANDS BASIC COMPUTER/TECHNOLOGY OPERATIONS AND ISSUES RELATED TO THE USE OF COMPUTER/TECHNOLOGY RESOURCES.

Skill 20.1   Demonstrates understanding of appropriate terminology related to computers and technology

SEE Skill 20.2

Skill 20.2   Demonstrates knowledge of how to use computer systems to run software; access, generate, and manipulate data; and publish results

The computer system can be divided into two main parts—the hardware and the software. Hardware can be defined as all the physical components that make up the machine. Software includes the programs (sets of instructions) that enable that machine to do a particular job.

HARDWARE
Input devices are those parts of the computer that accept information from the user. The most common input devices are the keyboard and the mouse. Other more specialized input devices might include joysticks, light pens, touch pads, graphic tablets, voice recognition devices, and optical scanners.

Output devices are the parts of the computer that display the results of processing for the user. These commonly include the monitor and printers, but a computer might also output information to plotters and speech synthesizers. Monitors and printers can vary greatly in the quality of the output displayed. Monitors are classified according to their resolution (dpi = dots per square inch). SVGA (Super Video Graphics Adapter) monitors are able to display a three dimensional picture that looks almost real.

Printers vary in the way they produce "hard copy" as well as in the quality of the resultant product. Dot matrix printers are the cheapest printers and form an image on the paper by actually impacting the paper much the way a typewriter does. Because the image is composed of dots on the paper, it is not considered "letter" quality, but is usually sufficient for classroom use. Ink jet printers are more expensive both to purchase and to maintain, but because they produce a much clearer image, they are often preferred when the quality of the hard copy is important. With market prices coming down, they are becoming much more affordable. The best hard copies are produced by laser printers, but laser printers are also the most expensive. They are usually found in offices where volume is not high but the best quality is desired.

Storage devices enable computers to save documents and other important files for future editing. Hard drives are built into most computers for the storage of the large programs used today. As programs increase in size and complexity to make use of the enhanced graphic and sound capabilities of today's computers, the amount of storage space on a hard drive has become increasingly important. Many schools avoid the limitations imposed by the hard drive's storage space by using networks to deliver programs to the individual systems. The CD ROM/DVD drives of multimedia computers that can access CD ROM/DVD disks containing large amounts of information and usually including sound, graphics and even video clips.

The last hardware component of a computer system is the Central Processing Unit or CPU along with all the memory chips on the motherboard. This "brain" of the computer is responsible for receiving input from the input or storage devices, placing it in temporary storage (RAM or Random Access Memory), performing any processing functions required by the program (like mathematical equations or sorting), and eventually retrieving the information from storage and displaying it by means of an output device.

SOFTWARE
Software consists of all the programs containing instructions for the computer and is stored on the hard drive, CD ROM, or DVD disks. Programs fall into two major groups—operating system and application programs. Operating system programs contain instructions that allow the computer to function. Applications are all the jobs that a user might wish to perform on the computer. These might include word processors, databases, spreadsheets, educational and financial programs, games, and telecommunications programs.

With a surplus of educational software on the market, it is important for an educator to be able to evaluate a program before purchasing it. There are three general steps to follow when evaluating a software program. First, one must read the instructions thoroughly to familiarize oneself with the program, its hardware requirements, and its installation. Once the program is installed and ready to run, the evaluator should first run the program as it would be run by a successful student, without deliberate errors but making use of all the possibilities available to the student. Thirdly, the program should be run making deliberate mistakes to test the handling of errors. One should try to make as many different kinds of mistakes as possible, including those for incorrect keyboard usage and the validity of user directions.

Many school districts have addressed this problem by publishing a list of approved software titles for each grade level in much the same way that they publish lists of approved text books and other classroom materials. In addition, most districts have developed a software evaluation form to be used by any instructor involved in the purchase of software that is not already on the "approved" list.

When dealing with large class sizes and at the same time trying to offer opportunities for students to use computers, it is often necessary to use a lot of ingenuity. If the number of computers available for student use is limited, the teacher must take a tip from elementary school teachers who are skilled at managing centers. Students can be rotated singly or in small groups to the computer centers as long as they are well oriented in advance to the task to be accomplished and with the rules to be observed. Rules for using the computer should be emphasized with the whole class prior to individual computer usage in advance and then prominently posted.

If a computer lab is available for use by the curriculum teacher, the problem of how to give each student the opportunity to use the computer as an educational tool might be alleviated, but a whole new set of problems must be dealt with. Again the rules to be observed in the computer lab should be discussed before the class ever enters the lab, and students should have a thorough understanding of the assignment. When a large group of students is visiting a computer lab, it is very easy for the expensive hardware to suffer from accidental or deliberate harm if the teacher is not aware of what is going on at all times. Students need to be aware of the consequences for not following the rules because it is so tempting to experiment and show off to their peers.

Unfortunately, students who have access to computers outside of school often feel like they know everything already and are reluctant to listen to instruction on lab etiquette or program usage. The teacher must be constantly on guard to prevent physical damage to the machines from foreign objects finding their way into disk drives, key caps from disappearing from keyboards (or being rearranged), or stray pencil or pen marks from appearing on computer systems.

Experienced students also get a lot of enjoyment from saving games on hard drives, moving files into new directories or eliminating them altogether, creating passwords to prevent others from using machines, etc. At the same time the other students need a lot of assistance to prevent accidents caused by their inexperience. It is possible to pair inexperienced students with more capable ones to alleviate some of the problem. Teachers must constantly rotate around the room and students must be prepared before their arrival in the lab so that they know exactly what to do when they get there to prevent them from exercising their creativity.

One way to take advantage of the computer's ability to store vast amounts of data is to utilize them in the classroom as a research tool. Entire encyclopedias, whole classical libraries, specialized databases in history, science, and the arts can be obtained on CD ROM disks to allow students to complete their research from the classroom computer.

With the "Search" feature of these programs, students can type in a one or two word description of the desired topic and the computer will actually locate all articles that deal with that topic. The student can either read the articles on the computer monitor or print them out. If the classroom computer has Internet access, the research possibilities are unlimited. When hooked up to the World Wide Web, students can actually talk to people from other parts of the globe or access libraries and journals from all over the world. For example, if students are studying weather, they might go on-line with students who live in different weather zones to discuss how weather affects their lives. Then they might access global weather reports and print out weather maps, and discuss their research with meteorologists—and all from a single computer station.

Once the research is completed, use of a desktop publishing program on the computer can produce professional quality documents enhanced by typed text, graphs, clip art, and even photos downloaded from the World Wide Web. Even primary grade students can use the computer to type and illustrate their stories on simple publishing programs like the Children's Writing and Publishing Center by The Learning Company. Spell check programs and other tools included in these publishing programs can assist students in producing top quality work.

The computer should not replace traditional research and writing skills taught to school-age children, but use of the computer as a tool must also be taught to children who live in a technological society.

Computers are as much a part of a child's life today as pencils and paper and the capabilities of computers need to be thoroughly explored to enable students to see computers as much more than a glorified "game machine." A major goal of education is to prepare students for their futures in business and the work place and if they are not taught how to use the available technology to its fullest advantage, educators will have failed in at least part of that purpose.

Networks

A network is composed of two or more computers, linked together. More specifically, a computer network is a data communications system made up of hardware and software that transmits data from one computer to another. In part, a computer network includes physical infrastructure like wires, cables, fiber optic lines, undersea cables, and satellites. The other part of a network is the software to keep it running. Computer networks can connect to other computer networks to create a vast computer network.

There are numerous configurations for computer networks, including:

- Local-area networks (LANS)--the computers are all contained within the same building
- Wide-area networks (WANS)--the computers are at a distance and are connected through telephone lines or radio waves
- Campus-area networks (CANs)--the computers are within a specific, geographic area, such as a school campus or military base
- Metropolitan-area networks (MANs)--a data network developed for a specific town or city
- Home-area networks (HANs)--a network contained within a private home which connects all the digital devices
- Internet—the communicating and sharing of data via shared routers and servers using common protocols

Depending on the type of network access, the teacher has productivity and instructional information and communications capabilities available from the next office or around the world.

Skill 20.3 Demonstrates understanding of methods for evaluating the performance of hardware and software components of computer systems and applying basic troubleshooting strategies

SEE Skill 22.1

Skill 20.4 Recognizes the social, ethical, legal, and human issues related to computing and technology, including the uses and effects of computers and technology in education, business and industry, and society.

SEE also Skill 21.5

Skill 20.5 Recognizes the historical development and important trends affecting the evolution of technology and its probable future roles in society.

Teachers' understanding and use of technology, as it has been developed over the past couple decades, has had a rocky start. There are two main reasons for this. First, school districts were not capable of paying the extraordinary amounts of money needed to set up schools for technology. Second, teachers have been skeptical of technology use in the classroom as there was a sense that technology would not add to student learning.

Both of these reasons, although not entirely resolved now, have faded away in some regard. First, the costs of technology have dropped enormously. Many grants have been available to schools to support the purchasing of technology. Additionally, school boards and districts have seen that the cost that is associated with technology is an important price to pay so that students can be better prepared for a technologically-advanced world.

The second reason that teachers have been skeptical of technology is the result of a disconnect between older methods of teaching and newer, more progressive methods of teaching. Technology may be irrelevant to education if the older models of teaching and learning with a focus on rote memorization, recall, and so on were the only expectations. However, more and more teachers are understanding the importance of differentiation, information literacy, technology literacy, and student-centered learning. Technology is critical in these regards.

The important point of this trend is that individuals, particularly educated individuals, are now expected to be able to use technology in their daily lives. And as we look into the future, we realize that technology will drive the globalization of our world. Therefore, it is crucial that students be technologically literate and proficient. Classrooms are, obviously, very important to this process.

Skill 20.6 Identifies strategies for facilitating consideration of ethical, legal, and human issues involving school purchasing and policy decisions.

Internet usage agreements define a number of criteria of technology use that a students must agree to in order to have access to school computers. Students must exercise responsibility and accountability in adhering to technology usage during the school day. Students who violate any parts of the computer usage agreement are subject to have all access to school computers or other educational technology denied or blocked, which, for the student needing to print a paper using the school computer and printer, could make the difference in handing assignments in on time or receiving a lower grade for late assignments.

District and school policies are developed to provide a consistent language of expectation for students using school technology. Districts are liable for the actions of students and teachers in school communities who use publicly-funded and legislatively-funded technology. The standards of usage for school computers are created to maximize student use for educational purposes and to minimize student surfing for non-educational sites that minimize learning during class times. The timeframes for computer usage are limited for students, since the numbers of computers being used in school communities are minimal to the users.

Technology use has policies that transcend from the district to school communities to students and staff. Federal and state funding to districts also carry technology expectations as conditions of funding, so the chain of expectation starts from top management to school communities. Given the predator nature of users on the Internet, the policies and procedures for school usage are necessary to keep students safe when they are using computers for educational purposes.

Beyond computer usage in schools, the use of other electronics like I-pods, Walkmans, and cell phones are prohibited in classrooms. The constant distractions of phones beeping, emitting loud noises, along with the choice of music that each generation listens to on a daily basis impede the educational access for students struggling to maintain focus on the lesson objectives. A student having trouble with inference in a reading passage could be easily distracted with the constant phone noises and electronic music coming from student earphones or computer downloads. An effective teacher underscores in the classroom that the focus on learning will be exclusive of electronic distractions and inappropriate computer use.

Students who have their computer privileges revoked due to abuse of the Internet agreements may find that academic progress may be jeopardized, especially if the students don't own computers or have Internet access beyond the classrooms. Teachers should monitor the activities of students who are using computers and actively respond to students who misuse public technology intended to enhance the learning process and access for all students.

COMPETENCY 21.0 UNDERSTANDS THE USE OF TECHNOLOGY FOR ENHANCING PERSONAL PROFESSIONAL GROWTH AND PRODUCTIVITY.

Skill 21.1 Demonstrates knowledge of how to use technology in communicating, collaborating, conducting research, and solving problems

Incorporating technology effectively into a fully content- and skill-based curriculum requires a good understanding of lesson objectives and how those objectives can be met with the technology. While teachers should definitely consider technological integration as an important aspect of their work in any subject and at any grade level, teachers should not include technology simply for the sake of technology. The best approach, considering all subjects can in certain ways be enhanced with technology, is for the teacher to consider a variety of lessons and units and decide which focus areas can be enhanced with technological tools.

Using technology in collaborative student group situations is considered to be the most effective method for a few reasons. Practically, most teachers cannot assign one computer to each student in the class whenever the teacher would like to utilize computers in the classroom. But that should not matter. As technological tools are complicated and complex, pair and small group work better facilitates stronger, social-based learning.

Even though teachers may assume all students know how to use various technological tools, they need to remember two very important things: First, not ALL students are proficient. Even though some highly-proficient students lead teachers to believe that the entire generation of kids in schools today already understands technology, many students actually never learned it at home. Some actually do not have the tools at home due to the high costs and therefore have no opportunity to practice. Second, not all technology skills transfer. While one student may navigate the web easily, he or she may not be able to use a word processing program with a similar level of expertise. Social opportunities to learn technology will help students to engage in a more productive, friendly, and help-centered fashion. Learning together, particularly in technology, can indeed reduce any anxiety or fear a student may have.

Teachers can consider technology learning as a method to also teach cooperation, decision-making skills, and problem-solving skills. For example, as a small group of students work together on a project on a computer, they must decide together how they will proceed and create. Teachers can instruct students in good cooperative decision-making skills to make the process easier. Students can also engage in activities where they are required to solve problems, build real-life solutions to situations, and create real-world products. Doing so will only enhance content-area instruction.

Finally, it is important to remember that as with all other learning, technological learning must be developmentally-appropriate. First, realize that while very young students can perform various functions on the computer, by virtue of development level, the time required for a particular activity may be greatly increased. Also, various technological tools are simply too advanced, too fast, and too complex for very young students. It may be best to introduce basic elements of technology in the earlier grades.

Skill 21.2   Identifies computer and other related technology resources for facilitating distance and lifelong learning.

Distance education is a method of education in which the student is physically separated from the teacher, the school or organization which supports the education forum. The design of distance education varies from correspondence-style courses to technologically based courses using the Internet.

Teachers should be aware of the benefits of distance education which serves as an alternative method for delivering academic course work to students unable to attend conventional campus-based classes. Educators are responsive to the knowledge that distance education offers students significant benefits, including increased access to learning, lifelong learning opportunities, and convenience of time and place. The teacher's use of various methods of electronic media increases time, effectiveness and improves the teaching of informational material.

Audio, video and computer-based learning applications are implemented and received by the independent student learner. Video/audio models of distance education include broadcast television, cable television and satellite. Computer technology through the use of the Internet or CD-ROM with television transmission provides a potentially new dimension to distance education.

Distance education encourages lifelong learning skills by reinforcing positive learning behaviors for student learners. These successful students develop persistence and skills in self-directing work. Students in distance education settings perform as well or better on assignments, class activities, and exams when compared to campus-based students (St. Pierre, 1998). Self-direction, a passion for learning, and strong individual responsibility are important influences on the achievement of lifelong learning, which can be accomplished through distance learning.

Garrels (1997) describes these elements for successful distance teaching.

- *Instructor enthusiasm* Teachers should feel comfortable in front of the camera, or with the technology utilized
- *Organization* Teaching materials must be prepared in advance; timing, variation, and smooth transitions must be planned
- *Strong commitment to student interaction* Teacher must encourage and facilitate ongoing communication between themselves and the students
- *Familiarity with technology* Teachers should be trained in computer use, video use, or other forms of instructional technology used

Skill 21.3   Demonstrates knowledge of how to use computers and other learning technologies to support problem solving, data collection, information management, communications, presentations, and decision making.

Teachers should be knowledgeable in the use of computers and applications, demonstrating an ability to use technology for research, problem solving, and communication. Students should be taught the fundamentals of locating, collecting, and processing information from a variety of electronic sources.

Students should be able to use computers creatively and purposefully, by recognizing the instructional material they need to learn. Learning to problem-solve enables the student to use the computer as part of the process of accomplishing their information management tasks. Individual computer skills take on a new meaning when they are integrated within this type of informational problem-solving process, and students develop true "computer literacy" due to genuinely applying various computer skills as part of the decision-making and consequently learning process.

Teachers should design and implement multiple lessons and units in which to utilize technology's unique capabilities in a variety of instructional roles (e.g., to provide information, to facilitate communication, and to manipulate or display data, etc.). Various software applications are now available which are beneficial to classroom instruction, including; ClarisWorks, Co-Writer, Power Point, Microsoft Word and Excel, Publisher, Print Shop Deluxe, and KidPix. Teachers can also integrate text, tables, graphs, drawings, diagrams, photographs, sounds, and animations within their presentations and communications.

The following skills provide a strategy for students to effectively and efficiently learn about processing informational needs (i.e. problem solving, decision making, and information management):

- Define the task
- Identify information needed in order to complete the task
- Brainstorm all possible informational sources
- Locate sources of information
- Extract relevant information
- Organize information from multiple sources
- Present the information
- Evaluation

Skill 21.4   Demonstrates knowledge of productivity tools used for word processing, database management, spreadsheet applications, and the creation of basic multimedia presentations.

The tools teachers have available to them to present information to students is always growing. Where just ten years ago, teachers needed to only know how to use word processing programs, grading programs, and overhead projectors, today, electronic slideshows (most people think of Power Point) are becoming the new "norm," and other methods of information distribution are expected by principals, parents, and students alike.

Many instructional programs include short video clips for students to help exemplify ideas. For example, many science programs include very short clips to demonstrate scientific principles. Or literature programs might include short dramatizations of stories or background information on a literature selection. These tools are particularly helpful to replace "prior knowledge" for students before embarking on new topics, and they are especially important for students who are strong visual learners.

In many schools, electronic and print information from teachers is necessary for communicating things to parents. For example, since many students' parents are at work all day long, it is more efficient for parents to look online for homework assignments rather than discuss certain homework issues. Many schools have instituted homework hotlines where teachers record homework for parents or absent students to call in and access.

In general, we know that the more a teacher communicates with parents, the more likely parents will trust the teacher and assist the teacher in his or her methods and strategies. And parents are impressed by teachers who take the time to put together something in a professional manner. So, teachers will earn much more respect from families by providing information in a timely and professional manner.

Many teachers now also have websites where they post assignments, as well as exemplary student work, helpful websites, and other useful information. While this is a good thing, teachers will want to double-check to ensure that sensitive student information is not included on the web. Although most people would say that it is fine to include possibly a picture of the students at work in the classroom, schools are finding that having NO pictures of students—individually or in a group—is better for the protection of students.

Teachers who do now know how to use these various tools have multiple learning options. Many community colleges specifically teach these skills, and many websites are available with video-based tutorials.

Skill 21.5 Recognizes socially responsible, ethical, and legal uses of technology, information, and software resources (e.g., application of copyright laws).

To a novice, computers might appear to be very complicated machines, but in reality it is not very difficult to operate one of today's "user-friendly" computers. Basically, all that is required is to attach the computer to the power source and turn it on. Most machines are configured to "boot up" into a menu of programs from which the user has merely to "point and click" at the desired choice.

For the computer to boot up from the hard drive to follow the instructions for which it has been configured, it is necessary to remove any diskettes from the floppy disk drive before turning on the power. Otherwise, the computer will not boot up into its menu from the hard drive, but rather will try to find the necessary boot up instructions on the floppy disk.

When preparing to shut down the computer, it is important to close all programs that are currently in use. This includes saving anything that needs to be kept for future sessions on the computer. When a program is not properly exited, important data might be lost and the computer might not boot up to the proper menu the next time it is turned on for use. It is just a matter of good housekeeping to put away everything in its proper place before leaving.

SEE also Skill 22.5

Skill 21.6 Applies information literacy skills to access, evaluate, and use information to improve teaching and learning.

Teachers have access to a variety of data to assist them in refining and improving their instruction. For example, most schools and/or districts have programs that allow teachers to access student achievement data. Additionally, many schools have programs that assist teachers in giving and analyzing classroom-based assessments. These assessments can show teachers the progress their students are making toward final year-end goals.

In addition to student achievement data, teachers can utilize information literacy skills to access instructional ideas through journals, books, and the internet. The range of teaching materials online, for example, is massive. Good information literacy skills would assist teachers in clarifying which materials are appropriate and which ones are not. Although a set of criteria for information that teachers can use to improve teaching would certainly not come close to covering the wide range of materials out there, teachers may want to look closely at these following considerations:

- *The source of the information.* Generally, better materials come from sources that have been vetted by experts in the field—or have been written by the experts, themselves.
- *Appropriateness.* There are many materials out there that may claim to work for a particular grade level and subject, but remember that all students are different. A third grade teacher that has a majority of students reading at the fourth or fifth grade levels may not want to blindly use third grade materials, for example.
- *Length.* Many resources out there are either very short or very long. It is important not to try to squeeze large lessons into small amounts of time, or vice versa.

COMPETENCY 22.0   UNDERSTANDS THE APPLICATION OF TECHNOLOGY IN INSTRUCTION.

Skill 22.1   Demonstrates knowledge of strategies and criteria for exploring, evaluating, and using computer and technology resources, including applications, tools, educational software, and associated documentation.

SEE Skill 20.2

Skill 22.2   Identifies current instructional principles, research, and appropriate assessment practices as related to the use of computers and technology resources in the curriculum.

There are a lot of computer programs available to enhance instruction in various curricula areas. Tutorials, educational programs, and games exist on almost every imaginable subject, but computers can also be used as a tool to enhance regular instruction.

Resources and materials for instruction are everywhere—in schools, on the web, in bookstores, and in adopted school programs. How does one decide where to get materials for instruction? And how does one evaluate materials for use in instruction?

The Internet and other research resources provide a wealth of information on thousands of interesting topics for students preparing presentations or projects. Using search engines like Google, Microsoft and Infotrac, student can search multiple Internet resources on one subject search. Students should have an outline of the purpose of a project or research presentation that includes:

- Purpose - Identity the reason for the research information
- Objective - Having a clear thesis for a project will allow the students opportunities to be specific on Internet searches
- Preparation - When using resources or collecting data, students should create folders for sorting through the information. Providing labels for the folders will create a system of organization that will make construction of the final project or presentation easier and less time consuming
- Procedure - Organized folders and a procedural list of what the project or presentation needs to include will create A+ work for students and A+ grading for teachers
- Visuals or artifacts - Choose data or visuals that are specific to the subject content or presentation. Make sure that poster boards or Power Point presentations can be visually seen from all areas of the classroom. Teachers can provide laptop computers for Power Point presentations.

When a teacher models and instructs students in the proper use of search techniques, the teacher can minimize wasted time in preparing projects and wasted paper from students who print every search. In some school districts, students are allowed a minimum number of printed pages per week. Since students have Internet accounts for computer usage, the monitoring of printing is easily done by the school's librarian and teachers in classrooms.

Having the school's librarian or technology expert as a guest speaker in classrooms provides another method of sharing and modeling proper presentation preparation using technology. Teachers can also appoint technology experts from the students in a classroom to work with students on projects and presentations. In high schools, technology classes provide students with upper-class teacher assistants who fill the role of technology assistants.

The wealth of resources for teachers and students seeking to incorporate technology and structured planning for student presentations and projects is as diverse as the presentations. There is an expert in every classroom who is always willing to offer advice and instruction. In school communities, that expert may begin with the teacher.

Many school districts have shared drives that contain multiple files of lesson and unit plans, curriculum maps, pacing guides, and assessment ideas. While these can be very beneficial, it is always a good idea to determine the intended use for such files and documents.

The best place to start is identifying the required materials that should be used in instruction. After that, many websites contain lesson plans and instructional ideas. Be careful, though, as some websites do not monitor the information placed on their servers. While a lesson may have a creative title and purpose, it may not always serve the best purpose for your instructional agenda. In fact, there is no guarantee that such lessons are any good! Consider how you would adapt it, if your students would get something out of it, and if it seems inappropriate for your particular group of students.

When looking through shared drives, remote devices, and other online databases, it is important to understand who has posted information and for what the information is intended. Often times, it might be for specialized programs within the district. It's always safest to ask.

Skill 22.3 **Demonstrates an understanding of methods for designing, implementing, and assessing student learning activities that integrate computers and technology for a variety of student-grouping strategies and for diverse student populations.**

There are two primary areas of equity issues related to technology. One is the level at which students come to school with proficiency in technology. The other is the fair distribution of technology exposure to all students in a class.

The first area, the level at which students come to school with a background in technology, is particularly important. First, teachers will need to understand that they have a variety of ability levels in their classrooms. Second, a lack of technology proficiency may actually be an embarrassment to students. Usually, not having technology skill can indicate that the student does not have much money—or even that the student is living in poverty.

When students come to school with a wide variety of skills, teachers need to find unique ways to provide students with fewer skills more opportunities to learn without compromising the ability of other students to still grow in their understandings of technology. Often, group-based work can be very helpful.

The second level is ensuring that all students have similar opportunities to use technology, particularly as the students with the least home exposure will need more time. Again, a good way of dealing with this is by having students work in groups. Specific rules should be put in place to ensure that students share actual keyboard/mouse control.

Skill 22.4 **Demonstrates awareness of resources for adaptive and assistive devices for students with special needs**

Technology has advanced so rapidly in the last decade that many learning disabilities can be addressed in part with unique tools. Furthermore, in various situations, other technological tools can enhance and broaden students' exposure to concepts and modalities of learning.

Tools for assisting students with disabilities:

- Amplification devices assist students with making computer content more clear.
- Speech recognition devices type in text as it's spoken by the student.
- Large print keys for students who have trouble with hand-eye coordination.
- Readers that read aloud alerts on screens.

Other tools that have become very helpful for students:

- Communication boards are "asynchronous" discussion or dialogue programs that allow students to post content in a discussion format. It is a particularly helpful way to encourage written discussion. It also is highly beneficial for students who have physical trouble getting to school.
- Wikis are tools that teachers are using more and more each day. Wikis are collaborative definitions, posted to computers, and often the web. After units, teachers might ask students in groups to post a wiki on a particular topic.
- Blogs, even though they are thought of as a tool for journalists, have become popular in the classroom. Teachers often ask students to maintain blogs, or web logs, on particular topics. Often, blogs are used for students to respond to classroom novels as students progress through books.

Many additional tools are becoming available around the clock. It is a good idea to keep up-to-date on technological tools that can assist teachers in meeting all students' needs.

Skill 22.5   Demonstrates knowledge of methods for designing policies and learning activities that foster equitable, ethical, and legal use of technology resources by students.

In this technological age, it is important that teachers be aware of their legal responsibilities when using computers in the classroom. As public employees, teachers are particularly vulnerable to public scrutiny. Not only are teachers more likely to be caught if they are unethical in the use of computers in the classroom, but it is also the responsibility of educators to model as well as teach ethical computer behaviors.

In 1980, P.L. 96-517, Section 117 of the copyright was amended to cover the use of computers. The following changes were made:

1. The definition of a "computer program" was inserted and is defined now as "a set of statements or instructions to be used directly in a computer in order to bring about a certain result.

2. The owner of a copy of a computer program is not infringing on the copyright by making or authorizing the making of or adaptation of that program if the following criteria are met:

a) The new copy or adaptation must be created in order to be able to use the program in conjunction with the machine and is used in no other manner.

b) The new copy or adaptation must be for archival purpose only and all archival copies must be destroyed in the event that continued possession of the computer program should cease to be rightful.

c) Any copies prepared or adapted may not be leased, sold, or otherwise transferred without the authorization of the copyright owner.

The intent of this amendment to the copyright act is to allow an individual or institutional owner of a program to make "backup" copies to avoid destruction of the original program disk, while restricting the owner from making copies in order to use the program on more that one machine at a time or to share with other teachers. Under the Software Copyright Act of 1980, once a program is loaded into the memory of a computer, a temporary copy of that program is made. Multiple machine loading (moving from machine to machine and loading a single program into several computers for simultaneous use) constitutes making multiple copies which is not permitted under the law. Since the same is true of a networked program, it is necessary to obtain permission from the owner of the copyright or purchase a license agreement prior to multiple use of a program in a school setting.

Infringement of copyright laws is a serious offense and can result in significant penalties if a teacher chooses to ignore the law. Not only does the teacher risk losing all personal computer equipment but he or she is also placing their job as an educator in jeopardy.

SEE also Skill 21.5

COMPETENCY 23.0   UNDERSTANDS THE USE OF TECHNOLOGY TO FACILITATE PRODUCTIVITY, COMMUNICATION, INFORMATION ACCESS, RESEARCH, PROBLEM SOLVING, AND PRODUCT DEVELOPMENT.

Skill 23.1   Recognizes advanced features and uses of technology-based productivity tools, including word processing, desktop publishing, graphics programs, spreadsheets, databases, and teacher utility and classroom management tools.

Technology-based productivity tools have become more user-friendly over the past few years, and increasingly, they are being used in schools for a variety of purposes. Below is an explanation of some tools and how they can be used in schools.

Word Processing. Word processing tools assist in typing, preparing, and presenting written text. Microsoft Word is the most famous word processing program; however, there are many others. Generally, when teachers have students compose on word processing programs, students get more practice in being able to edit and revise more fully than they could if they composed on paper. Moving, deleting, adding, and altering text is made very simple with such programs.

Desktop Publishing. Desktop publishing programs assist classroom teachers and students in presenting multimedia information. For example, a group of students could put together a newspaper "front page" with such a program.

Graphics Programs. Graphics programs assist in the development of graphics that can be used in a variety of other programs. Generally, students can use these programs to artistically portray information.

Spreadsheets. Spreadsheets help in organizing and analyzing numeric information. Microsoft Excel is the most famous spreadsheet program. Spreadsheets can be used to tabulate responses, organize long lists of numbers, etc. Mathematical functions can be used to interpret and analyze the information, once it is all organized.

Databases. Databases are electronic storage facilities. Often, schools will have databases on students. Sometimes, only administrators are allowed full viewing access to databases, as sensitive information can be seen. However, other databases, such as student achievement databases, can be viewed and used by teachers to help them understand their students' levels of achievement.

Teacher Utility and Classroom Management Tools. Electronic grade books, seat assignment charts, and other functions can be created with these tools. The options are endless, but in general, these types of tools assist teachers with their daily organization and management of teaching duties.

SEE also Skill 21.1

Skill 23.2 **Identifies features and applications of specific-purpose electronic devices (e.g., graphing calculator, language translator, scientific probeware, electronic thesaurus) in appropriate content areas.**

In addition to computers, there are a variety of types of technology that assist students and teachers in the teaching and learning process. Some of these devices, though not all—as there are many—are discussed below:

Graphing Calculator. A graphing calculator is a calculator that assists in geometric tasks, as well as area measurement tasks.

Language Translator. A language translator, usually is a small device, about the size of a calculator, that translates specific words or common phrases into other languages. Typically, each translator works for translating between two specific languages, say English and Spanish. Often, these translators have sound so that the user can actually hear pronunciation.

Electronic Thesaurus. An electronic thesaurus, like a language translator, is a small device the size of a calculator. The user can punch in a word (and sometimes speak a word), and the device will recall a variety of synonyms.

Skill 23.3 **Recognizes features and uses of telecommunications tools and resources (e.g., e-mail, Web browsers, online search tools) for information sharing, remote information access and retrieval, and multimedia and hypermedia publishing.**

Telecommunication tools are important in schools for two main reasons: (a) communication with parents, colleagues, administrators, and district support staff and (b) instructional purposes. Some of the types of tools are described below with explanations of how they might be useful in schools:

Email. Electronic mail, transported over internet lines. Email serves as a very convenient tool for bringing teachers on a spread-out campus closer together. It can also be useful for communication with parents who work during the day. Instructionally, teachers can assist students in learning how to write appropriate, professional emails for a variety of purposes and audiences.

Web Browsers. Web browsers support the electronic search for web pages, particularly when web addresses are already known. It is possible, then, to type into a web browser the web address and directly find a web site. Instructionally, teachers often will want students to go to a specific site, so that searching does not become burdensome. Web browsers can also assist in the publishing of multimedia and hypermedia. School websites often carry space for such endeavors.

Online Search Tools. When specific websites are not known, online search tools, such as Google or Yahoo allow students and teachers to find a lot of information on generalized topics.

Skill 23.4   Identifies basic principles of instructional design associated with the development of multimedia and hypermedia learning materials.

SEE Skill 21.4

Skill 23.5   Selects appropriate tools for communicating concepts, conducting research, and solving problems for an intended audience and purpose.

The tools that teachers have at their disposal to communicate concepts, conduct research, and solve problems are varied, yet as there are many, it is essential that teachers be skilled connoisseurs of resources so that they select the best ones.

While the space here is rather limited for the range of tools out there (and tools are described elsewhere in this section), we should consider some of the criteria teachers should employ when selecting tools.

The first thing to consider is whether or not the tool has pragmatic value for teaching and learning. In other words, will the tool actually help the teacher teach and the student learn? If not, then the tool may be worthless. Each teacher will have a fairly good idea of the answer to this question based on the specific students he or she has.

The next issue to consider is the feasibility of the tool. Feasibility of instructional tools consists of these following elements:

- Appropriateness for student level / age
- Appropriateness for subject matter / academic topic
- Ethical appropriateness (i.e., Is it acceptable for the age level?)
- Financial considerations (for teacher, school, and student)
- Time (i.e., Is the time it takes to utilize—or set up—the tool worth the trouble?)

In general, instructional tools must meet the above criteria in order to be successfully used in the classroom. Even then, teachers must be thoroughly familiar with the tools prior to use.

Skill 23.6 Demonstrates knowledge of strategies for collaborating with online workgroups to build bodies of knowledge about specific topics.

Online workgroups are internet-based discussion tools that bring together people with similar backgrounds and/or interests from a large geographical area. Think of an online workgroup as a discussion forum that takes place in a web-based "chat-room" or "message board." Let's consider a particular topic and audience as an example.

A group of 9th grade Biology teachers across the country have been interested in unique science laboratory teaching techniques. They met each other at a training held in a resort town in Florida one summer. After the one-week training, they decided that to really make use of this new training, they would stay in touch with each other throughout the school year. So, about once per week, each teacher goes online to view comments, post comments, and ask questions on this discussion board.

The positive thing about an online workgroup is that it provides teachers with a body of knowledge based on teachers from all areas of the country. Additionally, it provides teachers a convenient way to collaborate, get new teaching ideas, and seek assistance regarding teaching problems.

Overall, these groups are very beneficial for teachers. They can be found all over the internet, and they are also available and promoted through teaching conferences.

Sample Test

Directions: Read each item and select the best response

1. **When are students more likely to understand complex ideas?**

    (Average Rigor) (Skill 1.1)

    A. If they do outside research before coming to class

    B. Later when they write out the definitions of complex words

    C. When they attend a lecture on the subject

    D. When they are clearly defined by the teacher and are given examples and non-examples of the concept

2. **Mr. Smith is introducing the concept of photosynthesis to his class next week. In preparing for this lesson, he considers that this will be a new concept to many of his students. Mr. Smith understands that his students' brains are like filing cabinets and that there is currently no file for photosynthesis in those cabinets. What does Mr. Smith need to do to ensure his students acquire the necessary knowledge?**

    (Rigorous) (Skill 1.2)

    A. Help them create a new file

    B. Teach the students the information; they will organize it themselves in their own way

    C. Find a way to connect the new learning to other information they already know

    D. Provide many repetitions and social situations during the learning process

3. **What developmental patterns should a professional teacher assess to meet the needs of the student?**

    (Average Rigor) (Skill 1.3)

    A. Academic, regional, and family background

    B. Social, physical, academic

    C. Academic, physical, and family background

    D. Physical, family, ethnic background

4. **How many stages of intellectual development does Piaget define?**

    (Easy) (Skill 1.3)

    A. Two

    B. Four

    C. Six

    D. Eight

5. **Who developed the theory of multiple intelligences?**

    (Easy) (Skill 1.3)

    A. Bruner

    B. Gardner

    C. Kagan

    D. Cooper

6. **Discovery learning is to inquiry as direct instruction is to...**

    (Rigorous) (Skill 1.4)

    A. Scripted lessons

    B. Well-developed instructions

    C. Clear instructions which eliminate all misinterpretations

    D. Creativity of teaching

7. **Students who can solve problems mentally have...**

    (Average Rigor) (Skill 1.5)

    A. Reached maturity

    B. Physically developed

    C. Reached the pre-operational stage of thought

    D. Achieved the ability to manipulate objects symbolically

8. **Curriculum mapping is an effective strategy because it…**

   (Rigorous) (Skill 1.6)

   A. Provides an orderly sequence to instruction

   B. Provides lesson plans for teachers to use and follow

   C. Ties the curriculum into instruction

   D. Provides a clear map so all students receive the same instruction across all classes

9. **Mrs. Peck wants to justify the use of personalized learning community to her principal. Which of the following reasons should she use?**

   (Rigorous) (Skill 2.1)

   A. They build multiculturalism

   B. They provide a supportive environment to address academic and emotional needs

   C. They builds relationships between students which promote life long learning

   D. They are proactive in their nature

10. **Mrs. Potts has noticed an undercurrent in her classroom of an unsettled nature. She is in the middle of her math lesson, but still notices that many of her students seem to be having some sort of difficulty. Mrs. Potts stops class and decides to have a class meeting. She understands that even though her math objectives are important, it is equally important to address whatever is troubling her classroom. What is it Mrs. Potts knows?**

    (Rigorous) (Skill 2.3)

    A. Discipline is important

    B. Social issues can impact academic learning

    C. Maintaining order is important

    D. Social skills instruction is important

11. **Which of the following describes the functional approach to language acquisition?**

    (Average Rigor) (Skill 2.4)

    A. Communicative elements

    B. Conceptual purposes

    C. Grammar elements

    D. All of the above

12. How can the teacher establish a positive climate in the classroom?

(Average Rigor) (Skill 3.1)

A. Help students see the unique contributions of individual differences

B. Use whole group instruction for all content areas

C. Help students divide into cooperative groups based on ability

D. Eliminate teaching strategies that allow students to make choices

13. Which of the following could be an example of a situation which could have an effect on a student's learning and academic progress?

(Average Rigor) (Skill 3.2)

A. Relocation

B. Abuse

C. Both of the Above

D. Neither of the Above

14. When developing lessons it is imperative teachers provide equity in pedagogy so…

(Rigorous) (Skill 3.3)

A. Unfair labeling of students will not occur

B. Student experiences will be positive

C. Students will achieve academic success

D. All of the above

15. In successful inclusion of students with disabilities:

(Average Rigor) (Skill 3.4)

A. A variety of instructional arrangements are available

B. School personnel shift the responsibility for learning outcomes to the student

C. The physical facilities are used as they are

D. Regular classroom teachers have sole responsibility for evaluating student progress

16. **Which of the following is not a communication issue that is related to diversity within the classroom?**

(Average Rigor) (Skill 3.5)

A. Learning disorder

B. Sensitive terminology

C. Body language

D. Discussing differing viewpoints and opinions

17. **What does the validity of a test refer to?**

(Easy) (Skill 4.1)

A. Its consistency

B. Its usefulness

C. Its accuracy

D. The degree of true scores it provides

18. **What is the best definition for an achievement test?**

(Average Rigor) (Skill 4.2)

A. It measures mechanical and practical abilities

B. It measures broad areas of knowledge that are the result of cumulative learning experiences

C. It measures the ability to learn to perform a task

D. It measures performance related to specific, recently acquired information

19. **How are standardized tests useful in assessment?**

(Average Rigor) (Skill 4.2)

A. For teacher evaluation

B. For evaluation of the administration

C. For comparison from school to school

D. For comparison to the population on which the test was normed

20. **What is an effective way to prepare students for testing?**

(Average Rigor) (Skill 4.3)

A. Minimize the importance of the test

B. Orient the students to the test, telling them of the purpose, how the results will be used and how it is relevant to them

C. Use the same format for every test are given

D. Have them construct an outline to study from

21. **How will students have a fair chance to demonstrate what they know on a test?**

(Average Rigor) (Skill 4.3)

A. The examiner has strictly enforced rules for taking the test

B. The examiner provides a comfortable setting free of distractions and positively encourages the students

C. The examiner provides frequent stretch breaks to the students

D. The examiner stresses the importance of the test to the overall grade

22. **Safeguards against bias and discrimination in the assessment of children include:**

(Average Rigor) (Skill 4.4)

A. The testing of a child in standard English

B. The requirement for the use of one standardized test

C. The use of evaluative materials in the child's native language or other mode of communication

D. All testing performed by a certified, licensed, psychologist

23. **Which of the following is a presentation modification?**

(Easy) (Skill 4.5)

A. Taking an assessment in an alternate room

B. Providing an interpreter to give the test in American Sign Language

C. Allowing dictation of written responses

D. Extending the time limits on an assessment

24. **When a teacher wants to utilize an assessment which is subjective in nature, which of the following is the most effective method for scoring?**

(Easy) (Skill 4.6)

A. Rubric

B. Checklist

C. Alternative Assessment

D. Subjective measures should not be utilized

25. **Which of the following is the correct term for the alignment of the curriculum across all grades K-12?**

(Rigorous) (Skill 4.7)

A. Data Based Decision Making

B. Curriculum Mapping

C. Vertical Integration

D. Curriculum Alignment

26. **Which of the following describes why it is important and necessary for teachers to be able to analyze data on their students?**

(Rigorous) (Skill 4.7)

A. To provide appropriate instruction

B. To make instructional decisions

C. To communicate and determine instructional progress

D. All of the above

27. **What are critical elements of instructional process?**

(Average Rigor) (Skill 5.1)

A. Content, goals, teacher needs

B. Means of getting money to regulate instruction

C. Content, materials, activities, goals, learner needs

D. Materials, definitions, assignments

28. **What would improve planning for instruction?**

    (Average Rigor) (Skill 5.1)

    A. Describe the role of the teacher and student

    B. Evaluate the outcomes of instruction

    C. Rearrange the order of activities

    D. Give outside assignments

29. **What is one component of the instructional planning model that must be given careful evaluation?**

    (Rigorous) (Skill 5.1)

    A. Students' prior knowledge and skills

    B. The script the teacher will use in instruction

    C. Future lesson plans

    D. Parent participation

30. **The teacher states that the lesson the students will be engaged in will consist of a review of the material from the previous day, demonstration of the scientific of an electronic circuit, and small group work on setting up an electronic circuit. What has the teacher demonstrated?**

    (Rigorous) (Skill 5.2)

    A. The importance of reviewing

    B. Giving the general framework for the lesson to facilitate learning

    C. Giving students the opportunity to leave if they are not interested in the lesson

    D. Providing momentum for the lesson

31. **What steps are important in the review of subject matter in the classroom?**

    (Rigorous) (Skill 5.2)

    A. A lesson-initiating review, topic and a lesson-end review

    B. A preview of the subject matter, an in-depth discussion, and a lesson-end review

    C. A rehearsal of the subject matter and a topic summary within the lesson

    D. A short paragraph synopsis of the previous days lesson and a written review at the end of the lesson

32. **When is utilization of instructional materials most effective?**

    (Average Rigor) (Skill 5.2)

    A. When the activities are sequenced

    B. When the materials are prepared ahead of time

    C. When the students choose the pages to work on

    D. When the students create the instructional materials

33. **How can mnemonic devices be used to increase achievement?**

    (Rigorous) (Skill 5.2)

    A. They help the child rehearse the information

    B. They help the child visually imagine the information

    C. They help the child to code information

    D. They help the child reinforce concepts

34. **The teacher states, "We will work on the first page of vocabulary words. On the second page we will work on the structure and meaning of the words. We will go over these together and then you will write out the answers to the exercises on your own. I will be circulating to give help if needed". What is this an example of?**

    (Rigorous) (Skill 5.2)

    A. Evaluation of instructional activity

    B. Analysis of instructional activity

    C. Identification of expected outcomes

    D. Pacing of instructional activity

35. **If teachers attend to content, instructional materials, activities, learner needs, and goals in instructional planning, what could be an outcome?**

(Rigorous) (Skill 5.2)

A. Planning for the next year

B. Effective classroom performance

C. Elevated test scores on standardized tests

D. More student involvement

36. **What should a teacher do when students have not responded well to an instructional activity?**

(Average Rigor) (Skill 5.3)

A. Reevaluate learner needs

B. Request administrative help

C. Continue with the activity another day

D. Assign homework on the concept

37. **When planning instruction, which of the following is an organizational tool to help ensure you are providing a well balanced set of objectives?**

(Rigorous) (Skill 5.4)

A. Using a taxonomy to develop objectives

B. Determining prior knowledge skill levels

C. Determining readiness levels

D. Ensuring you meet the needs of diverse learners

38. **Which of the following is not one of the levels of Bloom's taxonomy?**

(Average Rigor) (Skill 5.4)

A. Synthesis

B. Evaluation

C. Understanding

D. Knowledge

39. Mr. Ryan has proposed to his classroom that the students may demonstrate understanding of the unit taught in a variety of ways including: taking a test, writing a paper, creating an oral presentation, or building a model/project. Which of the following areas of differentiation has Mr. Ryan demonstrated?

(Rigorous) (Skill 6.1)

A. Synthesis

B. Product

C. Content

D. Process

40. Louise is a first grade teacher. She is planning her instructional activities for the week. In considering her planning, she should keep in mind that activities for this age of child should change how often?

(Average Rigor) (Skill 6.2)

A. 25-40 minutes

B. 30-40 minutes

C. 5-10 minutes

D. 15-30 minutes

41. What is an example of formative feedback?

(Average Rigor) (Skill 6.3)

A. The results of an intelligence test

B. Correcting the tests in small groups

C. Verbal behavior that expresses approval of a student response to a test item

D. Scheduling a discussion prior to the test

42. Mr. Weiss understands that it is imperative that students who are struggling with acquiring concepts at a specific grade level can still benefit from participating in whole classroom discussions and lessons. In fact, such students should be required to be present for whole classroom lessons. Mr. Weiss's beliefs fall under which of the following principles?

(Rigorous) (Skill 6.5)

A. Self-fulfilling prophecy

B. Partial participation

C. Inclusion

D. Heterogeneous grouping

43. **When creating and selecting materials for instruction, teachers should complete which of the following steps:**

(Average Rigor) (Skill 7.2)

A. Relevant to the prior knowledge of the students

B. Allow for a variation of learning styles

C. Choose alternative teaching strategies

D. All of the above

44. **Which of following is not the role of the teacher in the instructional process:**

(Average Rigor) (Skill 7.5)

A. Instructor

B. Coach

C. Facilitator

D. Follower

45. **When considering the development of the curriculum, which of the following accurately describe the four factors which need to be considered?**

(Rigorous) (Skill 8.1)

A. Alignment, Scope, Sequence, and Design

B. Assessment, Instruction, Design, and Sequence

C. Data, Alignment, Correlation, and Score

D. Alignment, Sequence, Design and Assessment

46. **All of the following are true about phonological awareness EXCEPT:**

(Rigorous) (Skill 8.3)

A. It may involve print.

B. It is a prerequisite for spelling and phonics.

C. Activities can be done by the children with their eyes closed.

D. Starts before letter recognition is taught.

47. The arrangement and relationship of words in sentences or sentence structure best describes:

(Easy) (Skill 8.3)

A. Style.

B. Discourse.

C. Thesis.

D. Syntax.

48. Which of the following is not a technique of prewriting?

(Easy) (Skill 8.3)

A. Clustering

B. Listing

C. Brainstorming

D. Proofreading

49. Of the following choices, which would require the students to utilize the most complex algebraic thinking process?

(Rigorous) (Skill 8.3)

A. Red, blue, red, blue, _____

B. Red, yellow, green, red, yellow, green, _____

C. 2, 4, 6, 8, _____

D. 2, 4, _____, 8, 10

50. Suzy is given the following math problem to solve. There are five bicycles parked in front of the school. How many wheels are in front of the school? Which mathematical concept will help Suzy to solve the problem?

(Rigorous) (Skill 8.3)

A. Patterns

B. Relationships

C. Functions

D. Translation

51. How can student misconduct be redirected at times?

(Average Rigor) (Skill 9.1)

A. The teacher threatens the students

B. The teacher assigns detention to the whole class

C. The teacher stops the activity and stares at the students

D. The teacher effectively handles changing from one activity to another

52. **What is one way of effectively managing student conduct?**

    (Average Rigor) (Skill 9.1)

    A. State expectations about behavior

    B. Let students discipline their peers

    C. Let minor infractions of the rules go unnoticed

    D. Increase disapproving remarks

53. **While teaching, three students cause separate disruptions. The teacher selects the major one and tells that student to desist. What is the teacher demonstrating?**

    (Easy) (Skill 9.1)

    A. Deviancy spread

    B. Correct target desist

    C. Alternative behavior

    D. Desist major deviance

54. **Robert throws a piece of paper across the room. Dennis, sitting next to Robert, bats the piece of paper to the back of the room. The teacher ignores Dennis and reprimands Robert. What is the teacher demonstrating?**

    (Average Rigor) (Skill 9.1)

    A. Deviant disruption

    B. Correct target desist

    C. Alternative behavior

    D. Serious desist

55. **To maintain the flow of events in the classroom, what should an effective teacher do?**

    (Average Rigor) (Skill 9.4)

    A. Work only in small groups

    B. Use only whole class activities

    C. Direct attention to content, rather than focusing the class on misbehavior

    D. Follow lectures with written assignments

56. **The concept of efficient use of time includes which of the following?**

(Rigorous) (Skill 9.4)

A. Daily review, seatwork, and recitation of concepts

B. Lesson initiation, transition, and comprehension check

C. Review, test, review

D. Punctuality, management transition, and wait time avoidance

57. **What is a sample of an academic transition signal?**

(Average Rigor) (Skill 9.4)

A. "How do clouds form?"

B. "Today we are going to study clouds."

C. "We have completed today's lesson."

D. "That completes the description of cumulus clouds. Now we will look at the description of cirrus clouds."

58. **What has been established to increase student originality, intrinsic motivation, and higher order thinking skills?**

(Rigorous) (Skill 10.2)

A. Classroom climate

B. High expectations

C. Student choice

D. Use of authentic learning opportunities

59. **The success oriented classroom is designed to ensure students are successful at attaining new skills. In addition, mistakes are viewed as... in this type of classroom.**

(Rigorous) (Skill 10.3)

A. Motivations to improve

B. Natural part of the learning process

C. Ways to improve

D. Building blocks

60. **Mrs. Grant is providing her students with many extrinsic motivators in order to increase their intrinsic motivation. Which of the best explains this relationship?**

(Rigorous) (Skill 10.4)

A. This is a good relationship and will increase intrinsic motivation

B. The relationship builds animosity between the teacher and the students

C. Extrinsic motivation does not in itself help to build intrinsic motivation

D. There is no place for extrinsic motivation in the classroom

61. **What must be a consideration when a parent complains that he/she can't control their child's behavior?**

(Average Rigor) (Skill 10.5)

A. Consider whether the parent gives feedback to the child

B. Consider whether the parent's expectations for control are developmentally appropriate

C. Consider how much time the parent spends with the child

D. Consider how rigid the rules are that the parent sets

62. A parent has left an angry message on the teacher's voicemail. The message relates to a concern about a student and is directed at the teacher. The teacher should:

(Average Rigor) (Skill 10.5)

A. Call back immediately and confront the parent

B. Cool off, plan what to discuss with the parent, then call back

C. Question the child to find out what set off the parent

D. Ignore the message, since feelings of anger usually subside after a while

63. Which of the following should NOT be a purpose of a parent-teacher conference?

(Average Rigor) (Skill 10.5)

A. To involve the parent in their child's education

B. To establish a friendship with the child's parents

C. To resolve a concern about the child's performance

D. To inform parents of positive behaviors by the child

64. Which of the following can be measured utilizing the following types of assessments: direct observation, role playing, context observation, and teacher ratings?

(Easy) (Skill 11.1)

A. Social Skills

B. Reading Skills

C. Math Skills

D. Need for specialized instruction

65. Which of the following is a definition of an intercultural communication model?

(Average Rigor) (Skill 11.2)

A. Learning how different cultures engage in both verbal and nonverbal modes to communicate meaning.

B. Learning how classmates engage in both verbal and nonverbal modes to communicate meaning.

C. Learning how classmates engage in verbal dialogues

D. Learning how different cultures engage in verbal modes to communicate meaning.

66. **What do cooperative learning methods all have in common?**

    (Average Rigor) (Skill 11.3)

    A. Philosophy

    B. Cooperative task/cooperative reward structures

    C. Student roles and communication

    D. Teacher roles

67. **With the passage of the No Child Left Behind Act (NCLB), schools are required to develop action plans to improve student learning. Which of the following is not a part of this action plan?**

    (Rigorous) (Skill 12.1)

    A. Clearly defined goals for school improvement

    B. Clearly defined assessment plan

    C. Clearly defined timelines

    D. Clearly defined plans for addressing social skills improvement

68. **Which of the following can impact the desire of students to learn new material?**

    (Easy) (Skill 12.3)

    A. Assessments plan

    B. Lesson plans

    C. Enthusiasm

    D. School community

69. **Mrs. Graham has taken the time to reflect, complete observations, and asked for feedback about the interactions between her and her students from her principal. It is obvious by seeking this information out that Mrs. Graham understands which of the following?**

    (Rigorous) (Skill 12.4)

    A. The importance of clear communication with the principal

    B. She needs to analyze her effectiveness of classroom interactions

    C. She is clearly communicating with the principal

    D. She cares about her students

70. **Which statement is an example of specific praise?**

(Easy) (Skill 12.5)

A. "John, you are the only person in class not paying attention"

B. "William, I thought we agreed that you would turn in all of your homework"

C. "Robert, you did a good job staying in line. See how it helped us get to music class on time"

D. "Class, you did a great job cleaning up the art room"

71. **Which of the following is a good reason to collaborate with a peer:**

(Average Rigor) (Skill 13.1)

A. To increase your knowledge in areas where you feel you are weak, but the peer is strong

B. To increase your planning time and that of your peer by combining the classes and taking more breaks

C. To have fewer lesson plans to write

D. To teach fewer subjects

72. **Which of the following are ways a professional can assess his/her teaching strengths and weaknesses?**

(Rigorous) (Skill 13.1)

A. Examining how many students were unable to understand a concept

B. Asking peers for suggestions or ideas

C. Self-evaluation/Reflection of lessons taught

D. All of the above

73. Mr. German is a math coach within his building. He is the only math coach in his building and in fact within his district. Mr. German believes it is imperative he seek out the support of colleagues to work in a more collaborative manner. Which of the following would be an appropriate step for him to take?

(Rigorous) (Skill 13.2)

A. Collaborating with other teachers in his building regardless of their skill level knowledge in his area

B. Asking for the administration to find colleagues with which he can collaborate

C Joining a professional organization such as the NCTM

D. Searching the internet for possible collaboration opportunities

74. Family Systems Theory is a problem solving approach used to…

(Rigorous) (Skill 14.1)

A. Improving the relationships people have in their lives by blaming others for the difficulties they experience

B. Improving the relationships people have in their lives by accepting their responsibility for the problems of others

C. Improve the relationships people have in their lives by seeing their relationships with others

D. Improve the relationships people have in their lives by shifting away from blaming others and into accepting the responsibility for their own actions

75. **Which of the following is not one of the eight factors of the Family Systems Theory?**

(Average Rigor) (Skill 14.1)

A. Triangles

B. Peer Pressure

C. Differentiation of Self

D. Sibling Position

76. **Which of the following is an example of a restriction within the affective domain?**

(Easy) (Skill 14.2)

A. Unable to think abstractly

B. Inability to synthesize information

C. Inability to concentrate

D. Inability complete physical activities

77. **Mr. Brown wishes to improve his parent communication skills. Which of the following is a strategy he can utilize to accomplish this goal?**

(Easy) (Skill 14.3)

A. Hold parent-teacher conferences

B. Send home positive notes

C. Have parent nights where the parents are invited into his classroom

D. All of the above

78. **Tommy is a student in your class, his parents are deaf. Tommy is struggling with math and you want to contact the parents to discuss the issues. How should you proceed?**

(Easy) (Skill 14.3)

A. Limit contact due to the parents' inability to hear

B. Use a TTY phone to communicate with the parents

C. Talk to your administrator to find an appropriate interpreter to help you communicate with the parents personally

D. Both B and C but not A

79. **When communicating with parents for whom English is not the primary language you should:**

(Easy) (Skill 14.3)

A. Provide materials whenever possible in their native language

B. Use an interpreter

C. Provide the same communication as you would to native English speaking parents

D. All of the above

80. **Which of the following is NOT a sound educational practice for expanding the professional development opportunities for teachers?**

(Rigorous) (Skill 15.1)

A. Looking at multiple methods of classroom management strategies

B. Training teachers in understanding and applying multiple assessment formats and implementations in curriculum and instruction

C. Having the students complete professional development assessments on a regular basis

D. Teaching teachers how to disaggregate student data in improving instruction and curriculum implementation for student academic equity and access

81. **What is a benefit of frequent self-assessment?**

(Average Rigor) (Skill 15.2)

A. Opens new venues for professional development

B. Saves teachers the pressure of being observed by others

C. Reduces time spent on areas not needing attention

D. Offers a model for students to adopt in self-improvement

82. **Which of the following could be used to improve teaching skills?**

(Average Rigor) (Skill 15.3)

A. Developing a professional development plan

B. Use of self-evaluation and reflection

C. Building professional learning communities

D. All of the above

83. **Which of the following information can NOT be gained by examining school level data in an in-depth manner?**

(Average Rigor) (Skill 15.3)

A. Teacher effectiveness

B. Educational trends within a school

C. Student ability to meet state and national goals and objectives

D. Ways to improve student learning goals and academic success

84. **What would happen if a school utilized an integrated approach to professional development?**

(Rigorous) (Skill 15.4)

A. All stake holders needs are addressed

B. Teachers and administrators are on the same page

C. High quality programs for students are developed

D. Parents drive the curriculum and instruction

85. **Which description of the role of a teacher is no longer an accurate description?**

    (Rigorous) (Skill 15.5)

    A. Guide on the Side

    B. Authoritarian

    C. Disciplinarian

    D. Sage on the Stage

86. **In the past, teaching has been viewed as _____ while in more current society it has been viewed as _____.**

    (Rigorous) (Skill 15.6)

    A. Isolating....collaborative

    B. Collaborative....isolating

    C. Supportive.....isolating

    D. Isolating.... supportive

87. **A district superintendent's job is to:**

    (Easy) (Skill 16.1)

    A. Supervise senior teachers in the district

    B. Develop plans for school improvement

    C. Allocate community resources to individual schools

    D. Implement policies set by the board of education

88. **Teacher Unions are involved in all of the following EXCEPT:**

    (Average Rigor) (Skill 16.1)

    A. Updating teachers on current educational developments

    B. Advocating for teacher rights

    C. Matching teachers with suitable schools

    D. Developing professional codes and practices

89. **How may a teacher use a student's permanent record?**

(Average Rigor) (Skill 16.4)

A. To develop a better understanding of the needs of the student

B. To record all instances of student disruptive behavior

C. To brainstorm ideas for discussing with parents at parent-teacher conferences

D. To develop realistic expectations of the student's performance early in the year

90. **You receive a phone call from a person who indicates she is now tutoring a student in your class. She would like you to provide an overview of the academic areas which the student is having difficulties. What is the first thing you should do?**

(Rigorous) (Skill 16.4)

A. Find a time and talk with the tutor about issues you see within the classroom

B. Call the parents

C. Put together a packet of information to share with the tutor

D. Offer to invite the tutor in to have a discussion and observe the child

91. Andy shows up to class abusive and irritable. He is often late, sleeps in class, sometimes slurs his speech, and has an odor of drinking. What is the first intervention to take?

(Rigorous) (Skill 16.4)

A. Confront him, relying on a trusting relationship you think you have

B. Do a lesson on alcohol abuse, making an example of him.

C. Do nothing, it is better to err on the side of failing to identify substance abuse

D. Call administration, avoid conflict, and supervise others carefully.

92. A 16 year-old girl who has been looking sad writes an essay in which the main protagonist commits suicide. You overhear her talking about suicide. What do you do?

(Average Rigor) (Skill 16.4)

A. Report this immediately to school administration, talk to the girl, letting her know you will talk to her parents about it

B. Report this immediately to authorities

C. Report this immediately to school administration. Make your own report to authorities if required by protocol in your school. Do nothing else

D. Just give the child some extra attention, as it may just be that's all she's looking for

93. **Marco's mother is quite irate. She calls in and leaves a message on your voicemail. After listening to the voicemail, which of the following is the most appropriate response for you to make?**

(Easy) (Skill 16.5)

A. Have the principal return the call

B. Ask Marco's mother to come into school for a meeting

C. Ignore the phone call

D. Return the call and discuss the issue over the phone

94. **Marcus is a first grade boy of good developmental attainment. His learning progress is good the first half of the year. He shows no indicators of emotional distress. After the holiday break, he returns much changed. He is quieter, sullen even, tending to play alone. He has moments of tearfulness, sometimes almost without cause. He avoids contact with adults as often as he can. Even play with his friends has become limited. He has episodes of wetting not seen before, and often wants to sleep in school. What approach is appropriate for this sudden change in behavior?**

(Rigorous) (Skill 16.6)

A. Give him some time to adjust. The holiday break was probably too much fun to come back to school from

B. Report this change immediately to the administration. Do not call the parents until the administration decides a course of action

C. Document his daily behavior carefully as soon as you notice such a change, report to the administration next month or so in a meeting

D. Make a courtesy call to the parents to let them know he is not acting like himself, being sure to tell them he is not making trouble for others

95. **Which is true of child protective services?**

(Average Rigor) (Skill 16.6)

A. They have been forced to become more punitive in their attempts to treat and prevent child abuse and neglect

B. They have become more a means for identifying cases of abuse and less an agent for rehabilitation due to the large volume of cases

C. They have become advocates for structured discipline within the school

D. They have become a strong advocate in the court system

96. **Abigail has had intermittent hearing loss from the age of 1 through age 5 when she had tubes put in her ears. What is one area of development which may be affected by this?**

(Rigorous) (Skill 17.1)

A. Math

B. Language

C. Social skills

D. None

97. **Students who are learning English as a second language often require which of the following to process new information?**

(Rigorous) (Skill 17.1)

A. Translators

B. Reading tutors

C. Instruction in their native language

D. Additional time and repetitions

98. **Many of the current ESL approaches used in classrooms today are based on which approach?**

(Easy) (Skill 17.1)

A. Social Learning Methods

B. Native Tongue Methods

C. ESL Learning Methods

D. Special Education Methods

99. **Which of the following is the last stage of second language acquisition according to the theories of Stephen Krashen?**

(Easy) (Skill 17.1)

A. The affective filter hypothesis

B. The input hypothesis

C. The natural order hypothesis

D. The monitor hypothesis

100. **If a student has a poor vocabulary the teacher should recommend that:**

(Average Rigor) (Skill 17.4)

A. The student read newspapers, magazines and books on a regular basis.

B. The student enroll in a Latin class.

C. The student writes the words repetitively after looking them up in the dictionary.

D. The student use a thesaurus to locate synonyms and incorporate them into his/her vocabulary.

101. **When asking questions of students it is important to…**

(Easy) (Skill 18.2)

A. Use questions the students can answer

B. Provide numerous questions

C. Provide questions at various levels

D. Provide only a limited about of questions

102. **Wait-time has what effect?**

(Average Rigor) (Skill 18.2)

A. Gives structure to the class discourse

B. Fewer chain and low level questions are asked with more higher-level questions included

C. Gives the students time to evaluate the response

D. Gives the opportunity for in-depth discussion about the topic

103. **What is an effective amount of "wait time"?**

    (Average Rigor) (Skill 18.2)

    A. 1 second

    B. 5 seconds

    C. 15 seconds

    D. 10 seconds

104. **The use of technology in the classroom allows for...**

    (Easy) (Skill 18.3)

    A. More complex lessons

    B. Better delivery of instruction

    C. Variety of instruction

    D. Better ability to meet more individual student needs

105. **Active listening is an important skill for teachers to utilize with both students and teachers. Active listening involves all of the following strategies except...**

    (Rigorous) (Skill 18.4)

    A. Eye Contact

    B. Restating what the speaker has said

    C. Clarification of speaker statements

    D. Open and receptive body language

106. **What are the two ways concepts can be taught?**

    (Easy) (Skill 18.6)

    A. Factually and interpretively

    B. Inductively and deductively

    C. Conceptually and inductively

    D. Analytically and facilitatively

107. When using a kinesthetic approach, what would be an appropriate activity?

(Rigorous) (Skill 18.6)

A. List

B. Match

C. Define

D. Debate

108. One of the many ways in which a child can demonstrate comprehension of a story is by:

(Rigorous) (Skill 19.2)

A. Filling in a strategy sheet.

B. Retelling the story orally.

C. Retelling the story in writing.

D. All of the above.

109. Ms. Clark-is seen by outside observers from her district, seated in front of her class of sixth graders with a notebook in her lap and an easel. She reads aloud from a book and then writes down a series of questions. As she reads along, she sometimes writes down the answers to her own questions. This is most likely:

(Rigorous) (Skill 19.2)

A. A sign that Ms. Clark is uncertain of her own comprehension capacity.

B. She is modeling self questioning for the children.

C. She is aware that she is being watched and wants to make a good impression.

D. All of the above.

110. To help children with "main idea" questions, the teacher should:

    (Rigorous) (Skill 19.3)

    A. Give out a strategy sheet on the main idea for children to place in their reader's notebooks.

    B. Model responding to such a question as part of guided reading.

    C. Have children create "main idea questions" to go with their writings.

    D. All of the above.

111. Greg Ball went to an author signing where Faith Ringgold gave a talk about one of her many books. He was so inspired by her presence and by his reading of her book *TAR BEACH,* that he used the book for his reading and writing workshop activities. His supervisor wrote in his plan book, that he was pleased that Greg had used the book as an/a _____ book.

    (Easy) (Skill 19.3)

    A. Basic book.

    B. Feature book.

    C. Anchor book.

    D. Focus book

112. Which of the following is NOT a part of the hardware of a computer system?

    (Average Rigor) (Skill 20.2)

    A. Storage Device

    B. Input Devices

    C. Software

    D. Central Processing Unit

113. **What are three steps, in the correct order, for evaluating software before purchasing it for use within the classroom?**

(Rigorous) (Skill 20.2)

A. Read the instructions to ensure it will work with the computer you have, try it out as if you were a student, and examine how the program handles errors or mistakes the student may make

B. Try the computer program as if you were a student, read any online information about the program, have a student use the program and provide feedback

C. Read the instructions and load it onto your computer, try out the program yourself as if you were a student, have a student use the program and provide feedback

D. Read the instructions, have a student use the program, try it out yourself

114. **You are a classroom teacher in a building which does not have a computer lab for your class to use. However, knowing that you enjoy incorporating technology into the classroom, your principal has worked to find computers for your room. They are set up in the back of your classroom and have software loaded, but no access to the intranet or internet within your building. Which of the following is NOT an acceptable method for using these computers within your classroom instruction?**

(Rigorous) (Skill 20.2)

A. Rotating the students in small groups through the computers as centers

B. Putting students at the computers individually for skill based review or practice

C. Dividing your classroom into three groups and putting each group at one computer and completing a whole class lesson

D. Using the computers for students to complete their writing assignments with an assigned sign up sheet, so the students know the order in which they will type their stories

115. Which of the following statements is true about computers in the classroom?

(Average Rigor) (Skill 20.2)

A. Computers are simply a glorified game machine and just allow students to play games

B. The computer should replace traditional research and writing skills taught to school-age children.

C. Computers stifle the creativity of children.

D. Computers allow students to be able to access information they may otherwise be unable to

116. Which of the following is NOT a consideration of using technology within the school setting?

(Rigorous) (Skill 20.6)

A. Federal and State policies regarding use policies

B. Most up-to-date and current technology

C. Technology literacy of the students

D. Internet usage agreements

117. While an asset to students, technology is also important for teachers. Which of the following can be taught using technology to students?

(Average Rigor) (Skill 21.1)

A. Cooperation skills

B. Decision-Making skills

C. Problem Solving Skills

D. All of the above

118. As a classroom teacher, you have data on all of your students which you must track over the remainder of the school year. You will need to keep copies of the scores students receive and then graph their results to share progress with the parents an administrators. Which of the following software programs will be most useful in this manner?

(Easy) (Skill 21.4)

A. Word processing program

B. Spreadsheet

C. Database

D. Teacher Utility and Classroom Management Tools

119. **Which of the following statements is NOT true?**

    (Average Rigor) (Skill 21.5)

    A. Printing and distributing material off of the internet breaks the copyright law

    B. Articles are only copyrighted when there is a © in the article

    C. Email messages that are posted online are considered copyrighted

    D. It is not legal to scan magazine articles and place on your district web site.

120. **Which of the follow statements is NOT true?**

    (Rigorous) (Skill 21.5)

    A. You must contact the owner of the material before you use it for permission in order to not break the copyright law

    B. Copying CD's is against copyright laws

    C. It is illegal to make a backup copy of a computer program

    D. Placing information from one CD on more than one computer without a specific license to do so, is against the copyright laws

Answer Key

1.	D	31.	A	61.	B	91.	D
2.	C	32.	A	62.	B	92.	C
3	B	33.	B	63.	B	93.	B
4	B	34.	B	64.	A	94.	B
5	B	35.	B	65.	A	95.	B
6.	C	36.	A	66.	B	96.	B
7.	D	37.	A	67.	D	97.	D
8.	A	38.	C	68.	C	98.	A
9.	B	39.	B	69.	B	99.	A
10.	B	40.	D	70.	C	100.	A
11.	A	41.	C	71.	A	101.	C
12.	A	42.	B	72.	D	102.	B
13.	C	43.	D	73.	C	103.	B
14.	D	44.	D	74.	D	104.	D
15.	A	45.	A	75.	B	105.	B
16.	A	46.	A	76.	C	106.	B
17.	B	47.	D	77.	D	107.	B
18.	B	48.	D	78.	D	108.	D
19.	D	49.	A	79.	D	109.	B
20.	B	50.	B	80.	C	110.	D
21.	B	51.	D	81.	A	111.	C
22.	C	52.	A	82.	D	112.	C
23.	B	53.	D	83.	A	113.	A
24.	A	54.	B	84.	C	114.	C
25.	C	55.	C	85.	D	115.	D
26.	D	56.	D	86.	A	116.	B
27.	C	57.	D	87.	D	117.	D
28.	B	58.	C	88.	C	118.	B
29.	A	59.	B	89.	A	119.	B
30.	B	60.	C	90.	B	120.	C

Rigor Table

Question #	Easy %20	Average Rigor %40	Rigorous %40
Question #	4, 5, 17, 23, 24, 47, 48, 53, 64, 68, 70, 76, 77, 93, 98, 99, 104, 111, 118	1, 3, 7, 11, 12, 13, 15, 16, 18, 19, 20, 21, 22, 27, 28, 32, 36, 38, 40, 41, 43, 44, 51, 52, 54, 55, 57, 61, 62, 63, 65, 66, 71, 74, 75, 112, 115, 117, 119	2, 6, 8, 9, 10, 14, 25, 26, 29, 30, 31, 33, 34, 35, 37, 39, 42, 45, 46, 49, 50, 56, 58, 59, 60, 67, 69, 72, 73, 84, 85, 86, 96, 97, 105, 108, 109, 110, 113, 114, 116, 120

Rationales for Sample Questions

1. **When are students more likely to understand complex ideas?**

   (Average Rigor) (Skill 1.1)

a. If they do outside research before coming to class

b. Later when they write out the definitions of complex words

c. When they attend a lecture on the subject

d. When they are clearly defined by the teacher and are given examples and non-examples of the concept

Answer: D. When they are clearly defined by the teacher and are given examples and non-examples of the concept

Several studies have been carried out to determine the effectiveness of giving examples as well as the difference in effectiveness of various types of examples. It was found conclusively that the most effective method of concept presentation included giving a definition along with examples and non-examples and also providing an explanation of them. These same studies indicate that boring examples were just as effective as interesting examples in promoting learning. Additional studies have been conducted to determine the most effective number of examples that will result in maximum student learning. These studies concluded that a few thoughtfully selected examples are just as effective as many examples. It was determined that the actual number of examples necessary to promote student learning was relative to the learning characteristics of the learners. It was again ascertained that learning is facilitated when examples are provided along with the definition.

2. **Mr. Smith is introducing the concept of photosynthesis to his class next week. In preparing for this lesson, he considers that this will be a new concept to many of his students. Mr. Smith understands that his students' brains are like filing cabinets and that there is currently no file for photosynthesis in those cabinets. What does Mr. Smith need to do to ensure his students acquire the necessary knowledge?**

   (Rigorous) (Skill 1.2)

   a. Help them create a new file

   b. Teach the students the information; they will organize it themselves in their own way

   c. Find a way to connect the new learning to other information they already know

   d. Provide many repetitions and social situations during the learning process

Answer: C. Find a way to connect the new learning to other information they already know

While behavioral theories indicate that it is through socialization and multiple repetitions that students acquire new information, new research into the brain and how it works indicates that students learn best by making connections. Therefore, it is imperative when teaching new concepts that teachers find a way to connect new information to previously learned material.

3. **What developmental patterns should a professional teacher assess to meet the needs of the student?**

   (Average Rigor) (Skill 1.3)

   a.   Academic, regional, and family background

   b.   Social, physical, academic

   c.   Academic, physical, and   family background

   d.   Physical, family, ethnic background

Answer: B. Social, physical, academic.

The effective teacher applies knowledge of physical, social, and academic developmental patterns and of individual differences, to meet the instructional needs of all students in the classroom and. The most important premise of child development is that all domains of development (physical, social, and academic) are integrated. The teacher has a broad knowledge and thorough understanding of the development that typically occurs during the students' current period of life. More importantly, the teacher understands how children learn best during each period of development. An examination of the student's file coupled with ongoing evaluation assures a successful educational experience for both teacher and students.

4. **How many stages of intellectual development does Piaget define?**

(Easy) (Skill 1.3)

a. Two

b. Four

c. Six

d. Eight

Answer: B. Four

The stages are:
1. Sensorimotor stage: from birth to age 2 years (children experience the world through movement and senses).
2. Preoperational stage: from ages 2 to 7(acquisition of motor skills).
3. Concrete operational stage: from ages 7 to 11 (children begin to think logically about concrete events).
4. Formal Operational stage: after age 11 (development of abstract reasoning).

5. **Who developed the theory of multiple intelligences?**

(Easy) (Skill 1.3)

a. Bruner

b. Gardner

c. Kagan

d. Cooper

Answer: B. Gardner

Howard Gardner's most famous work is probably Frames of Mind, which details seven dimensions of intelligence (Visual/Spatial Intelligence, Musical Intelligence, Verbal Intelligence, Logical/Mathematical Intelligence, Interpersonal Intelligence, Intrapersonal Intelligence, and Bodily/Kinesthetic Intelligence). Gardner's claim that pencil and paper IQ tests do not capture the full range of human intelligences has garnered much praise within the field of education but has also met criticism, largely from psychometricians. Since the publication of Frames of Mind, Gardner has additionally identified the 8th dimension of intelligence: Naturalist Intelligence, and is still considering a possible ninth—Existentialist Intelligence.

6.   Discovery learning is to inquiry as direct instruction is to...

        (Rigorous) (Skill 1.4)

a.   Scripted lessons

b.   Well-developed instructions

c.   Clear instructions which eliminate all misinterpretations

d.   Creativity of teaching

Answer: C. Clear instructions which eliminate all misinterpretations

Direct instruction is a technique which relies on carefully well developed instructions and lessons which eliminate misinterpretations. In this manner, all students have the opportunity to acquire and learn the skills presented to the students. This approach limits teacher creativity to some extent, but has a good solid research based following with much ability to replicate its results.

7.   Students who can solve problems mentally have...

        (Average Rigor) (Skill 1.5)

a.   Reached maturity

b.   Physically developed

c.   Reached the pre-operational stage of thought

d.   Achieved the ability to manipulate objects symbolically

Answer: D. Achieved the ability to manipulate objects symbolically

When students are able to solve mental problems, it is an indication to the teacher that they have achieved the ability to manipulate objects symbolically and should be instructed to continue to develop their cognitive and academic skills.

8.   **Curriculum mapping is an effective strategy because it...**

      (Rigorous) (Skill 1.6)

a.   Provides an orderly sequence to instruction

b.   Provides lesson plans for teachers to use and follow

c.   Ties the curriculum into instruction

d.   Provides a clear map so all students receive the same instruction across all classes

Answer: A. Provides an orderly sequence to instruction

Curriculum mapping is a strategy used to tie the actual curriculum with the support materials (text books) being utilized to support the teaching of said curriculum. Mapping is usually done to the month or quarter and provides a logical sequence to instruction so that all necessary skills and topics are covered in an appropriate fashion.

9.   **Mrs. Peck wants to justify the use of personalized learning community to her principal. Which of the following reasons should she use?**

      (Rigorous) (Skill 2.1)

a.   They build multiculturalism

b.   They provide a supportive environment to address academic and emotional needs

c.   They builds relationships between students which promote life long learning

d.   They are proactive in their nature

Answer: B. They provide a supportive environment to address academic and emotional needs

While professional learning communities do all of the choices provided, this question asks for a justification statement. The best justification of those choices provided for implementing a personalized learning community in a classroom is to provide a supportive environment to help address the academic and emotional needs of her students.

10. **Mrs. Potts has noticed an undercurrent in her classroom of an unsettled nature. She is in the middle of her math lesson, but still notices that many of her students seem to be having some sort of difficulty. Mrs. Potts stops class and decides to have a class meeting. She understands that even though her math objectives are important, it is equally important to address whatever is troubling her classroom. What is it Mrs. Potts knows?**

   (Rigorous) (Skill 2.3)

   a.   Discipline is important

   b.   Social issues can impact academic learning

   c.   Maintaining order is important

   d.   Social skills instruction is important

Answer: B. Social issues can impact academic learning

Mrs. Potts understands that as long as there is a social situation or issue in the classroom, it is unlikely that any academics she presents will be learned. All of those areas instructed are important; however, it is this understanding of the fact that the academics will be impacted that is important in this particular situation as she is interrupting her math instruction.

11. **Which of the following describes the functional approach to language acquisition?**

   (Average Rigor) (Skill 2.4)

   a.   Communicative elements

   b.   Conceptual purposes

   c.   Grammar elements

   d.   All of the above

Answer: A. Focus on communicative elements

In the functional approach to language acquisition students learn practical functional daily phrases rather than words in isolation. For example, young children might learn colors, letters and numbers, while travelers may learn restaurant words, bathroom words, and other travel related words.

12. **How can the teacher establish a positive climate in the classroom?**

(Average Rigor) (Skill 3.1)

a.   Help students see the unique contributions of individual differences

b.   Use whole group instruction for all content areas

c.   Help students divide into cooperative groups based on ability

d.   Eliminate teaching strategies that allow students to make choices

Answer: A. Help students see the unique contributions of individual differences

In the first place, an important purpose of education is to prepare students to live successfully in the real world, and this is an important insight and understanding for them to take into that world. In the second place, the most fertile learning environment is one in which all viewpoints and backgrounds are respected and where everyone has equal respect.

13. **Which of the following could be an example of a situation which could have an effect on a student's learning and academic progress?**

(Average Rigor) (Skill 3.2)

a.   Relocation

b.   Abuse

c.   Both of the Above

d.   Neither of the Above

Answer: C. Both of the Above

There are an unlimited amount of situations which can affect a student's learning. Teachers need to keep in mind this when teaching. Students are whole people and just as stress affects us as adults, children experience the same feelings. They usually do not have the same tool box that adults have to deal with the feelings and may require some additional guidance.

14. **When developing lessons it is imperative teachers provide equity in pedagogy so...**

   (Rigorous) (Skill 3.3)

a.   Unfair labeling of students will not occur

b.   Student experiences will be positive

c.   Students will achieve academic success

d.   All of the above

Answer: D. All of the above

Providing equity of pedagogy allows for students to have positive learning experiences, achieve academic success, and helps to prevent the labeling of students in an unfair manner.

15. **In successful inclusion of students with disabilities:**

   (Average Rigor) (Skill 3.4)

a.   A variety of instructional arrangements are available

b.   School personnel shift the responsibility for learning outcomes to the student

c.   The physical facilities are used as they are

d.   Regular classroom teachers have sole responsibility for evaluating student progress

Answer: A. A variety of instructional arrangements are available

Here are some support systems and activities that are in evidence where successful inclusion has occurred:

Attitudes and beliefs
- the regular teacher believes the student can succeed.
- school personnel are committed to accepting responsibility for the learning outcomes of students with disabilities.
- school personnel and the students in the class have been prepared to receive a student with disabilities

Services and Physical accommodations

- services needed by the student are available (e.g. health, physical, occupational, or speech therapy).
- accommodations to the physical plant and equipment are adequate to meet the students' needs (e.g. toys, building and playground facilities, learning materials, assistive devices).

School support

- the principal understands the needs of students with disabilities
- adequate numbers of personnel, including aides and support personnel, are available
- adequate staff development and technical assistance, based on the needs of the school personnel, are being provided (e.g. information on disabilities, instructional methods, awareness and acceptance activities for students and team-building skills).
- appropriate policies and procedures for monitoring individual student progress, including grading and testing are in place

Collaboration

- special educators are part of the instructional or planning team
- teaming approaches are used for program implementation and problem solving
- regular teachers, special education teachers, and other specialists collaborate (e.g. co-teach, team teach, work together on teacher assistance teams).

Instructional methods

- teachers have the knowledge and skills needed to select and adapt curricular and instructional methods according to individual student needs
- a variety of instructional arrangements is available (e.g. team teaching, cross-grade grouping, peer tutoring, teacher assistance teams).
- teachers foster a cooperative learning environment and promote socialization.

16. **Which of the following is not a communication issue that is related to diversity within the classroom?**

    (Average Rigor) (Skill 3.5)

a. Learning disorder

b. Sensitive terminology

c. Body language

d. Discussing differing viewpoints and opinions

Answer: A. Learning disorders

Learning disorders, while they may have a foundation in the specific communication skills of a student, are not in and of themselves a communication issue related to diversity within the classroom.

17. **What does the validity of a test refer to?**

    (Easy) (Skill 4.1)

a. Its consistency

b. Its usefulness

c. Its accuracy

d. The degree of true scores it provides

Answer: B. Its usefulness

The Joint technical standards for educational and psychological testing (APA, AERA, NCME, 1985) states: "Validity is the most important consideration in test evaluation. The concept refers to the appropriateness, meaningfulness and usefulness of the specific inferences made from test scores. Test validation is the process of accumulating evidence to support such inferences. A variety of inferences may be made from scores produced by a given test, and there are many ways of accumulating evidence to support any particular inference. Validity, however, is a unitary concept. Although evidence may be accumulated in many ways, validity always refers to the degree to which that evidence supports the inferences that are made from test scores."

18. **What is the best definition for an achievement test?**

    (Average Rigor) (Skill 4.2)

a.   It measures mechanical and practical abilities

b.   It measures broad areas of knowledge that are the result of cumulative learning experiences

c.   It measures the ability to learn to perform a task

d.   It measures performance related to specific, recently acquired information

Answer: B. It measures broad areas of knowledge that are the result of cumulative learning experiences

The ways that a teacher uses test data is a meaningful aspect of instruction and may increase the motivation level of the students especially when this information is available in the form of feedback to the students. This feedback should indicate to the students what they need to do in order to improve their achievement. Frequent testing and feedback is most often an effective way to increase achievement.

19. **How are standardized tests useful in assessment?**

    (Average Rigor) (Skill 4.2)

a.   For teacher evaluation

b.   For evaluation of the administration

c.   For comparison from school to school

d.   For comparison to the population on which the test was normed

Answer: D. For comparison to the population on which the test was normed

While the efficacy of the standardized tests that are being used nationally has come under attack recently, they are, actually the only device for comparing where an individual student stands with a wide range of peers. They also provide a measure for a program or a school to evaluate how their own students are doing as compared to the populace at large. Even so, they should not be the only measure upon which decisions are made or evaluations drawn. There are many other instruments for measuring student achievement that the teacher needs to consult and take into account.

20. **What is an effective way to prepare students for testing?**

    (Average Rigor) (Skill 4.3)

a.   Minimize the importance of the test

b.   Orient the students to the test, telling them of the purpose, how the results will be used and how it is relevant to them

c.   Use the same format for every test are given

d.   Have them construct an outline to study from

Answer: B: Orient the students to the test, telling them of the purpose, how the results will be used and how it is relevant to them

If a test is to be an accurate measure of achievement, it must test the information, not the format of the test itself. If students know ahead of time what the test will be like, why they are taking it, what the teacher will do with the results, and what it has to do with them, the exercise is more likely to result in a true measure of what they've learned.

21. **How will students have a fair chance to demonstrate what they know on a test?**

    (Average Rigor) (Skill 4.3)

a.   The examiner has strictly enforced rules for taking the test

b.   The examiner provides a comfortable setting free of distractions and positively encourages the students

c.   The examiner provides frequent stretch breaks to the students

d.   The examiner stresses the importance of the test to the overall grade

Answer: B. The examiner provides a comfortable setting free of distractions and positively encourages the students

Taking a test is intimidating to students at best. In addition, some students are unable to focus when there are distractions. Feeling that the teacher is on their side helps students relax and truly demonstrate what they have learned on a test.

22. **Safeguards against bias and discrimination in the assessment of children include:**

   (Average Rigor) (Skill 4.4)

   a.   The testing of a child in standard English

   b.   The requirement for the use of one standardized test

   c.   The use of evaluative materials in the child's native language or other mode of communication

   d.   All testing performed by a certified, licensed, psychologist

Answer: C.   The use of evaluative materials in the child's native language or other mode of communication

The law requires that the child be evaluated in his native language, or mode of communication. The idea that a licensed psychologist evaluates the child does not meet the criteria if it is not done in the child's normal mode of communication.

23. **Which of the following is a presentation modification?**

   (Easy) (Skill 4.5)

   a.   Taking an assessment in an alternate room

   b.   Providing an interpreter to give the test in American Sign Language

   c.   Allowing dictation of written responses

   d.   Extending the time limits on an assessment

Answer: B. Providing an interpreter to give the test in American Sign Language

There are numerous types of modifications which can be provided to students in the classroom and for assessments. All of the described choices are appropriate modifications, but the only one which effects the presentation of the items is the one related to providing an interpreter.

24. **When a teacher wants to utilize an assessment which is subjective in nature, which of the following is the most effective method for scoring?**

    (Easy) (Skill 4.6)

a. Rubric

b. Checklist

c. Alternative Assessment

d. Subjective measures should not be utilized

Answer: A. Rubric

Rubrics are the most effective tool for assessing items which can be considered subjective. They provide the students with a clearer picture of teacher expectations and provide the teacher with a more consistent method of comparing this type of assignment.

25. **Which of the following is the correct term for the alignment of the curriculum across all grades K-12?**

    (Rigorous) (Skill 4.7)

a. Data Based Decision Making

b. Curriculum Mapping

c. Vertical Integration

d. Curriculum Alignment

Answer: C. Vertical Integration

Curriculum mapping is the process of taking the curriculum and deciding when the information needs to be taught throughout the school year. Curriculum alignment involves the process of connecting the curriculum to something else (typically standards) to ensure all areas are being taught. Vertical integration is the process of ensuring that the curriculum flows in an appropriate manner from the lowest levels to the highest levels in a logical and responsible manner.

26. **Which of the following describes why it is important and necessary for teachers to be able to analyze data on their students?**

(Rigorous) (Skill 4.7)

a.   To provide appropriate instruction

b.   To make instructional decisions

c.   To communicate and determine instructional progress

d.   All of the above

Answer: D. All of the above

Especially in today's high stakes environment, it is critical teachers have a complete understanding of the process involved in examining student data in order to make instructional decisions, prepare lessons, determine progress, and report progress to stakeholders.

27. **What are critical elements of instructional process?**

(Average Rigor) (Skill 5.1)

a.   Content, goals, teacher needs

b.   Means of getting money to regulate instruction

c.   Content, materials, activities, goals, learner needs

d.   Materials, definitions, assignments

Answer: C. Content, materials, activities, goals, learner needs

Goal-setting is a vital component of the instructional process. The teacher will, of course, have overall goals for her class, both short-term and long-term. However, perhaps even more important than that is the setting of goals that take into account the individual learner's needs, background, and stage of development. Making an educational program child-centered involves building on the natural curiosity children bring to school, and asking children what they want to learn. Student-centered classrooms contain not only textbooks, workbooks, and literature but also rely heavily on a variety of audiovisual equipment and computers. There are tape recorders, language masters, filmstrip projectors, and laser disc players to help meet the learning styles of the students. Planning for instructional activities entails identification or selection of the activities the teacher and students will engage in during a period of instruction.

28.   What would improve planning for instruction?

(Average Rigor) (Skill 5.1)

a.   Describe the role of the teacher and student

b.   Evaluate the outcomes of instruction

c.   Rearrange the order of activities

d.   Give outside assignments

Answer: B. Evaluate the outcomes of instruction

Important as it is to plan content, materials, activities, goals taking into account learner needs and to base what goes on in the classroom on the results of that planning, it makes no difference if students are not able to demonstrate improvement in the skills being taught. An important part of the planning process is for the teacher to constantly adapt all aspects of the curriculum to what is actually happening in the classroom. Planning frequently misses the mark or fails to allow for unexpected factors. Evaluating the outcomes of instruction regularly and making adjustments accordingly will have a positive impact on the overall success of a teaching methodology.

29.   What is one component of the instructional planning model that must be given careful evaluation?

(Rigorous) (Skill 5.1)

a.   Students' prior knowledge and skills

b.   The script the teacher will use in instruction

c.   Future lesson plans

d.   Parent participation

Answer: A. Students' prior knowledge and skills

The teacher will, of course, have certain expectations regarding where the students will be physically and intellectually when he/she plans for a new class. However, there will be wide variations in the actual classroom. If he/she doesn't make the extra effort to understand where there are deficiencies and where there are strengths in the individual students, the planning will probably miss the mark, at least for some members of the class. This can be obtained through a review of student records, by observation, and by testing.

30. **The teacher states that the lesson the students will be engaged in will consist of a review of the material from the previous day, demonstration of the scientific of an electronic circuit, and small group work on setting up an electronic circuit. What has the teacher demonstrated?**

   (Rigorous) (Skill 5.2)

a. The importance of reviewing

b. Giving the general framework for the lesson to facilitate learning

c. Giving students the opportunity to leave if they are not interested in the lesson

d. Providing momentum for the lesson

Answer: B. Giving the general framework for the lesson to facilitate learning

If children know where they're going, they're more likely to be engaged in getting there. It's important to give them a road map whenever possible for what is coming in their classes.

31.   **What steps are important in the review of subject matter in the classroom?**

(Rigorous) (Skill 5.2)

a.   A lesson-initiating review, topic and a lesson-end review

b.   A preview of the subject matter, an in-depth discussion, and a lesson-end review

c.   A rehearsal of the subject matter and a topic summary within the lesson

d.   A short paragraph synopsis of the previous days lesson and a written review at the end of the lesson

Answer: A. A lesson-initiating review, topic, and a lesson-end review

The effective teacher utilizes all three of these together with comprehension checks to make sure the students are processing the information. Lesson-end reviews are restatements (by the teacher or teacher and students) of the content of discussion at the end of a lesson. Subject matter retention increases when lessons include an outline at the beginning of the lesson and a summary at the end of the lesson. This type of structure is utilized in successful classrooms. Moreover, when students know what is coming next, and what is expected of them, they feel more a part of their learning environment and deviant behavior is lessened.

32.   **When is utilization of instructional materials most effective?**

(Average Rigorous) (Skill 5.2)

a.   When the activities are sequenced

b.   When the materials are prepared ahead of time

c.   When the students choose the pages to work on

d.   When the students create the instructional materials

Answer: A. When the activities are sequenced

Most assignments will require more than one educational principle. It is helpful to explain to students the proper order in which these principles must be applied to complete the assignment successfully. Subsequently, students should also be informed of the nature of the assignment (i.e., cooperative learning, group project, individual assignment, etc). This is often done at the start of the assignment.

33. How can mnemonic devices be used to increase achievement?

   (Rigorous) (Skill 5.2)

a. They help the child rehearse the information

b. They help the child visually imagine the information

c. They help the child to code information

d. They help the child reinforce concepts

Answer: B: They help the child visually imagine the information

Mnemonics are often verbal, something such as a very short poem or a special word used to help a person remember something, particularly lists. Mnemonics rely not only on repetition to remember facts, but also on associations between easy-to-remember constructs and lists of data, based on the principle that the humanistic mind much more easily remembers insignificant data attached to spatial, personal, or otherwise meaningful information than that occurring in meaningless sequences (like Kool-Aid). The sequences must make sense, though. If a random mnemonic is made up, it is not necessarily a memory aid.

34. The teacher states, "We will work on the first page of vocabulary words. On the second page we will work on the structure and meaning of the words. We will go over these together and then you will write out the answers to the exercises on your own. I will be circulating to give help if needed". What is this an example of?

   (Rigorous) (Skill 5.2)

a. Evaluation of instructional activity

b. Analysis of instructional activity

c. Identification of expected outcomes

d. Pacing of instructional activity

Answer: B. Analysis of instructional activity

The successful teacher carefully plans all activities to foresee any difficulties in executing the plan. This also assures that the directions being given to students will be clear, avoiding any misunderstanding.

35. **If teachers attend to content, instructional materials, activities, learner needs, and goals in instructional planning, what could be an outcome?**

   (Rigorous) (Skill 5.2)

a.   Planning for the next year

b.   Effective classroom performance

c.   Elevated test scores on standardized tests

d.   More student involvement

Answer: B. Effective classroom performance

Another outcome will be teacher satisfaction in a job well-done and in the performance of the students. Days will have far fewer disruptions and the classroom will be easy to manage.

36. **What should a teacher do when students have not responded well to an instructional activity?**

(Average Rigor) (Skill 5.3)

a. Reevaluate learner needs

b. Request administrative help

c. Continue with the activity another day

d. Assign homework on the concept

Answer: A. Reevaluate learner needs

The value of teacher observations cannot be underestimated. It is through the use of observations that the teacher is able to informally assess the needs of the students during instruction. These observations will drive the lesson and determine the direction that the lesson will take based on student activity and behavior. After a lesson is carefully planned, teacher observation is the single most important component of an instructional presentation. If the teacher observes that a particular student is not on-task, she will change the method of instruction accordingly. She may change from a teacher-directed approach to a more interactive approach. Questioning will increase in order to increase the participation of the students. If appropriate, the teacher will introduce manipulative materials to the lesson. In addition, teachers may switch to a cooperative group activity, thereby removing the responsibility of instruction from the teacher and putting it on the students.

37. **When planning instruction, which of the following is an organizational tool to help ensure you are providing a well balanced set of objectives?**
    (Rigorous) (Skill 5.4)

a. Using taxonomy to develop objectives

b. Determining prior knowledge skill levels

c. Determining readiness levels

d. Ensuring you meet the needs of diverse learners

Answer: A. Using taxonomy to develop objectives

The use of taxonomy, such as Bloom's, allows teachers to ensure the students are receiving instruction at a variety of different levels. It is important students are able to demonstrate skills and knowledge at a variety of different levels.

38. **Which of the following is <u>not</u> one of the levels of Bloom's taxonomy?**

(Average Rigor) (Skill 5.4)

a. Synthesis

b. Evaluation

c. Understanding

d. Knowledge

Answer: C. Understanding

Bloom's taxonomy consists of the following levels: knowledge, comprehension, application, analysis, synthesis, evaluation. These levels are in order from the most basic level to the more complex.

39. **Mr. Ryan has proposed to his classroom that the students may demonstrate understanding of the unit taught in a variety of ways including: taking a test, writing a paper, creating an oral presentation, or building a model/project. Which of the following areas of differentiation has Mr. Ryan demonstrated?**

(Rigorous) (Skill 6.1)

a. Synthesis

b. Product

c. Content

d. Process

Answer: B. Product

There are three ways to differentiate instruction: content, process, product. In the described case, Mr. Ryan has chosen to provide the students with alternate opportunities to produce knowledge; therefore, the product is the area being differentiated.

40. Louise is a first grade teacher. She is planning her instructional activities for the week. In considering her planning, she should keep in mind that activities for this age of child should change how often?

(Average Rigor) (Skill 6.2)

a. 25-40 minutes

b. 30-40 minutes

c. 5-10 minutes

d. 15-30 minutes

Answer: D. 15-30 minutes

For young children, average activities should change about every twenty minutes.

41. What is an example of formative feedback?

(Average Rigor) (Skill 6.3)

a. The results of an intelligence test

b. Correcting the tests in small groups

c. Verbal behavior that expresses approval of a student response to a test item

d. Scheduling a discussion prior to the test

Answer: C. Verbal behavior that expresses approval of a student response to a test item

Standardized testing is currently under great scrutiny but educators agree that any test that serves as a means of gathering and interpreting information about children's learning and which can provide accurate, helpful input for nurturing children's further growth, is acceptable. All testing must be formative in nature. Formative evaluation is the basic, everyday kind of assessment that teachers continually do to understand students' growth and to help them learn further.

42. **Mr. Weiss understands that it is imperative that students who are struggling with acquiring concepts at a specific grade level can still benefit from participating in whole classroom discussions and lessons. In fact, such students should be required to be present for whole classroom lessons. Mr. Weiss's beliefs fall under which of the following principles?**

    (Rigorous) (Skill 6.5)

a.   Self-fulfilling prophecy

b.   Partial participation

c.   Inclusion

d.   Heterogeneous grouping

Answer: B. Partial participation

The concept of partial participation indicates that children, even those struggling, can participate in complex concepts at least to a partial degree. While they may not be able to complete all of the requirements of a lesson objective, they may be able complete portions of the objective and will benefit from that additional learning in a positive manner.

43. **When creating and selecting materials for instruction, teachers should complete which of the following steps:**

    (Average Rigor) (Skill 7.2)

a.   Relevant to the prior knowledge of the students

b.   Allow for a variation of learning styles

c.   Choose alternative teaching strategies

d.   All of the above

Answer: D. All of the above

It is imperative that when creating and selecting materials for instruction that teachers consider many different factors. This makes the planning for instruction a difficult and somewhat time consuming process. There are numerous factors which must always be balanced in order to deliver the most appropriate and beneficial instruction to students.

44. Which of following is <u>not</u> the role of the teacher in the instructional process:

    (Average Rigor) (Skill 7.5)

    a. Instructor

    b. Coach

    c. Facilitator

    d. Follower

Answer: D. Follower

The teacher demonstrates a variety of roles within the classroom. Teachers, however, should not be followers. They must balance all of their roles in an efficient way to ensure that instruction is delivered to meet the needs of his/her students.

45. When considering the development of the curriculum, which of the following accurately describe the four factors which need to be considered?

    (Rigorous) (Skill 8.1)

    a. Alignment, Scope, Sequence, and Design

    b. Assessment, Instruction, Design, and Sequence

    c. Data, Alignment, Correlation, and Score

    d. Alignment, Sequence, Design and Assessment

Answer: A. Alignment, Scope, Sequence, and Design

When developing curriculum, it is important to first start with alignment. Alignment to state, national or other standards is the first step. Next, the scope of the curriculum involves looking at the amount of material covered within a grade level or subject. Next, the sequence of material needs to be considered. Finally, it is important to look at the design of the units individually from beginning to end.

46. **All of the following are true about phonological awareness EXCEPT:**

(Rigorous) (Skill 8.3)

a. It may involve print.

b. It is a prerequisite for spelling and phonics.

c. Activities can be done by the children with their eyes closed.

d. Starts before letter recognition is taught.

Answer: A. It may involve print

The key word here is EXCEPT which will be highlighted in upper case on the test as well. All of the options are correct aspects of phonological awareness except the first one, because phonological awareness DOES NOT involve print.

47. **The arrangement and relationship of words in sentences or sentence structure best describes:**

(Easy) (Skill 8.3)

a. Style.

b. Discourse.

c. Thesis.

d. Syntax.

Answer: D. Syntax

Syntax is the grammatical structure of sentences.

48.   **Which of the following is not a technique of prewriting?**

(Easy) (Skill 8.3)

a.   Clustering

b.   Listing

c.   Brainstorming

d.   Proofreading

Answer: D. Proofreading

Proofreading cannot be a method of prewriting, since it is done on already written texts only.

49.   **Of the following choices, which would require the students to utilize the most complex algebraic thinking process?**

(Rigorous) (Skill 8.3)

a.   Red, blue, red, blue, _____

b.   Red, yellow, green, red, yellow, green, _____

c.   2, 4, 6, 8, _____

d.   2, 4, _____, 8, 10

Answer: A. She is trying to help Maria expand her algebraic thinking

Having students make changes to patterns, build their own patterns, or converting patterns into new formats help students begin to think in more complex ways. This is one way to develop and build concepts of algebraic thinking.

50. **Suzy is given the following math problem to solve.**
    There are five bicycles parked in front of the school. How many
    wheels are in front of the school?
    Which mathematical concept will help Suzy to solve the problem?

    (Rigorous) (Skill 8.3)

a. Patterns

b. Relationships

c. Functions

d. Translation

Answer: B. Relationships

In order for Suzy to determine how many wheels are in front of the school, she must understand the relationship between a bicycle and wheels. She needs to understand that each bicycle will have two wheels. Once she accepts and identifies this relationship, she can determine that there will be ten wheels in front of the school.

51.   How can student misconduct be redirected at times?

(Average Rigor) (Skill 9.1)

a.   The teacher threatens the students

b.   The teacher assigns detention to the whole class

c.   The teacher stops the activity and stares at the students

d.   The teacher effectively handles changing from one activity to another

Answer: D. The teacher effectively handles changing from one activity to another.

Appropriate verbal techniques include a soft non-threatening voice void of undue roughness, anger, or impatience regardless of whether the teacher is instructing, providing student alerts, or giving a behavior reprimand. Verbal techniques that may be effective in modifying student behavior, include simply stating the student's name, explaining briefly and succinctly what the student is doing that is inappropriate and what the student should be doing. Verbal techniques for reinforcing behavior include both encouragement and praise delivered by the teacher. In addition, for verbal techniques to positively affect student behavior and learning, the teacher must give clear, concise directives while implying her warmth toward the students.

52. **What is one way of effectively managing student conduct?**

(Average Rigor) (Skill 9.1)

a.   State expectations about behavior

b.   Let students discipline their peers

c.   Let minor infractions of the rules go unnoticed

d.   Increase disapproving remarks

Answer: A. State expectations about behavior

The effective teacher demonstrates awareness of what the entire class is doing and is in control of the behavior of all students even when the teacher is working with only a small group of the children. In an attempt to prevent student misbehaviors the teacher makes clear, concise statements about what is happening in the classroom directing attention to content and the students' accountability for their work rather than focusing the class on the misbehavior. It is also effective for the teacher to make a positive statement about the appropriate behavior that is observed. If deviant behavior does occur, the effective teacher will specify who the deviant is, what he or she is doing wrong, and why this is unacceptable conduct or what the proper conduct would be. This can be a difficult task to accomplish as the teacher must maintain academic focus and flow while addressing and desisting misbehavior. The teacher must make clear, brief statements about the expectations without raising his/her voice and without disrupting instruction.

53. While teaching, three students cause separate disruptions. The teacher selects the major one and tells that student to desist. What is the teacher demonstrating?

(Easy) (Skill 9.1)

a. Deviancy spread

b. Correct target desist

c. Alternative behavior

d. Desist major deviance

Answer: D. Desist major deviance

When the teacher attempts to desist a deviancy, what he/she says and how it is said directly influence the probability of stopping the misbehavior. The effective teacher demonstrates awareness of what the entire class is doing and is in control of the behavior of all students even when the teacher is working with only a small group of children. In an attempt to prevent student misbehaviors the teacher makes clear, concise statements about what is happening in the classroom directing attention to content and the students' accountability for their work rather than focusing the class on the misbehavior. It is also effective for the teacher to make a positive statement about the appropriate behavior that is observed. If deviant behavior does occur, the effective teacher will specify who the deviant is, what he or she is doing wrong, and why this is unacceptable conduct or what the proper conduct would be. When more than one student is disrupting the class, it is wise to focus on the one that is causing the greatest problem. This is usually sufficient to bring the others into line. This can be a difficult task to accomplish as the teacher must maintain academic focus and flow while addressing and desisting misbehavior. The teacher must make clear, brief statements about the expectations without raising his/her voice and without disrupting instruction.

54. **Robert throws a piece of paper across the room. Dennis, sitting next to Robert, bats the piece of paper to the back of the room. The teacher ignores Dennis and reprimands Robert. What is the teacher demonstrating?**

    (Average Rigor) (Skill 9.1)

    a. Deviant disruption

    b. Correct target desist

    c. Alternative behavior

    d. Serious desist

Answer: B. Correct target desist

Students expect fairness from their teacher. By focusing on the student who initiated the misbehavior, the teacher demonstrates fairness in dealing with rule-breakers.

55. **To maintain the flow of events in the classroom, what should an effective teacher do?**

    (Average Rigor) (Skill 9.4)

    a. Work only in small groups

    b. Use only whole class activities

    c. Direct attention to content, rather than focusing the class on misbehavior

    d. Follow lectures with written assignments

Answer: C. Direct attention to content, rather than focusing the class on misbehavior

Students who misbehave often do so to attract attention. By focusing the attention of the misbehaver as well as the rest of the class on the real purpose of the classroom sends the message that misbehaving will not be rewarded with class attention to the misbehaver. Engaging students in content by using the various tools available to the creative teacher goes a long way in ensuring a peaceful classroom.

56. **The concept of efficient use of time includes which of the following?**

(Rigorous) (Skill 9.4)

a. Daily review, seatwork, and recitation of concepts

b. Lesson initiation, transition, and comprehension check

c. Review, test, review

d. Punctuality, management transition, and wait time avoidance

Answer: D. Punctuality, management transition, and wait time avoidance

The concept of efficient use of time includes which of the following? (Rigorous) (Skill 9.4)

The "benevolent boss" described in the rationale for question 34 applies here. One who succeeds in managing a business follows these rules; so does the successful teacher.

57. **What is a sample of an academic transition signal?**

(Average Rigor) (Skill 9.4)

a. "How do clouds form?"

b. "Today we are going to study clouds."

c. "We have completed today's lesson."

d. "That completes the description of cumulus clouds. Now we will look at the description of cirrus clouds."

Answer: D. "That completes the description of cumulus clouds. Now we will look at the description of cirrus clouds."

Transitions are language bridges between one topic and another. The teacher should thoughtfully plan transitions when several topics are going to be presented in one lesson to be sure that students are carried along. Without transitions, sometimes students are still focused on a previous topic and are lost in the discussion.

58. **What has been established to increase student originality, intrinsic motivation, and higher order thinking skills?**

(Rigorous) (Skill 10.2)

a.   Classroom climate

b.   High expectations

c.   Student choice

d.   Use of authentic learning opportunities

Answer: C. Student choice

While all of the descriptors are good attributes for students to demonstrate, it has been shown through research that providing student choice can increase all of the described factors.

59. **The success oriented classroom is designed to ensure students are successful at attaining new skills. In addition, mistakes are viewed as… in this type of classroom.**

(Rigorous) (Skill 10.3)

a.   Motivations to improve

b.   Natural part of the learning process

c.   Ways to improve

d.   Building blocks

Answer: B. Natural part of the learning process.

In the success oriented classroom, mistakes are viewed as a natural part of learning. In this way, mistakes continue the learning. Students have the ability to continually improve their grades or learning by correcting mistakes, rather than the mistake being a penalty.

60. **Mrs. Grant is providing her students with many extrinsic motivators in order to increase their intrinsic motivation. Which of the best explains this relationship?**

    (Rigorous) (Skill 10.4)

a. This is a good relationship and will increase intrinsic motivation

b. The relationship builds animosity between the teacher and the students

c. Extrinsic motivation does not in itself help to build intrinsic motivation

d. There is no place for extrinsic motivation in the classroom

Answer: C. Extrinsic motivation does not in itself help to build intrinsic motivation

There are some cases where it is necessary to utilize extrinsic motivation; however, the use of extrinsic motivation is not alone a strategy to use to build intrinsic motivation. Intrinsic motivation comes from within the student themselves, while extrinsic motivation comes from outside parties.

61. **What must be a consideration when a parent complains that he/she can't control their child's behavior?**

    (Average Rigor) (Skill 10.5)

a. Consider whether the parent gives feedback to the child

b. Consider whether the parent's expectations for control are developmentally appropriate

c. Consider how much time the parent spends with the child

d. Consider how rigid the rules are that the parent sets

Answer: B. Consider whether the parent's expectations for control are developmentally appropriate.

The teacher is the expert when it comes to developmental expectations. This is one area where a concerned and helpful teacher can be invaluable in helping a family through a crisis. Parents often have unrealistic expectations about their children's behavior simply because they don't know what is normal and what is not. Some stages tend to be annoying, especially if they are not understood. A teacher can help to defuse the conflicts in these cases.

62. **A parent has left an angry message on the teacher's voicemail. The message relates to a concern about a student and is directed at the teacher. The teacher should:**

(Average Rigor) (Skill 10.5)

a.   Call back immediately and confront the parent

b.   Cool off, plan what to discuss with the parent, then call back

c.   Question the child to find out what set off the parent

d.   Ignore the message, since feelings of anger usually subside after a while

Answer: B. Cool off, plan what to discuss with the parent, then call back

It is professional for a teacher to keep her head in the face of emotion and respond to an angry parent in a calm and objective manner. The teacher should give herself time to cool off and plan the conversation with the parent with the purpose of understanding the concern and resolving it, rather than putting the parent in their place. Above all the teacher should remember that parent-teacher interactions should aim to benefit the student.

63. **Which of the following should NOT be a purpose of a parent-teacher conference?**

(Average Rigor) (Skill 10.5)

a.   To involve the parent in their child's education

b.   To establish a friendship with the child's parents

c.   To resolve a concern about the child's performance

d.   To inform parents of positive behaviors by the child

Answer: B. To establish a friendship with the child's parents

The purpose of a parent teacher conference is to involve parents in their child's education, address concerns about the child's performance and share positive aspects of the student's learning with the parents. It would be unprofessional to allow the conference to degenerate into a social visit to establish friendships.

64. **Which of the following can be measured utilizing the following types of assessments: direct observation, role playing, context observation, and teacher ratings?**

(Easy) (Skill 11.1)

a. Social Skills

b. Reading Skills

c. Math Skills

d. Need for specialized instruction

Answer: A. Social Skills

Social skills can be measured using the listed types of assessments. They can also be measured using sociometric measures including: peer nomination, peer rating, paired-comparison.

65. **Which of the following is a definition of an intercultural communication model?**

(Average Rigor) (Skill 11.2)

A. Learning how different cultures engage in both verbal and nonverbal modes to communicate meaning.

B. Learning how classmates engage in both verbal and nonverbal modes to communicate meaning.

C. Learning how classmates engage in verbal dialogues

D. Learning how different cultures engage in verbal modes to communicate meaning.

Answer: A. Learning how different cultures engage in both verbal and nonverbal modes to communicate meaning.

This process allows students to begin to understand the process of communicating with each other in a multicultural manner, which helps them to better understand their own learning. It provides for a more global learning process for all students.

66. **What do cooperative learning methods all have in common?**

(Average Rigor) (Skill 11.3)

a.   Philosophy

b.   Cooperative task/cooperative reward structures

c.   Student roles and communication

d.   Teacher roles

Answer: B. Cooperative task/cooperative reward structures.

Cooperative learning situations, as practiced in today's classrooms, grew out of searches conducted by several groups in the early 1970's. Cooperative learning situations can range from very formal applications such as STAD (Student Teams-Achievement Divisions) and CIRC (Cooperative Integrated Reading and Composition) to less formal groupings known variously as "group investigation," "learning together," and "discovery groups." Cooperative learning as a general term is now firmly recognized and established as a teaching and learning technique in American schools. Since cooperative learning techniques are so widely diffused in the schools, it is necessary to orient students in the skills by which cooperative learning groups can operate smoothly, and thereby enhance learning. Students who cannot interact constructively with other students will not be able to take advantage of the learning opportunities provided by the cooperative learning situations and will furthermore deprive their fellow students of the opportunity for cooperative learning.

67. **With the passage of the No Child Left Behind Act (NCLB), schools are required to develop action plans to improve student learning. Which of the following is not a part of this action plan?**

    (Rigorous) (Skill 12.1)

    a.   Clearly defined goals for school improvement

    b.   Clearly defined assessment plan

    c.   Clearly defined timelines

    d.   Clearly defined plans for addressing social skills improvement

Answer: D. Clearly defined plans for addressing social skills improvement

The school action plan as related to NCLB should address all of the following areas:

- Clearly defined goals and objects for student learning and school improvement
- Clear alignment of goals and objectives
- Developing clear timelines and accountability for goal implementation steps
- Constructing an effective evaluation plan for assessing data around student performance and established objectives for student learning outcomes.
- Defining a plan B in case plan A falls short of meeting the goals and objectives for student achievement and school improvement.

68. **Which of the following can impact the desire of students to learn new material?**

    (Easy) (Skill 12.3)

a. Assessments plan

b. Lesson plans

c. Enthusiasm

d. School community

Answer: C. Enthusiasm

The enthusiasm a teacher exhibits can not only have positive effects on students' desire to learn, but also on on-task behaviors as well.

69. **Mrs. Graham has taken the time to reflect, complete observations, and asked for feedback about the interactions between her and her students from her principal. It is obvious by seeking this information out that Mrs. Graham understands which of the following?**

    (Rigorous) (Skill 12.4)

a. The importance of clear communication with the principal

b. She needs to analyze her effectiveness of classroom interactions

c. She is clearly communicating with the principal

d. She cares about her students

Answer: B. She needs to analyze her effectiveness of classroom interactions

Utilizing reflection, observations and feedback from peers or supervisors, teachers can help to build their own understanding of how they interact with students. In this way, they can better analyze their effectiveness at building appropriate relationships with students.

70. **Which statement is an example of specific praise?**

(Easy) (Skill 12.5)

a. "John, you are the only person in class not paying attention"

b. "William, I thought we agreed that you would turn in all of your homework"

c. "Robert, you did a good job staying in line. See how it helped us get to music class on time"

d. "Class, you did a great job cleaning up the art room"

Answer: C. "Robert, you did a good job staying in line. See how it helped us get to music class on time?"

Praise is a powerful tool in obtaining and maintaining order in a classroom. In addition, it is an effective motivator. It is even more effective if the positive results of good behavior are included.

71. **Which of the following is a good reason to collaborate with a peer:**

(Average Rigor) (Skill 13.1)

a. To increase your knowledge in areas where you feel you are weak, but the peer is strong

b. To increase your planning time and that of your peer by combining the classes and taking more breaks

c. To have fewer lesson plans to write

d. To teach fewer subjects

Answer: A. To increase your knowledge in areas where you feel you are weak, but the peer is strong

Collaboration with a peer allows teachers to share ideas and information. In this way, the teacher is able to improve his/her skills and share additional information with each other.

72. **Which of the following are ways a professional can assess his/her teaching strengths and weaknesses?**

    (Rigorous) (Skill 13.1)

a. Examining how many students were unable to understand a concept

b. Asking peers for suggestions or ideas

c. Self-evaluation/Reflection of lessons taught

d. All of the above

Answer: D. All of the above

It is important for teachers to involve themselves in constant periods of reflection and self-reflection to ensure they are meeting the needs of the students.

73. **Mr. German is a math coach within his building. He is the only math coach in his building and in fact within his district. Mr. German believes it is imperative he seek out the support of colleagues to work in a more collaborative manner. Which of the following would be an appropriate step for him to take?**

    (Rigorous) (Skill 13.2)

a. Collaborating with other teachers in his building regardless of their skill level knowledge in his area

b. Asking for the administration to find colleagues with which he can collaborate

c. Joining a professional organization such as the NCTM

d. Searching the internet for possible collaboration opportunities

Answer: C. Joining a professional organization such as the NCTM

Joining a professional organization, such as NCTM would provide Mr. German with the ability to learn and update his own knowledge specifically in his field of study and also open up the opportunity for him to interact with colleagues in his field from across the country.

74. **Family Systems Theory is a problem solving approach used to...**

(Rigorous) (Skill 14.1)

A.   Improving the relationships people have in their lives by blaming others for the difficulties they experience

B.   Improving the relationships people have in their lives by accepting their responsibility for the problems of others

C.   Improve the relationships people have in their lives by seeing their relationships with others

d.   Improve the relationships people have in their lives by shifting away from blaming others and into accepting the responsibility for their own actions

Answer: D. Improve the relationships people have in their lives by shifting away from blaming others and into accepting the responsibility for their own actions

Family systems theory was developed and popularized by Dr. Bowen. It helps people to understand and accept their own responsibility for their actions as opposed to blaming others for problems they may be experiencing.

75. **Which of the following is not one of the eight factors of the Family Systems Theory?**

    (Average Rigor) (Skill 14.1)

a. Triangles

b. Peer Pressure

c. Differentiation of Self

d. Sibling Position

Answer: B. Peer Pressure

The eight factors of the Family Systems Theory are:

- Triangles
- Differentiation of Self
- Nuclear Family Emotional System
- Multigenerational Transmission Process
- Emotional Cutoff
- Sibling Position
- Family Projection Process
- Societal Emotional Process

76. **Which of the following is an example of a restriction within the affective domain?**

   (Easy) (Skill 14.2)

a.   Unable to think abstractly

b.   Inability to synthesize information

c.   Inability to concentrate

d.   Inability complete physical activities

Answer: C. Inability to concentrate

The affective domain refers to such things as concentration, focus, lack of participation, inability to express themselves, and inconsistent behavior. Areas of the affective domain may affect other domains such as the cognitive or physical.

77. **Mr. Brown wishes to improve his parent communication skills. Which of the following is a strategy he can utilize to accomplish this goal?**

   (Easy) (Skill 14.3)

a.   Hold parent-teacher conferences

b.   Send home positive notes

c.   Have parent nights where the parents are invited into his classroom

d.   All of the above

Answer: D. All of the above

Increasing parent communication skills is important for teachers. All of the listed strategies are methods a teacher can utilize to increase his skills.

78.   Tommy is a student in your class, his parents are deaf. Tommy is struggling with math and you want to contact the parents to discuss the issues. How should you proceed?

(Easy) (Skill 14.3)

a.   Limit contact due to the parents' inability to hear

b.   Use a TTY phone to communicate with the parents

c.   Talk to your administrator to find an appropriate interpreter to help you communicate with the parents personally

d.   Both B and C but not A

Answer: D. Both B and C but not A

You should never avoid communicating with parents for any reason; instead you should find strategies to find an effective way to communicate in various methods, just as you would with any other student in your classroom.

79.   When communicating with parents for whom English is not the primary language you should:

(Easy) (Skill 14.3)

a.   Provide materials whenever possible in their native language

b.   Use an interpreter

c.   Provide the same communication as you would to native English speaking parents

d.   All of the above

Answer: D. All of the above

When communicating with non English speaking parents it is important to treat them as you would any other parent and utilize any means necessary to ensure they have the ability to participate in their child's educational process.

80. **Which of the following is NOT a sound educational practice for expanding the professional development opportunities for teachers?**

    (Rigorous) (Skill 15.1)

a. Looking at multiple methods of classroom management strategies

b. Training teachers in understanding and applying multiple assessment formats and implementations in curriculum and instruction

c. Having the students complete professional development assessments on a regular basis

d. Teaching teachers how to disaggregate student data in improving instruction and curriculum implementation for student academic equity and access

Answer: C. having the students complete professional development assessments on a regular basis

Giving teachers tests on a regular basis, while providing information on what knowledge they may have does not expand the professional development opportunities for teachers.

81. **What is a benefit of frequent self-assessment?**

    (Average Rigor) (Skill 15.2)

a. Opens new venues for professional development

b. Saves teachers the pressure of being observed by others

c. Reduces time spent on areas not needing attention

d. Offers a model for students to adopt in self-improvement

Answer: A. Opens new venues for professional development

When a teacher is involved in the process of self-reflection and self-assessment, one of the common outcomes is that the teacher comes to identify areas of skill or knowledge that require more research or improvement on her part. She may become interested in overcoming a particular weakness in her performance or may decide to attend a workshop or consult with a mentor to learn more about a particular area of concern.

82.   **Which of the following could be used to improve teaching skills?**

(Average Rigor) (Skill 15.3)

a.   Developing a professional development plan

b.   Use of self-evaluation and reflection

c.   Building professional learning communities

d.   All of the above   .

Answer: D. All of the above

Creating a personalized plan for increasing your professional development, using self reflection and working with other teachers in a professional learning community are all excellent strategies for improving ones teaching skills.

83.   **Which of the following information can NOT be gained by examining school level data in an in-depth manner?**

(Average Rigor) (Skill 15.3)

a.   Teacher effectiveness

b.   Educational trends within a school

c.   Student ability to meet state and national goals and objectives

d.   Ways to improve student learning goals and academic success

Answer: A. Teacher effectiveness

While to some degree student progress can provide information on the effectiveness of a teacher, looking only at statistical information may not provide a clear and accurate representation of the effectiveness of a teacher. For example, if the data examined indicates that 75% of the students achieved the state goals. This may indicate the teacher was not very effective. However, if in the previous year, only 10% of these same students achieved the state goals, it would provide a completely different picture on the effectiveness of this teacher.

84. **What would happen if a school utilized an integrated approach to professional development?**

   (Rigorous) (Skill 15.4)

a. All stake holders' needs are addressed

b. Teachers and administrators are on the same page

c. High quality programs for students are developed

d. Parents drive the curriculum and instruction

Answer: C. High quality programs for students are developed

The implementation of an integrated approach to professional development is a critical component to ensuring success of programs for students. It involves teachers, parents and other community members working together to develop appropriate programs to ensure students are receiving the necessary instruction to be successful in the future workforce.

85. **Which description of the role of a teacher is no longer an accurate description?**

   (Rigorous) (Skill 15.5)

a. Guide on the Side

b. Authoritarian

c. Disciplinarian

d. Sage on the Stage

Answer: D. Sage on the Stage

The old phrase of describing a teacher as a sage on the stage is no longer accurate. It is not the responsibility of the teacher to impart his/her knowledge on students. Teachers do not, nor should it be thought that they, have all of the answers. In contrast, it is the responsibility of the teacher to guide students through the learning process.

86. In the past, teaching has been viewed as _____ while in more current society it has been viewed as _____.

(Rigorous) (Skill 15.6)

a.   Isolating....collaborative

b.   Collaborative....isolating

c.   Supportive.....isolating

d.   Isolating.... supportive

Answer: A. Isolating....collaborative

In the past, teachers often walked into their own classrooms and closed the door. They were not involved in any form of collaboration and were responsible for only the students within their classrooms. However, in today's more modern schools, teachers work in collaborative teams and are responsible for all of the children in a school setting.

87. A district superintendent's job is to:

(Easy) (Skill 16.1)

a.   Supervise senior teachers in the district

b.   Develop plans for school improvement

c.   Allocate community resources to individual schools

d.   Implement policies set by the board of education

Answer: D. Implement policies set by the board of education

A district superintendent is the chief officer of the school district and has the responsibility of overseeing that policies set forth by the Board of Education are implemented by the schools in the district. He does not have the responsibility of directly supervising teachers or students or developing individual school improvement plans.

88. **Teacher Unions are involved in all of the following EXCEPT:**

    (Average Rigor) (Skill 16.1)

    a.   Updating teachers on current educational developments

    b.   Advocating for teacher rights

    c.   Matching teachers with suitable schools

    d.   Developing professional codes and practices

Answer: C. Matching teachers with suitable schools

The role of Teacher Unions is to work with teachers to develop and improve the profession of teaching by advocating for higher wages and improved conditions for teachers, developing professional codes and practices and keeping teachers up to date on current educational developments. It is not the role of Teacher Unions to find suitable employment for teachers.

89. **How may a teacher use a student's permanent record?**

    (Average Rigor) (Skill 16.4)

    a.   To develop a better understanding of the needs of the student

    b.   To record all instances of student disruptive behavior

    c.   To brainstorm ideas for discussing with parents at parent-teacher conferences

    d.   To develop realistic expectations of the student's performance early in the year

Answer: A. To develop a better understanding of the needs of the student

The purpose of a student's permanent record is to give the teacher a better understanding of the student's educational history and provide her with relevant information to support the student's learning. Permanent records may not be used to arrive at preconceived judgments, or to build a case against the student. Above all, the contents of a student's permanent record are confidential.

90. You receive a phone call from a person who indicates she is now tutoring a student in your class. She would like you to provide an overview of the academic areas which the student is having difficulties. What is the first thing you should do?

(Rigorous) (Skill 16.4)

a. Find a time and talk with the tutor about issues you see within the classroom

b. Call the parents

c. Put together a packet of information to share with the tutor

d. Offer to invite the tutor in to have a discussion and observe the child

Answer: B. Call the parents

Before you share any information with anyone about a student, you should always secure parental permission in writing.

91. **Andy shows up to class abusive and irritable. He is often late, sleeps in class, sometimes slurs his speech, and has an odor of drinking. What is the first intervention to take?**

    (Rigorous) (Skill 16.4)

    a. Confront him, relying on a trusting relationship you think you have

    b. Do a lesson on alcohol abuse, making an example of him.

    c. Do nothing, it is better to err on the side of failing to identify substance abuse

    d. Call administration, avoid conflict, and supervise others carefully.

Answer: D. Call administration, avoid conflict, and supervise others carefully

Educators are not only likely to, but often do face students who are high on something. Of course, they are not only a hazard to their own safety and those of others, but their ability to be productive learners is greatly diminished, if not non-existent. They show up instead of skip, because it's not always easy or practical for them to spend the day away from home, but not in school. Unless they can stay inside they are at risk of being picked up for truancy. Some enjoy being high in school, getting a sense of satisfaction by putting something over on the system. Some just don't take drug use seriously enough to think usage at school might be inappropriate. The first responsibility of the teacher is to assure the safety of all of the children. Avoiding conflict with the student who is high and obtaining help from administration is the best course of action.

92. **A 16 year-old girl who has been looking sad writes an essay in which the main protagonist commits suicide. You overhear her talking about suicide. What do you do?**

    (Average Rigor) (Skill 16.4)

a. Report this immediately to school administration, talk to the girl, letting her know you will talk to her parents about it

b. Report this immediately to authorities

c. Report this immediately to school administration. Make your own report to authorities if required by protocol in your school. Do nothing else

d. Just give the child some extra attention, as it may just be that's all she's looking for

Answer: C. Report this immediately to school administration. Make your own report to authorities if required by protocol in your school. Do nothing else.

A child who is suicidal is beyond any help that can be offered in a classroom. The first step is to report the situation to administration. If your school protocol calls for it, the situation should also be reported to authorities.

93. **Marco's mother is quite irate. She calls in and leaves a message on your voicemail. After listening to the voicemail, which of the following is the most appropriate response for you to make?**

    (Easy) (Skill 16.5)

a. Have the principal return the call

b. Ask Marco's mother to come into school for a meeting

c. Ignore the phone call

d. Return the call and discuss the issue over the phone

Answer: B. Ask Marco's mother to come into school for a meeting

It is best to discuss difficult situations in person rather than over the phone. First, it is sometimes helpful to involve other parties, which is often difficult to do on the phone. Second, the personal connection allows you to show appropriate documentation or other information which cannot be done over the phone.

Finally, having other parties present can help to avoid, he said/ she said situations at a later time.

94. **Marcus is a first grade boy of good developmental attainment. His learning progress is good the first half of the year. He shows no indicators of emotional distress. After the holiday break, he returns much changed. He is quieter, sullen even, tending to play alone. He has moments of tearfulness, sometimes almost without cause. He avoids contact with adults as often as he can. Even play with his friends has become limited. He has episodes of wetting not seen before, and often wants to sleep in school. What approach is appropriate for this sudden change in behavior?**

    (Rigorous) (Skill 16.6)

    a.   Give him some time to adjust. The holiday break was probably too much fun to come back to school from

    b.   Report this change immediately to administration. Do not call the parents until administration decides a course of action

    c.   Document his daily behavior carefully as soon as you notice such a change, report to administration the next month or so in a meeting

    d.   Make a courtesy call to the parents to let them know he is not acting like himself, being sure to tell them he is not making trouble for others

Answer: B. Report this change immediately to administration. Do not call the parents until administration decides a course of action

Anytime a child's disposition, attitude, or habits change significantly, teachers and parents need to seriously consider the existence of emotional difficulties. Emotional disturbances in childhood are not uncommon and take a variety of forms. Usually these problems show up in the form of uncharacteristic behaviors. Most of the time, children respond favorably to brief treatment programs of psychotherapy. At other times, disturbances may need more intensive therapy and are harder to resolve. All stressful behaviors need to be addressed, and any type of chronic antisocial behavior needs to be examined as a possible symptom of deep-seated emotional upset. In a case where the change is sudden and dramatic, administration needs to become involved.

95. **Which is true of child protective services?**

 (Average Rigor) (Skill 16.6)

a. They have been forced to become more punitive in their attempts to treat and prevent child abuse and neglect

b. They have become more a means for identifying cases of abuse and less an agent for rehabilitation due to the large volume of cases

c. They have become advocates for structured discipline within the school

d. They have become a strong advocate in the court system

Answer: B. They have become more a means for identifying cases of abuse and less an agent for rehabilitation due to the large volume of cases.

Nina Bernstein, who wrote The Lost Children of Wilder told of a long-running lawsuit in New York City that attempted to hold the city and its child-care services responsible for meeting the needs of abused children. Unfortunately, while it is an extreme case, it is not untypical of the plight of children all across the country. The only thing a teacher can do is attempt to provide a refuge of concern and stability during the time such children are in her care, hoping that they will, somehow, survive.

96. **Abigail has had intermittent hearing loss from the age of 1 through age 5 when she had tubes put in her ears. What is one area of development which may be affected by this?**

 (Rigorous) (Skill 17.1)

a. Math

b. Language

c. Social skills

d. None

Answer: B. Language

Frequent ear infections and intermittent hearing loss can significantly impair the development of language skills.

97. **Students who are learning English as a second language often require which of the following to process new information?**

    (Rigorous) (Skill 17.1)

a. Translators

b. Reading tutors

c. Instruction in their native language

d. Additional time and repetitions

Answer: D. Additional time and repetitions

While there are varying thoughts and theories into the most appropriate instruction for ESL students, much ground can be gained by simply providing additional repetitions and time for new concepts. It is important to include visuals and the other senses into every aspect of this instruction.

98. **Many of the current ESL approaches used in classrooms today are based on which approach?**

    (Easy) (Skill 17.1)

a. Social Learning Methods

b. Native Tongue Methods

c. ESL Learning Methods

d. Special Education Methods

Answer. A. Social Learning Methods

Placing students in mixed groups and pairing them with native speakers, ESL students are given the opportunities to practice English in a more natural setting.

99.   **Which of the following is the last stage of second language acquisition according to the theories of Stephen Krashen?**

       (Easy) (Skill 17.1)

a.   The affective filter hypothesis

b.   The input hypothesis

c.   The natural order hypothesis

d.   The monitor hypothesis

Answer: A. The affective filter hypothesis

According to Stephen Krashen's theories the five principles are:
The acquisition-learning hypothesis
The monitor hypothesis
The natural order hypothesis
The input hypothesis
The affective filter hypothesis

100.   **If a student has a poor vocabulary the teacher should recommend that:**

       (Average Rigor) (Skill 17.4)

A.   The student read newspapers, magazines and books on a regular basis.

B.   The student enroll in a Latin class.

C.   The student writes the words repetitively after looking them up in the dictionary.

D.   The student use a thesaurus to locate synonyms and incorporate them into his/her vocabulary.

Answer: A. the student read newspapers, magazines and books on a regular basis

It is up to the teacher to help the student choose reading material, but the student must be able to choose where s/he will search for the reading pleasure indispensable for enriching vocabulary.

101. **When asking questions of students it is important to...**

(Easy) (Skill 18.2)

a.   Use questions the students can answer

b.   Provide numerous questions

c.   Provide questions at various levels

d.   Provide only a limited about of questions

Answer: C. Provide questions at various levels

Providing questions at various levels is essential to encourage deeper thinking and reflective thought processes.

102. **Wait-time has what effect?**

(Average Rigor) (Skill 18.2)

a.   Gives structure to the class discourse

b.   Fewer chain and low level questions are asked with higher level questions included

c.   Gives the students time to evaluate the response

d.   Gives the opportunity for in-depth discussion about the topic

Answer: B. Fewer chain and low level questions are asked with higher level questions included

One part of the questioning process for the successful teacher is wait-time: the time between the question and either the student response or your follow-up. Many teachers vaguely recommend some general amount of wait-time (until the student starts to get uncomfortable or is clearly perplexed), but we focus here on wait-time as a specific and powerful communicative tool that speaks through its structured silences. Embedded in wait-time are subtle clues about your judgments of a student's abilities and your expectations of individuals and groups. For example, the more time you allow a student to mull through a question, the more you trust his or her ability to answer that question without getting flustered. As a rule, the practice of prompting is not a problem. Giving support and helping students reason through difficult conundrums is part of being an effective teacher.

103. **What is an effective amount of "wait time"?**

(Average Rigor) (Skill 18.2)

a.   1 second

b.   5 seconds

c.   15 seconds

d.   10 seconds

Answer: B. 5 seconds

In formal training, most preservice teachers are taught the art of questioning. One part of the questioning process is wait-time: the time between the question and either the student response or your follow-up. Many teachers vaguely recommend some general amount of wait-time (until the student starts to get uncomfortable or is clearly perplexed), but we focus here on wait-time as a specific and powerful communicative tool that speaks through its structured silences. Embedded in wait-time are subtle clues about your judgments of a student's abilities and your expectations of individuals and groups. For example, the more time you allow a student to mull through a question, the more you trust his or her ability to answer that question without getting flustered.
As a rule, the practice of prompting is not a problem. Giving support and helping students reason through difficult conundrums is part of being an effective teacher.

104. **The use of technology in the classroom allows for...**

(Easy) (Skill 18.3)

a.   More complex lessons

b.   Better delivery of instruction

c.   Variety of instruction

d.   Better ability to meet more individual student needs

Answer: D. Better ability to meet more individual student needs

The utilization of technology provides the teacher with the opportunity to incorporate more than one learning style into a lesson. In this way, the teacher is better able to meet the individual needs of his/her students.

105. Active listening is an important skill for teachers to utilize with both students and teachers. Active listening involves all of the following strategies except...

(Rigorous) (Skill 18.4)

a.   Eye Contact

b.   Restating what the speaker has said

c.   Clarification of speaker statements

d.   Open and receptive body language

Answer: B. Restating what the speaker has said

While it is often taught that it is important to restate conversations during meetings, when you are active listening it is more appropriate to seek clarification rather than simply restating.

106. What are the two ways concepts can be taught?

(Easy) (Skill 18.6)

a.   Factually and interpretively

b.   Inductively and deductively

c.   Conceptually and inductively

d.   Analytically and facilitatively

Answer: B. Inductively and deductively.

Induction is reasoning from the particular to the general—that is, looking at a feature that exists in several examples and drawing a conclusion about that feature. Deduction is the reverse: it's the statement of the generality and then supporting it with specific examples.

107. **When using a kinesthetic approach, what would be an appropriate activity?**

   (Rigorous) (Skill 18.6)

   a.   List

   b.   Match

   c.   Define

   d.   Debate

Answer: B. Match

Brain lateralization theory emerged in the 1970s and demonstrated that the left hemisphere appeared to be associated with verbal and sequential abilities whereas the right hemisphere appeared to be associated with emotions and with spatial, holistic processing. Although those particular conclusions continue to be challenged, it is clear that people concentrate, process, and remember new and difficult information under very different conditions. For example, auditory and visual perceptual strengths, passivity, and self-oriented or authority-oriented motivation often correlate with high academic achievement, whereas tactual and kinesthetic strengths, a need for mobility, nonconformity, and peer motivation often correlate with school underachievement (Dunn & Dunn, 1992, 1993). Understanding how students perceive the task of learning new information differently is often helpful in tailoring the classroom experience for optimal success.

108. **One of the many ways in which a child can demonstrate comprehension of a story is by:**

   (Rigorous) (Skill 19.2)

   a.   Filling in a strategy sheet.

   b.   Retelling the story orally.

   c.   Retelling the story in writing.

   d.   All of the above.

Answer: D. All of the above.

All of the choices provided show different ways in which students can demonstrate the comprehension of a story.

109. **Ms. Clark is seen by outside observers from her district, seated in front of her class of sixth graders with a notebook in her lap and an easel. She reads aloud from a book and then writes down a series of questions. As she reads along, she sometimes writes down the answers to her own questions. This is most likely:**

(Rigorous) (Skill 19.2)

a. A sign that Ms. Clark is uncertain of her own comprehension capacity.

b. She is modeling self questioning for the children.

c. She is aware that she is being watched and wants to make a good impression.

d. All of the above.

Answer: B. She is modeling self questioning for the children.

This is a technique children are taught and Ms. Clark is modeling it. "C" is insulting to Ms. Clark and "A" is insulting as well.

110. **To help children with "main idea" questions, the teacher should:**

(Rigorous) (Skill 19.3)

a. Give out a strategy sheet on the main idea for children to place in their reader's notebooks.

b. Model responding to such a question as part of guided reading.

c. Have children create "main idea questions" to go with their writings.

d. All of the above.

Answer: D. All of the above.

All of the above options are ways a teacher can help students begin to be able to answer main idea questions.

111. Greg Ball went to an author signing where Faith Ringgold gave a talk about one of her many books. He was so inspired by her presence and by his reading of her book *TAR BEACH,* that he used the book for his reading and writing workshop activities. His supervisor wrote in his plan book, that he was pleased that Greg had used the book as an/a _____ book.

    (Easy) (Skill 19.3)

a.   Basic book.

b.   Feature book.

c.   Anchor book.

d.   Focus book

Answer: C. Anchor book.

A book that is used to teach reading and writing is called an Anchor book.

112.   Which of the following is NOT a part of the hardware of a computer system?

    (Average Rigor) (Skill 20.2)

a.   Storage Device

b.   Input Devices

c.   Software

d.   Central Processing Unit

Answer: C. Software

Software is not a part of the hardware of a computer, but instead consists of all of the programs which allow the computer to run. Software is either an operating system or an application program.

113. **What are three steps, in the correct order, for evaluating software before purchasing it for use within the classroom?**

     (Rigorous) (Skill 20.2)

a.   Read the instructions to ensure it will work with the computer you have, try it out as if you were a student, and examine how the program handles errors or mistakes the student may make

b.   Try the computer program as if you were a student, read any online information about the program, have a student use the program and provide feedback

c.   Read the instructions and load it onto your computer, try out the program yourself as if you were a student, have a student use the program and provide feedback

d.   Read the instructions, have a student use the program, try it out yourself

Answer: A. Read the instructions to ensure it will work with the computer you have, try it out as if you were a student, and examine how the program handles errors or mistakes the student may make

You should not have students use the program until you have read all of the material related to the use, tried it out yourself as if you were a student and made many different types of mistakes when using it. You should try to make as many different types of errors as possible, so that you can see how the program responds and ensure it is how you want your students errors handled.

114.   You are a classroom teacher in a building which does not have a computer lab for your class to use. However, knowing that you enjoy incorporating technology into the classroom, your principal has worked to find computers for your room. They are set up in the back of your classroom and have software loaded, but no access to the intranet or internet within your building. Which of the following is NOT an acceptable method for using these computers within your classroom instruction?

(Rigorous) (Skill 20.2)

a.   Rotating the students in small groups through the computers as centers

b.   Putting students at the computers individually for skill based review or practice

c.   Dividing your classroom into three groups and putting each group at one computer and completing a whole class lesson

d.   Using the computers for students to complete their writing assignments with an assigned sign up sheet, so the students know the order in which they will type their stories

Answer: C. Dividing your classroom into three groups and putting each group at one computer and completing a whole class lesson

Three computers are not enough for a typical class size across the country. This would involve too many students at one computer and could result in behavioral issues. Additionally, it would be difficult for the students to all have the ability to interact in a meaningful way with the software. If you would like to complete a whole class lesson using the technology, it would be best to find a projector which connects to the computer so all students have equal opportunity to participate and see.

115. **Which of the following statements is true about computers in the classroom?**

(Average Rigor) (Skill 20.2)

a. Computers are simply a glorified game machine and just allow students to play games

b. The computer should replace traditional research and writing skills taught to school-age children.

c. Computers stifle the creativity of children.

d. Computers allow students to be able to access information they may otherwise be unable to

Answer: D. Computers allow students to be able to access information they may otherwise be unable to

Computers, particularly those connected to the Internet; provide students with the ability to research information school libraries might otherwise be unable to provide due to funding issues. It opens the doors and pathways for students to increase the amount of information they acquire in school.

116. **Which of the following is NOT a consideration of using technology within the school setting?**

(Rigorous) (Skill 20.6)

a. Federal and State policies regarding use policies

b. Most up-to-date and current technology

c. Technology literacy of the students

d. Internet usage agreements

Answer: B. Most up-to-date and current technology

It is rarely neither feasible, nor necessary for schools to have the most up-to-date and current technology available. However, it is important to understand the Federal and State policies regarding use of the technology within the school for funding purposes. It is also necessary to provide students with the knowledge base to become technologically literate. Internet usage agreements were developed to protect the students and schools.

117. While an asset to students, technology is also important for teachers. Which of the following can be taught using technology to students?

(Average Rigor) (Skill 21.1)

a. Cooperation skills

b. Decision-Making skills

c. Problem Solving Skills

d. All of the above

Answer: D. All of the above

Having students work together on a project using the technology available to you within your school can not only teach the content you wish them to learn, but can also provide them with skills in: cooperation, decision-making, and problem solving.

118. As a classroom teacher, you have data on all of your students which you must track over the remainder of the school year. You will need to keep copies of the scores students receive and then graph their results to share progress with the parents an administrators. Which of the following software programs will be most useful in this manner?

(Easy) (Skill 21.4)

a. Word processing program

b. Spreadsheet

c. Database

d. Teacher Utility and Classroom Management Tools

Answer: B. Spreadsheet

Spreadsheets help a teacher to organize numeric information and can easily take that data and transfer it into a graph for a visual representation to administrators or parents.

119. **Which of the following statements is NOT true?**

    (Average Rigor) (Skill 21.5)

a.   Printing and distributing material off of the internet breaks the copyright law

b.   Articles are only copyrighted when there is a © in the article

c.   Email messages that are posted online are considered copyrighted

d.   It is not legal to scan magazine articles and place on your district web site.

Answer: B. Articles are only copyrighted when there is a © in the article

Articles, even without the symbol are considered copyrighted material. This includes articles from newspapers, magazines, or even posted online.

120. **Which of the follow statements is NOT true?**

    (Rigorous) (Skill 21.5)

a.   You must contact the owner of the material before you use it for permission in order to not break the copyright law

b.   Copying CD's is against copyright laws

c.   It is illegal to make a backup copy of a computer program

d.   Placing information from one CD on more than one computer without a specific license to do so, is against the copyright laws

Answer: C. It is illegal to make a backup copy of a computer program

Under the amendment to the copyright act, it is allowable to make a copy of an original program disk in case of destruction or damage. It is not allowable to make copies for friends, family, home use, etc.

SAMPLE CONSTRUCTED ESSAY

Essay 1 – Instruction and Assessment

SAMPLE ASSIGNMENT

In an essay written for a group of educators, frame your response by identifying a grade level and/or subject area for which you are prepared to teach; then:

- Explain the importance of using a variety of instructional approaches so that all students can learn and master the standards.
- Describe two strategies to meet this goal.
- Explain why the strategies you have chosen would be effective.

Be sure to specify a grade level/subject area in your essay, and frame your ideas so that an educator at your level will be able to understand the basis for your response.

SAMPLE RESPONSE

As a future high school English teacher, I understand the importance of tailoring instruction of difficult concepts to meet the needs of all students. To describe the importance of utilizing various instructional strategies and then to provide examples of useful strategies, I will illustrate with a hypothetical ninth grade Language Arts class.

When teachers vary instructional strategies, they do many things for their students. First, since we know that all students have different styles of learning, some instructional strategies will not necessarily be as effective for some students. By utilizing a wide range of strategies to teach the same concept, for example, teachers ensure that as many learning styles as possible are satisfied. Let's consider a visual learner in a Language Arts classroom who only receives instruction orally. The teacher focuses on texts abstractly, and often discussion is utilized. The teacher rarely uses the board and never uses PowerPoint and never allows students to demonstrate learning in artistic ways. While this visual learner may have the potential to achieve at a higher level, this may not occur as the instruction has missed his or her learning style entirely.

A second reason for varying instructional strategies is based on the concept of constructivism. Constructivism, as a learning theory, suggests that people develop concepts in their minds in highly personalized ways. Take a concept that might be taught in a ninth grade Language Arts class: hyperbole, a literary term for exaggeration. Strategies for teaching this concept include lecturing, pointing out examples in a text, and allowing students to develop their own examples of hyperbole. Certainly, students may understand hyperbole from lecture alone, yet if they were given the opportunity to experience the concept in those multiple ways, they are sure to have a more complete mental construct of the concepts.

A third reason for varying instructional strategies is based on student engagement. While ninth grade English teachers may enjoy talking about hyperbole, their students may not be so fascinated. By varying instructional strategies, students get opportunities to learn actively and in many different modalities. They experience concepts in different ways and involve themselves in various contexts of the concepts. A classroom with varied instructional strategies is sure to be more interesting to most students than a classroom that relies on lecture or reading alone.

To illustrate how instructional strategies can be varied in a ninth grade Language Arts class, I will provide an example on research report writing. A research report is a very standard assignment in ninth grade Language Arts. This assignment teaches students valuable skills in writing and research, including developing thesis statements, analyzing sources, and developing bibliographies.

While a teacher could simply assign a research report and provide lectures on the various methods of designing and carrying out a research report, students would be much more successful if they experience a variety of instructional strategies throughout the unit. I will briefly describe two unique strategies that a teacher might use to promote student learning of the concepts involved in developing and writing a research report.

The first strategy in this unit on research report writing comes at an early stage. As students are settling on topics and looking into books they might use to inform their reports, a teacher might have students conduct a first-hand investigation on their own. For example, a student interested in writing a report on an historical figure might interview a history teacher at the school. Or a student interested in writing about air pollution might conduct a small science experiment by testing the air quality on the side of a highway. While the evidence collected does not have to be extensive, just the act of having students go out into the "field" and gather data helps them learn about the ways in which knowledge is generated. It gives them a deeper understanding about the ways in which the books and articles they will use in the report were developed. This strategy also promotes active, hands-on learning. It gives students who may be troubled about embarking on a large research report project the opportunity to see an aspect of their topic firsthand. It makes the experience more real for them, and it allows them to become more engaged in the process.

A second strategy in this unit comes at the end of the process, as students' rough drafts are written. On the day students come to class with their rough drafts, students would work in groups of no more than four. Each student would have to read his or her paper aloud to the other students in the group. The group members listen and write comments. Then, each group member gets the opportunity to comment on the paper for two to three minutes. After one student's paper is complete, then the group rotates to the next group member. This strategy is beneficial for many reasons. While many classrooms utilize peer review for student writing, by having students read their papers aloud, students experience a performance-type setting to the process, which is more engaging.

Also, when students review peers' papers, they often focus on grammar and spelling, rather than more important aspects of clarity, content, and focus.

Utilizing various instructional strategies provides students with richer opportunities to learn concepts. It allows simplistic standards to come alive, and it promotes deep learning. In general, teachers who use various instructional strategies will have more lively, learning-centered classrooms.

EVALUATION

This paper would earn a high score for a variety of reasons. First, most importantly, it answers all parts of the question. It provides a framing grade level and subject. It focuses on a general conception of why utilizing various instructional strategies is beneficial for students. It provides two rich and well explained strategies as examples. And finally, it explains why those strategies would be effective for student learning. The examples focus on multiple areas of importance in instruction: student engagement, multiple learning styles, conceptual understanding, and student achievement.

Essay 2 – Student Learning

SAMPLE ASSIGNMENT

In an essay written for a group of educators, frame your response by identifying a grade level and/or subject area for which you are prepared to teach; then:

- Explain the importance of helping students learn to be critical learners in the classroom who exert higher-order thinking skills.
- Describe two strategies to meet this goal.
- Explain why the strategies you have chosen would be effective.

Be sure to specify a grade level/subject area in your essay, and frame your ideas so that an educator at your level will be able to understand the basis for your response.

SAMPLE RESPONSE

I believe that students truly start to become critical thinkers by about the fourth or fifth grades. For that reason, I desire to be a teacher in the upper elementary grades. As such, I have been prepared as a general subjects elementary teacher. My goal in teaching fourth or fifth grade is, above and beyond helping my students master state standards, to help them become conscious of the deeper issues in academic subjects, to appreciate the complexity of academic learning, and to become life-long learners.

The level of knowledge available to us in our society is immense. Knowledge is produced daily, and the number of books, journals, magazines, and websites at our disposal increases every minute. With so much knowledge, it is hard for students to understand how to discern between important and unimportant knowledge, factual and "made-up" information, and useful or irrelevant texts. Messages bombard us constantly, from advertising in places we would likely not expect to opinions that masquerade as news.

To meet those needs, and to assist our students in finding intrinsic motivation to learn, teachers need to be cognizant of the competing demands of information both in school and out of school. They must be aware that students have to make hard choices about the knowledge they receive. Finally, they must realize that sustaining a level of critical awareness about knowledge takes a lot of effort. We don't want our students to hate learning or despise being critical thinkers because it is so hard. Instead, we want them to enjoy the excitement, creativity, and stimulation of sifting through knowledge for the best answer or the most appealing opinion.

To do so, it is extremely important that teachers help their students become highly critical thinkers who use higher-order thinking skills. Attaining this goal in the classroom is not hard, but it does take considerable effort in utilizing effective strategies. One such strategy is in teaching students to develop their own questions about texts. For example, we might start by having students in small team develop comprehension questions (for the purpose of clarification and simple reading skills), as well as analytic questions (for the purpose of interpretation, argumentation, and analysis). First, by having students come up with their own questions, teachers can ensure that students focus on the issues that are most interesting and important to them in the texts they read. Second, by differentiating comprehension from analytic questions, we reinforce to students that there is a distinct difference between re-telling and interpreting. This difference is critical in helping students to understand the complexity of texts, as well as to find enjoyment in the discussion of reading.

Another strategy for encouraging critical thinking skills is to use problem-based learning. Problem-based learning sets up problems for students to solve; through the process of solving problems, students are forced to learn new information in more relevant ways. For example, students can learn about meteorology by studying current weather patterns and predicting the weather for later in the day. The problem is a real one: "What will the weather be like later today?" But the method is focused on relevant learning: Students will be forced to learn about cloud types and wind direction, for example, in order to make predictions. This type of learning is authentic, and it allows for students to create their own questions, be critical of the knowledge they receive, and examine all evidence for the best solutions.

In conclusion, it is critical for teachers to utilize multiple strategies in helping students to become better connoisseurs of information, text, and knowledge. In doing so, we can foster a love of learning, as we demonstrate that learning is not all about correct and incorrect answers, memorization, and tests.

EVALUATION

This essay would earn the highest score possible, as it not only answers the prompt, displays in-depth knowledge regarding the standards, and comes across clearly; but it also provides an in-depth explanation as to why this topic is important and shows good examples of real and effective teaching practices.

STATE MAJOR COMPONENTS RETAINED AND CHANGES OF IDEA 2004

The second revision of IDEA occurred in 2004, IDEA was re-authorized as the Individuals with Disabilities Education Improvement Act of 2004 (IDEIA 2004) is commonly referred to as IDEA 2004. IDEA 2004 was effective July 1, 2005. It was the intention to improve IDEA by adding the philosophy and understanding that special education students need preparation for further study beyond the high school setting by teaching compensatory methods. Accordingly, IDEA 2004 provided a close tie to PL 89-10, the Elementary and Special Education Act of 1965, and stated that students with special needs should have maximum access to the general curriculum. This was defined as the amount for an individual student to reach his fullest potential. Full inclusion was stated not to be the only option by which to achieve this, and specified that skills should be taught to compensate students later in life in cases where inclusion was not the best setting.

IDEA 2004 added a new requirement for special education teachers on the secondary level enforcing NCLBs "Highly Qualified" requirements in the subject area of their curriculum. The rewording in this part of IDEA states that they shall be "no less qualified" than teachers in the core areas.

Free and Appropriate Public Education (FAPE), was revised by mandating that students have maximum access to appropriate general education. Additionally, LRE placement for those students with disabilities must have the same school placement rights as those students who are not disabled. IDEA 2004 recognizes that due to the nature of some disabilities, appropriate education may vary in the amount of participation / placement in the general education setting. For some students, FAPE will mean a choice as to the type of educational institution they attend (private school for example), any of which must provide the special education services deemed necessary for the student through the IEP.

The definition of *Assistive technology devices* was amended to exclude devices that are surgically implanted (i.e. cochlear implants), and clarified that students with assistive technology devices shall not be prevented from having special education services. Assistive technology devices may need to be monitored by school personnel, but schools are not responsible for the implantation or replacement of such devices surgically. An example of this would be a cochlear implant.

The definition of *Child with a disability* is the term used for children ages 3-9 with a developmental delay now has been was changed to allow for the inclusion of Tourettes Syndrome.

IDEA 2004 recognized that all states must follow the National Instructional Materials Accessibility Standards which states that students who need materials in a certain form will get those at the same time their non-disabled peers receive their materials. Teacher recognition of this standard is important.

Changes in Requirements for Evaluations

The clock/time allowance between the request for an initial evaluation and the determination if a disability is present may be requested has been changed to state the finding/determination must occur within 60 calendar days of the request. This is a significant change as previously it was interpreted to mean 60 school days. Parental consent is also required for evaluations and prior to the start of special education services.

No single assessment or measurement tool may now be used to determine special education qualification. Assessments and measurements used should be in *language and form* that will give the most accurate picture of the child's abilities.

IDEA 2004's recognized that there exists a disproportionate representation of minorities and bilingual students and that pre-service interventions that are *scientifically based on early reading programs, positive behavioral interventions and support, and early intervening services*) may prevent some of those children from needing special education services. This understanding has led to a child not being considered to have a disability if he/she has not had appropriate education in math or reading, nor shall a child be considered to have a disability if the reason for his/her delays is that English is a second language.

When determining a specific learning disability, the criteria may or may not use a discrepancy between *achievement and intellectual ability* but whether or not the child responds to scientific research-based intervention. In general, children who may not have been found eligible for special education (via testing) but are known to need services (via functioning, excluding lack of instruction) are still eligible for special education services. This change now allows input for evaluation to include state and local testing, classroom observation, academic achievement, and *related developmental needs,*

Changes in Requirements for IEPs

Individualized Education Plans (IEPS) continue to have multiple sections. One section, *present levels,* now addresses *academic achievement and functional performance.* Annual IEP goals must now address the same areas.

IEP goals should be aligned to state standards, thus short term objectives are not required on every IEP. Students with IEPs must not only participate in regular education programs to the full extent possible, they must show progress in those programs. This means that goals should be written to reflect academic progress. For students who must participate in alternate assessment, there must be alignment to *alternate achievement standards*.

Significant change has been made in the definition of the IEP team as it now includes *not less than 1* teacher from each of the areas of special education and regular education be present.

IDEA 2004 recognized that the amount of required paperwork placed upon teachers of students with disabilities should be reduced if possible, for this reason a pilot program has been developed in which some states will participate using multi-year IEPs. Individual student inclusion in this program will require consent by both the school and the parent.

XAMonline, INC. 21 Orient Ave. Melrose, MA 02176

Toll Free number 800-509-4128

TO ORDER Fax 781-662-9268 OR www.XAMonline.com

ILLINOIS TEACHER CERTIFICATION SYSTEM -

PO#   Store/School:

Address 1:

Address 2 (Ship to other):

City, State Zip

Credit card number_____-_____-_____-_____   expiration_____

EMAIL _____

PHONE   FAX

ISBN	TITLE	Retail	Total
978-1-58197-975-6	ICTS Special Education Learning Behavior Specialist I 155		
978-1-58197-998-5	ICTS Special Education General Curriculum Test 163		
978-1-58197-976-3	ICTS Basic Skills 096		
978-1-58197-293-1	ICTS Assessment of Professional Teaching Tests 101-104		
978-1-58197-978-7	ICTS Science- Biology 105		
978-1-58197-979-4	ICTS Science- Chemistry 106		
978-1-58197-673-1	ICTS Science- Earth and Space Science 108		
978-1-58197-996-1	ICTS Elementary-Middle Grades 110		
978-1-58197-666-3	ICTS Early Childhood Education 107		
978-1-58197-981-7	ICTS English Language Arts 111		
978-1-58197-982-4	ICTS Social Science- History 114		
978-1-58197-983-1	ICTS Mathematics 115		
978-1-58197-999-2	ICTS Science: Physics 116		
978-1-58197-985-5	ICTS Social Science- Political Science 117		
978-1-58197-987-9	ICTS Foreign Language- French Sample Test 127		
978-1-58197-988-6	ICTS Foreign Language- Spanish 135		
978-1-58197-989-3	ICTS Physical Education 144		
978-1-58197-990-9	ICTS Visual Arts Sample Test 145		
978-1-58197-992-3	ICTS Library Information Specialist 175		
978-1-58197-993-0	ICTS Reading Teacher 177		
978-1-58197-994-7	ICTS School Counselor 181		
978-1-58197-995-4	ICTS Principal 186		
		SUBTOTAL	
		Ship	$8.25
		TOTAL	

LaVergne, TN USA
18 November 2010

205323LV00001B/21/P